Proposal Of Solution On The Chaotic Political Situation In DRC

Proposal Of Solution On The Chaotic Political Situation In DRC

HONORE MATAMBA

To order additional copies of this book, contact:
Amazon.com

303009

CONTENTS

DEDICATION

To you the Congolese people, i dedicate this book.
It is for you a source of hope wherever you are.

ACKNOWLEDGEMENTS

A finger can not pick better a louse, they say.
To carry out the work under your hand, this saying was tested.

This book is the first book since i left university.
I say thank you to all who contributed to my education from primary school to university.

It became a reality thanks to the kindness and mercy of the Lord who protected me, fortified, has opened my mind to get to do what i could do today.

In addition to the protection and grace of God, the moral, physical support of my family, was a necessity for me. Here i quote my wife Astrid K. MWIKA MATAMBA who could sometimes cope with me, my daughters DIANE KASEKA MATAMBA, PRISCA MASENGU MATAMBA, MERDI MPUNGA MATAMBA.

My family where i come from, is my deep gratitude. This is CELESTIN KABANGA TSHIBAMBA, great sisters ASTRID KAYOWA, THERESE TSHIBWABWA, JOSEPHINE MASENGU, brothers TSHIMANGA GERARD, JEAN MBUYI SABWA, and young sister MARTE NGALULA KALENGA.

May the souls of my father DAVID KATOMBA WA NTUMBA and my mother BERNADETTE KASEKA NSANZA, my big brothers CRISPIN (TOM) MUTOMBO-KAZADI KOLESHA, JEAN-PIERRE NTUMBA KAZADI, DAVID MBUYI-KATOMBE, my little brother KABANGE NZENGU and my twin sister MBUYI KALENGA with which we were born, but who unfortunately passed away so soon, rest in peace.

May all members of my extended family and friends that i shut the names here, find my deep gratitude.

In Namibia (Osire), my thanks go to:

–SIMON KASHINDI who helped me to have access to a book that helped me for informational purposes.

–JEAN PIERRE DWANI, for helping me with a typing machine for writing this work in the secondary stage.

–RICKY UMBA with technical input (initiation in the handling of the computer) was crucial for the preparation of this work in the tertiary stage.

–PATRICK MUKANYA for his assistance in the handling of the laptop.

–Teacher ESAI BASHALA for his assistance in the handling of the laptop.

–Doctor FABIEN NGOY MANGA for moral support, his contribution is significant for me.

–ROBERT KAZINGA, KIPONDA ANZULUNI, NGOYI JEAN DE LA CROIX and MIOMI JEAN DE DIEU, Pastor JOSUE KAYEMBE MUTSHINAY for facilitating the loading of the battery of the laptop.

All those i shut the names here are the expression of my gratitude.

HONORE MATAMBA MATAMBA LUKASU.

INTRODUCTION

At this time, while nations are making efforts, mobilize their various resources to develop, Congo is driven to sink into indescribable misery. Contemporary life in Congo contrast with the potential found in this country. Indeed, there is a huge contrast between the potential in men, natural resources, basements, soil, climate, hydrography, flora fauna etc . . . , in Congo, and the life of the majority of Congolese living in the country.

And in the words of MKANDAWIRE T., quoted by Professor André Mbata B. MANGO and MPRARISENI BUDELI, lecturer at the University of South Africa "since its independence June 30, 1960, the history of the Democratic Republic of Congo has been a succession of coups, attempted secessions, attacks by foreign troops, civil wars, rebellions, plundering, authoritarian regimes, interventions of the United Nations (UN) and national conferences or dialogues". [1]

Given the above, it is necessary to ask questions: Why this paradox?
What constitutes the obstacle to achieve the well-being of the Congolese?

In response to these questions, several answers have been proposed: the economic disintegration, lack of capital, lack of developmental political structures, etc . . . In this regard, we believe that the lack of developmental political structures would be the main cause of the chaotic situation in the Congo (DRC).Came then the major issues: how to change the policy in the Congo (DRC)? What to do to get the legitimate aspirations of the people?

---

[1]   MKANDAWIRE T.: Introduction in MBAHYA Kankonde (Ed)
To Zaire for what? (1992) ix-x

This book is an answer to these questions. And since we know that the Congo (DRC) has a crisis of structures, credible political institutions, which could lead and support the democratic culture conducive to the development, almost anyone can be of the opinion that the real political institutions that can facilitate, promote democratic culture can only come from democratic elections.

And it happened after the death of Laurent Desire Kabila who took power by force, that Joseph Kabila found himself at the head of the country by mechanisms unknown to the Congolese people.

Given the above, to hold transparent, reliable, credible, democratic elections, was a necessity to save the Congo from the abyss. But as a process, the essence of democracy, to achieve the results of democracy, elections should be legitimate, provide guarantees in terms of transparency and credibility. And this from: 1. Pre-electoral phase (including the identification and registration of voters and candidates to be elected including the campaign period). 2. Election phase itself. 3. And the post election (including the counting of votes, the results to be announced by the competent institution including confirmation of results by the Supreme Court of Justice.

It's based on this philosophy that some sons of the country refused to believe in the 2006 elections in Congo. This was the case of the UDPS's leader Mr. Etienne Tshisekedi who had "called members of his party to boycott the vote in 2006". [2]

But it seems, determined to help the Congo in its efforts to establish political structures conducive to development, different organizations, the

---

[2]   ANDRE MBATA B. Mangu and MPRARISENI BUDEL: Democracy and elections in Africa in the Republic of Congo: lessons for Africa.

Listen
Read phonetically
Rate translation

international community, "primarily the United Nations and European Union had contributed about $ 460 million to finance the electoral process.UN had deployed the world's largest contingent for peace. Individually, countries such as RSA, Canada, Britain, Belgium and France had contributed materially and financially. Most of the found for DRC's 2006 elections was funded from outside." [3]

"Many commentators, actors in the international community, the organization of the United Nations, European Union, African Union and individual countries that had supported the electoral process, considered these elections as a fresh start for DRC's democracy." [4]

And in general, most international organizations involved in the electoral process did not conceal their satisfaction with the results, although there were also some negative critics before, during and after the election results.

For example:
1. The observation Mission of the 2006 elections in the DRC in July 2006, sent by the SADC at the invitation of the Independent Electoral Commission had said in conclusion that "the elections were conducted in an environment that was given to the Congolese people opportunity to express their free will to vote for candidates of their choice for the first time in forty years.And this in line with the electoral norms and standards in the SADC region". [5]

2.   "On September 1, the Carter Center released its report on the first round of elections saying that it was" credible "without evidence widespread or systematic manipulation. "But it pointed to important shortcomings of procedures that weakened the transparency of the process." [6]

---

3.   ANDRE MBATA B. Mangu and MPRARISENI BUDELI: idem
4.   ANDRE MBATA B. Mangu and MPRARISENI BUDELI: ibidem
5.   Electoral Observer Mission to the 2006 Elections in the Democratic Republic of Congo, Google.Doc.
6.   Voice of America.Septembre 1, 2006.

3. "Former Canadian Prime Minister Joe Clark, leader of the Carter Center observer mission said that the attempts to manipulate the electoral process, while very serious in some cases appear isolated and unlikely to affect the overall success of the election." [7]

4. "MONUC said Sept. 6 that it is satisfied with the electoral process, but expressed concern about the humanitarian situation." [8]

5. "The African Union hailed driving smoothly, elections and called for calm as the counting of votes began ." [9]

But there were also complaints from different personalities, from political and civil organizations. The case of: "−the leader of the UDPS, Mr. Etienne Tshisekedi who had asked his party members to boycott the elections". [10]

−   Three Vice-Presidents of the outgoing government and presidential candidates, complained on the election's day about rigging the vote. Bemba, Ruberwa and Z'Ahidi said "may be we are currently leading ourselves into an election farce and parody. [11]

−   The powerful bishop of the Roman Catholic church in Kinshasa, Cardinal Frederic Etsou had denounced the election results of 2006 in the Congo, calling it a Western conspiracy to monopolize the mineral

---

7.   DRC Observers seek transparency in vote counting. La Voix de l'Amerique Novembre 1st, 2006.

8.   MONUC satisfied with DRC electoral process but concerned by «humanitarian situation» MONUC septembre 6, 2006.

9.   «A.U, Hails DRC polls appeal for calm». Mail and Guardian October 31, 2006.

10. Republic of Congo, General elections in 2006, from Wikipedia, the free encyclopedia.

11. Interim results (second round).

wealth of the country. [12] He told Radio France Internationale (RFI) that "real results are not those who are being published." [13]

While South African observers approved the election results, other instructors expressed concerns including the Carter Center. [14]

MONUC had also reported that on August 3, the third day of chaotic counting the votes, a suspicious fire at the Kinshasa's main elections center had aggravated the concern about the transparency of results. According to her, while the elections themselves can have met the requirements, "the process of collecting results from 50,000 polling stations had become chaotic". [15]

As the reason of the strongest is always the best, they say, President Joseph Kabila was again guaranteed secure found at the head of the country. And the international community and some Congolese hoped the democratic culture, peace and national security, respect and promotion of human rights, national reconciliation . . . will become a reality in the Congo or at least begin to take shape, and therefore make significant observed progress in different areas in a short time, given the support would have given the Congolese people through elections and the expected support of the international community as was the case for the electoral process.

But now almost five years after the 2006 elections, not counting the year that President Joseph Kabila is the head of the country since 2001, the Congo (DRC) shines among the two last countries, D.R.C is the 168th out

---

12. Chris: MC Greal in Kinshasa. The Guardian, Wednesday, November 15, 2006.

13. Chris: Ibid

14. Carter Center Finds DRC credible, objective Warns of Flaws PROCEDURAL important, Voice of America September 1, 2006.

15. "Congo ballots go up in flames" MONUC, August 6, 2006.

of 169 according to the classification of the human development index and its components in 2010. [16]

And, we can reach an agreement that the elections of 2006 reinforced the power of President Joseph Kabila, who although the support* he had from his supporters, showed its inability to bring democracy, to ensure security, peace and national harmony, respect for human rights . . . . But rather enhance the regime of arbitrariness, impunity, disregarding human rights, intolerance . . . as you will see in the pages that follow.

At this level to hold transparent, credible, democratic elections is even a need for the Congo (DRC). And as after the five-year term, elected in 2006, it is anticipated general elections, the Congo and the international community may wish seriously to see the holding of these elections.

But in the light of what happened during and after the elections of 2006, especially in light of the results and given that, the facts do not lie, if we look at the management of the country, to organize the elections with Joseph Kabila as head of the country, it is to use the trick against the Congolese people. For the regime of Joseph Kabila will probably confuse the issue during the elections to his advantage, or will never leave actual results to be published.

To see this, let see the following.During the 2006 elections, among the complaints, there was: "the electoral act was developed for the benefit of Joseph Kabila. The electoral commission was not independent of President Joseph Kabila who had named its president. Abbe Malu Malu, The president of the Independent Electoral Commission, was an ally of President Joseph Kabila, recruited from civil society. This commission (CEI) did not always act as an independent, impartial body.The veil that hid the impartiality of the CEI fell when it tried to discredit Alex and Dominique Kanku Kande, opposition candidates to the positions of governors in the provinces of

---

16.   (16) Human Development Report 2010. Calculated on the basis of GNP per
      capita according to a ranking and HDI.
*   We will discuss in the following pages.

Kasai Occidental and Kasai Oriental". [17] While such committee "should be impartial". [18]

Also the "judicial system was subjected to President because he had the power to appoint and remove members of their duties. In the absence of an independent judicial commission, court members were appointed and could be suspended, revoked by the President making them unable to sustain the results that do not declare him a winner of presidential elections." [19]

Yet "an electoral process can be totally derailed at the end if the court is biased. The court plays a crucial role in determining whether or not the elections were democratic." [20] To hold elections in such a regime (that of Joseph Kabila) is a utopia.

And today, what can assure the whole world that, what is said in the lines above can not be repeated? Especially since the world can still observe, as it says, "after Laurent Kabila, President of the Democratic Republic of Congo was assassinated ten years later, with Joseph Kabila as head of the country, democracy and stability in the country are still involved (in default). As we approach the general elections in November 2011, Kabila seems to return to some of the characteristics of his father. In the past months, many journalists and politicians were arrested, the opposition rallies were interrupted many times with deadly force. And one of those responsible for human rights was killed, apparently with the complicity of senior officials of the national police." [21]

President Joseph Kabila can pretend to be zealous to organize elections, while in fact he wants by all means to avoid elections and continue to lead the country. Elections are a threat to Kabila and his group as aware of their fraudulent victory in the 2006 election—"In 2006, he won the presidential

---

17. Andrew B. Mbata Mangu and Mprariseni Budel: Ibid
18. Andrew B. Mbata Mangu and Mprariseni Budel: Same
19. Andrew B. Mbata Mangu and Mprariseni Budel: Same
20. Andrew B. Mbata Mangu and Mprariseni Budel: Ibid
21. Jason Stearns, Wednesday, January 19, 2011, Guardio.Co.UK

elections fraud amid reports of violence across the country contesting the elections" [22]–, afraid of losing their lucrative positions in case there are real elections. For this, the Kabila regime is involved in finding all the tricks, all possible reasons to justify not holding elections, or if forced by the pressure for the elections, to look for opportunities to invest in fake elections to his advantage, or otherwise if the rigging is not successful even consider war as what he wanted in 2006, as we read: "August 16, Angola deployed four battalions along the border of the DRC. The deputy head of the Angolan army, General Geraldo Nunda Sachipendo, said that these are the steps that have been taken to ensure the security of our borders," while there was speculation that Angola is ready to intervene if necessary in support of Kabila. (23[23])

And we have taken the passages above as examples among many others, to illustrate what is happening in Congo. It is in the following chapters that we will discover together the abuse of human rights, insecurity, tension, by the military clashes here and there, wars and so on.

At this level, it should be understood that the elections in the Congo (DRC), are needed. But to be credible, democratic, they should be run by a transitional government different from that of Joseph Kabila. And speaking of the political transition, the Congo has known since 1990 a so long transition, so that when it comes to the political transition in Congo, people are tired. But to achieve a real political change, credible elections, democratic political transition is necessary.

So, how to establish political transitional's institutions capable of preparing credible and democratic elections?

That's where this book offers a solution that you will discover in Chapter 5.

---

22.   Gustavemoke's blog. Africa-Power: Fathers to sound: a game in rising Dictatorship.
23.   "Angola Reinforce Troops on DRC border," Mail & Guardian, August 17, 2006, taken from Democratic Republic of Congo, general elections 2006.

Jason Stearns is the former coordinator of United Nations experts on the Congo.

The aim of our research was to first try to understand the real political situation in the Congo and then propose a solution of hope. The Congo needs reliable political institutions and men willing to serve the country. For although perfect political structures, even established by the angels, we need men with a willing heart for the well-being of the community, knowing that it is from the welfare of the community that they can find their own well-being. There are inter–influence between institutions and leadership.

There is abundant literature about the politic in the Congo, it is the case of:
1. Democracy and elections in Africa in the Democratic Republic of Congo; lessons for Africa. [24]
2. Zaire, towards which destiny ? [25]
3. Reflection on the crisis in the DRC, published by Ibbo Mandaza in 1993. [26]
4. Africa can win, Pierre Merlin. [27]
5. African Guerilas, published by Christopher Claphan. [28]
6. Peace and Security in Africa borealis. By Ibbo Mandaza. [29]

---

24. Andrew B. Mbata Mangu (professor in the department of constitutional rights, international and indigenous. University of South Africa) and Mprariseni Budel (responsible for education rights mercantile.University of South Africa).

25. T. Mkandawire: Quoted by Professor André Mbata B. Mangu and lecturer Mprariseni Budel.

26. Ibbo Mandaza: Reflections on the crisis in the DRC. Saps Trust 1999 Zimbabwe.

27. Pierre Merlin: Africa can win. Paris Karthala 2001.

28. Christopher claphan: African Guerilas.Eritrea, Tigray, Sudan, Somalia, Uganda, Rwanda, DRC, Liberia and Sierra Leone. James Currey Ltd., 1998.

29. Ibbo Mandaza: Peace and Security in Africa Boreal (English) Sapes Trust 1996.

7. Towards creating a sustainable culture of Human Rights. by Lumumba-Kasongo, Tukumbi. [30]

8. And many others that i have not been able to access such as the one of Honoré Gbanda: the death knell has sounded

Although some of these publications do not speak specifically of the Congo, some of the facts of which they speak are real in the Congo. In most of these publications, although they speak of the involvement of Western powers, they don't show however clearly the interest that have these powers to support the political change in Congo.

But in our book, we want more of the solution we offer, to use this important aspect, the interest of Western powers to support political change in Congo. And this aspect seems to be neglected in almost all the literature in solving the political problems of Congo.

We want to show here that not only the involvement of Western powers in the resolution of political problems in the Congo is important to the Congo, but also be as to such powers, the interest they have to support political change in supporting credible, democratic transitional political institutions.

METHODOLOGICAL FRAMEWORK

To justify the need to end the regime of President Joseph Kabila and establish a transitional government able to organize credible, democratic elections, we will first base ourselves not only on the irregularities, complaints recorded during the electoral process of 2006 but also the evaluation of the regime of President Joseph Kabila in terms of democratic culture, respect for human rights, national security, the consideration of the work, protection of human life, etc . . . We will examine the independence of state institutions: the executive in relation to the presidency, the

[30] Lumumba-Kasongo, Tukumbi: Towards Creating s sustainable culture of Human Rights.Individual contributors 1998 Windhoek, Gamsberg MacMillan 1998.

legislature in relation to the presidency, the judiciary in relation to the presidency. We look to see if while being independent of each other, these institutions work as a system whose elements are interdependent within constitutional limits.

Governance seems more important because the key to our work is the well-being, development in the Congo (DRC). And among the main actors of national development, public institutions play a leadership role. As a system, these institutions need to interact within the limits set by law, and the management of these institutions opens doors or not to the progress and development. Therefore we will examine the governance in the regime of President Joseph Kabila to justify his disqualification in respect of the hope of making the well-being in the Congo.

It may be recalled that the 2006's constitution has taken "governance as a central priority". [31] And the PRGSP (Poverty Reduction and Growth Strategy Paper) "declared the governance its pillar". [32]

In 2007, "Belgium decided to focus almost a quarter of its aid on governance in the Congo-Kinshasa. DFID (Department for International Development) decided to focus its support on governance. Sweden had spent one third of its budget for the same coutry on governance" [33], etc . . .

The DRC is among countries mostly receving from international aid. "First in 2002 and 2003 in Africa, and seventh in the world in 2006". [34]

But after all this support, the DRC is 168eme/169 according to the Human Development Index in 2010. [35] Yet if one believes the results of

---

[31] World is Witness.Voices on Genocide Prevention. Google, Human Rights on DRC, page 66.

[32] Idem, page 79.

[33] Idem, page 79.

[34] Idem, page 71.

[35] Human Development Report 2010. Institute for Statistics (2010a), the World Bank (2010g) and IMF (2010a)

2006 elections, 58.05% [36], and if governance was rational and efficient, President Joseph Kabila would succeed brilliantly because in addition to international financial, material, technique . . . support, he had the driving force "the trust of the people". When reading the constitution promulgated in February 18, 2006 [37], to hear the inaugural address of Joseph Kabila (38), good governance was a priority. Democracy and respect for human rights were not at rest. Was it a genuine expression, sincere or pure demagogy? The facts and observations in Chapter 3, will say more.

Considering the Congo as one of the countries that make up the world system we used in this work, the systems approach, based on the concept of the system. It states that the world consists of different elements that interact, inter–influence. And the malfunction of one affects the rest of the system.

We will consider the Congo as a whole in a large whole world. As a whole country, Congo is composed of various bodies including (economic, political and ideological or cultural). And speaking of the political forum we will focus on the relationship between the executive, legislature and judiciary in relation to the presidency. And the malfunction of one component affects the rest of the system as a whole Congo.

Understand that all these components inter–influence themselves so that the malfunctioning of the political, economic or cultural, the malfunction of the Presidency, the executive, legislative, and judicial system will drive towards the dysfunction Congo.

As a component of the world, Congo is one of countries that make up the world, and the malfunction of the Congo microsystem can cause the malfunction of the macro-system world.

Speaking of the techniques, we used direct observation, observation indirectly, the free interview, documentation, statistics and so on.

---

36. In part I got it Tuesday, 5/25/2011 from page 126
37. Idem, same page (38).Idem same page 139

We are talking about the political crisis in Congo. Our study will focus on the political crisis, his influence on others. We focus our study more about the current crisis.

Given the multiple meanings of words, we believe our readers determine the meaning we give to words:

Solution: result of a reflection, to solve a problem, to overcome a difficulty.
Politic: that relates to public affairs of a State, on a way to govern.
Change: The fact to move from one state to another.
Transition: Intermediate.
Structure: organization of the various elements of a concrete whole.
Credible: reliable.
Potential: expresses the potential.
Imperialism: politics of a state that seeks to expand its political and economic domination at the expense of other states.

CHAPTER. 1.

BACK GROUND ON THE CONGO

Although several authors have written about the Congo on various aspects and generalizations such as geographic location, economic potential have been presented, we believe it is important to have a chapter on generalities, not only to give an idea of what Congo is to the reader, but also to cause the shock that can feel any human being having a sense of humanity in relation with the life in the Congo that is in contrast of the potentialities in human, land, sub-soil, climate, flora, fauna , hydrography, electricity . . .

1.1 A LITTLE HISTORY ON CONGO

We can not talk about the Congo without even a little about the history of the country which is the subject of our study. Certainly the history of Congo is known, but we still want to remind the reader.

Since we are talking about power, we will focus more on political history.

As they say DEANNA Swaney and DAVID WILLETT: pygmies are original inhabitants of Zaire, then came the influx of migrants from the north. At 14th century, the first great kingdoms have emerged, including the Kongo kingdom. Farther south were the most important kingdoms Luba, Kuba, and Lunda. In the 17th century, the Portuguese's need in slaves for their Brazilian plantations increased even more to the point that slavery came to Congo in the west [38].

---

[38]. Deanna Swaney, David Willett: Africa, Lonely Planet is a shoestring. LONELY PLANET 1995. NATIONAL LIBRARY of Australia Cataloguing in publication.

Continuing with DEANNA Swaney and DAVID WILLETT: although centuries
of trade with European powers, there was no direct penetration with the
interior of the country until 19th century. It was the English journalist Henry
Morton Stanley in the search of David Livingstone, turned its attention in
the exploration of the place and opened the way for the colonization of
this part of Africa. In 1878, King Leopold II through the study committee
for the Upper–CONGO, persuaded Stanley to an expedition to Central
Africa. [39]

Formally, Léopold II acquired rights to the Congo territory at the Berlin's
conference in 1885, and made it his private property (Congo Free State).
He began various infrastructure projects such as the rail way's construction.
[40] However these were first for the King's business interest: to convey the
raw materials oversea through the coast.

Léopold II's regime, brutalized local population to produce rubber, for
which the spread of automobiles and the development of rubber tires
created a growing international market. And the worl can remember that
millions Congolese died from it.

We can say here with the professor Isango Idi that Léopold II admired
the colonial system applied to the Dutch East Indies (Islands of Java), it
inspired him to govern the future Independent State of Congo (ISC). The
principle of this policy was as follows:" the colonial state is to recognize
the ownership of a fith of arable land and requires that as a tax, local
people cultivate freely this land of export products (coffee, cane sugar,
etc) that will be passed on metropolitan markets. A portion of profits cover
the cost of administering the colony. The surplus (surplus colonial) is used
exclusively for the benefit of the metropolis. The settlement's exploitation
seemed justified as a return of the civilization. [41]

---

39. Deanna Swaney, David Willett, op cit.
40. Democratic Republic of Congo. From Wikipedia: the free encyclopeadia.
41. Professor Isango IDI WANZILA: op cit.

The actions of the Léopold II's administration sparked international protests led by British reporter Edmund Dene Morel and British diplomat/Irish rebel Roger Casement, whose 1904 report on the Congo condemned the practice. In 1908 the Belgian parliament, despite initial reluctance, bowed to international pressure (especially that from Great Britain) and took over the Free State as Belgian colony from the King. Under the elected Belgian government, it became Belgian Congo. [42] This was not without interest. In fact initially relactant the Belgian opinion could understand that the Congo business would be profitable to Belgium when looking at different resources found in Congo and knowing that those resources would have good market in Europe at that time, the case of the rubber with the sprout of the automobile's industry.

"On 18 October 1908 Belgian Parliament voted for the Congo's annexation as a Belgian colony after king Leopold II had finally given up any hope to maintain the Congo Free State as separate crown property. The government of Belgian Congo was arranged by the 1908 charter. Executive power rested with the Belgian Minister of Colonial Affairs, assisted by a colonial council. Both resided in Brussels. The Belgian Parliament exercised legislative authority over the Belgian Congo. The highest-ranking representative of the colonial administration in the Congo was the Governor-General posted in Boma and moved later to Leopoldville.

Initially, the Belgian Congo was administratively divided into four provinces: Léopoldville (Congo-Kasaï), Equateur, Oriental and Katanga, each under a vice-Governor-General. In 1932 the number of provinces was six. The territorial service was the true backbone of the colonial administration. Each province was divided into districts (24 districts), and each district into 120 territories. A territory was managed by a territorial administrator, assisted by one or more assistants. The territories were further subdivided into numerous chiefdoms, at the head of which the Belgian administration appointed "traditional chiefs." [43]

---

42.   Democratic Republic of Congo: op cit.

43.   Belgian Congo, from Wikipedia, the free encyclopedia.

The Belgian authorities made efforts to improve education and health of people in the settlement but refused to give their voice in government. [44]

About education, let us say with professor Isango Idi that the principle was "no elites, no trouble." There were two separate systems of lessons: "one for whites and another for blacks. The colonizers had shown great reluctance to give blacks access to secondary education and higher education. The first was introduced to them in 1948 and the second in 1954." [45] At the independence the country had inched a dozen national holding a university degree.

As a logic consequence, the discrimination in employement matters was real. Blacks limited by education qualification were excluded to hold certain positions one could think. However let us continu with Professor Isango, saying that:"this discrimination was institutionalized. What so ever their qualifications, blacks could not access some fonctions.

In the public service there were two different status one for whites and another for blacks. The two status were entitled to different scales for similar functions. Their unity was not taken until 13/01/1959. There was difference between the employment contract signed by blacks and the contract of employment for whites. The first provided criminal penalties for violations by the natives, which was not the case of the contract of employment." [46]

When reading the history of this country we can understand that even in justice matters the discrimination was present. Only 50 years later due to internal pressures supported by movement of independence which blew in other African countries that the Belgian authorities felt obliged to mitigate their paternalistic governance and allowed the existence of political parties.

---

44. Deanna Swaney, David Willett: Africa Lonely is shoestring, Lonely Planet 1995. National Library of Australia Cataloguing in publication.
45. Prof. IDI Isango WANZILA: op cit
46. Prof. Isango IDI WANZILA: ibid

One can read in the encyclopedia: Belgium in 1957 allowed indigenous people to elect their representatives on boards of certain cities. But the demand for independence continued. [47]

DEANNA and David go on to say that the main force to emerge was the Mouvement National Congolais (MNC) of Patrice Lumumba, which organized to form a strong central government able to resist secessionist tendencies of regional parties based (tribal). In 1959 the looting broke out in Kinshasa (Léopoldville at the time) against the Belgian governance. Because of this, Belgium was deeply shocked that independence was abruptly given the following year. [48]

However the Belgian authorities did not intend to give a true and complete independence directly, but "framed" independence. We can say with Professor Isango Idi, that this conception of independence "supervised by Belgium is, "moreover, in certain provisions of the Basic Law. For example Article 51, paragraph 2 of this law stipulates for the interpretation of this Act, the Chambers may request the Belgian parliament the interpretation that it gives. For their part, Articles 253 and 254 respectively assigned to the council of state and at the court of accounts of Belgium the powers conferred on the Constitutional Court and the Court of Auditors of the Congo, until this country has the institutions." [49]

"The nation becomes independent on 30 june 1960 as the Democratic Republic of Congo, with Joseph Kasavubu as President of the Republic and Patrice E. Lumumba as Prime Minister. Four days later there are early signs of mutiny in the army. The reason is the fury of the African soldiers that in spite of independence the officers in the Congolese army are without exception white. The fact is not surprising (in the colonial army Africans could not rise higher than the rank of sergeant-major, and in the rush to independence the first Congolese officer cadets have not yet completed their courses).

---

47. ENCYCLOPEDIA w-x-yz 21.
48. Deanna and David: Ibidem
49. Professor Isango Idi: Ibidem

Lumumba gives in as the tention rises during the first week of July. He agrees to the dismissial of the Belgian officers and the appointment of Congolese in their place. The role of hastily issuing the new commissions falls to Joseph Mobutu, the minister of defence.

In the short term no one can control the unfolding chaos. Without any effective chain of command, the army goes berserk in riots against the Belgian population. Priests and nuns in particular are singled out for violence and rape. Before the middle of July 25,000 Belgians flee the country. In the other direction nearly 10,000 Belgian troops fly in to protect European live and property, particularly in wealthy Katanga." [50]

"On July, the richest province, Katanga, seceded under Moise Tshombe. The United Nations sent 20,000 peacekeepers to protect Europeans in the country and try to restore order. In the same periode Congo's second richest province, Kasaï, also announced its independence." [51]

"On September 4 President Kasavubu announced that he has dismissed Lumumba as prime minister. In response, Lumumba also has dismissed Kasavubu as president. The resulting confusion is only resolved when Mobutu declared on September 14 that he is "neutralizing" all politicians and is temporarily taking over the duties of government. Mobutu was secretly in Kasavubu's camp (both acted with the encouragement of the CIA, alarmed by Lumumba's soviet policy). Later he retuned the government to Kasavubu, who appointed him commander of the army." [52]

Let us talk a bit with the professor Isango Idi about this revocation that one may find controversial, that raised cons paid for its legal value. "Belgium recognize in article 22 (Basic Law) :to the leader in state, the right to appoint and dismiss the Prime Minister, the President's decision however,

50. History World, Convergence Africa. www. Historyworld.Net /wrldhs/plai Text histories.asp ? historyid=ad34THE DEMOCRATIC REPUBLIC OF CONGO.
51. History of the Democratic Republic of the Congo. From Wikipedia, the free encyclopedia.
52. History World, Convergence Africa: op cit.

was against the practices imposed in this matter by the parliamentary political system that was in force at the time in the Congo. Because such a dismissal is related to the withdrawal of confidence from the head of government in parliament, but it was not the case of Lumumba." [53]

Here we can reflect on the true meaning of the independence supervised by Belgiumas stipulated in certain provisions of the Basic Law. Here not only Belgium but also the UN could come to the rescue using diplomatic means or other known means to put pressure on President Kasavubu to stay in the line of the legality. Belgium and the United Nations would help the young country had not derailed because in view of the law, they (Belgium, United States of America and the United Nations) knew where was the reason, where was the legality. But the silence of Belgium, USA, UN etc . . . , surprised at the time more than one and allow the chaos that gripped the country since then.

This leads many to say that the Congo has suffered and is suffering from an international poitical conspiracy. And since then, the Congo is suffering from extreme lack to respecte the constitutional and caused the political jungle in Congo. The act of signing was emptied of its true meaning. That is how later, you can sign the morning but in the afternoon things are declared contrary to the signature.

"In 1965, as in 1960 the division of power between president and prime minister led to a stalemate and threatened the country's stability, Joseph-Désiré Mobutu seized again power (backed by United States).

By 1967, Mobutu had consolidated his rule and proceeded to give the country a new constitution and a single party. The new constitution was submitted to popular referendum in june 1967 and approved by 98 % of voters. It provided that executive powers be centralized in the president, who was to be head of state, head of government, commander in chief of the armed forces and the police, and in charge of foreign policy. The president was to appoint and dismiss cabinet members and determine

---

53.　Professor Isango Idi: Ibidem.

their areas of responsibility. The ministers, as heads of their respective departments, were to execute the programs and decisions of the president. The president also was to have the power to appoint and dismiss the governors of the provinces and the judges of all courts, including those of the supreme court of justice.

The bicameral parliament was replaced by a unicameral legislative body. The president had the power to issue autonomous regulations on matters other than those pertaining to the domain of law, without prejudice to other provisions of the constitution. Under certain conditions, the president was empowered to govern by executive order, which carried the force of law.

Relative peace and stability prevailed until 1977 and 1978 when Katangan rebels, based in Angola, launched a series of invasions, sometimes known as Shaba I. The rebels were driven out only with the aid of the French and Belgian paratroopers." [54]

Trying to comply with the critics from his backers (regime's supporters), and forced by the invasions of rebels (the war of 80 days), the president Mobutu tried to engage some reforms to democratize the country. On the 1st July 1977, he made a speech in which he proclaimed some democratic reforms. That is how he introduced the election within some organs of PMR (Popular Movement of the Revolution) the sole party. The case of the political Bureau where 18 members would be elected by people, while 12 would be nominated by him self. The legislative counsel where the members would be elected by people directly, contrarily to what was done before, and so on . . .

Besides what is said below, among the important innovations brought in 1977, announced in the speech of the 1st July 1977 there is the latitude accorded to parliamentarians to question the executive board members and the para-etatique responsibles in the accomplishement of their duties. Many were found guilty and arrested because of mismanagement and misappropriation of public funds. As the regime was not used to this kind

---

54.   Zaïre, from Wikipedia, the free encyclopedia.

of democratic culture, Mobutu had to stop the questioning. The democratic measures in election were squized until the return of the usual authoritarian regime, to show that those democratic measures were not coming from the heart of the president Mobutu.

However, although it was difficult to talk about internal opposition, it should be noted that an informal opposition could already be in the hearts, minds of people, but not as a formal body. It is at the end of 1980 that the decision of stopping the liberalization process of parliamentary activity will provide an opportunity for the birth of the first open political opposition initiated within the country by 13 parliamentarians who created later 1982 UDPS (Union for Democracy and Social Progress).

With the single party, the MPR (Mouvement Populaire de la Revolution), cynicism pushed further by making the party over the state, Mobutu institutionalized the party-state. However, towards the 90s, with corruption becoming common place, the continual decline in prices of raw materials like copper and cobalt, transport infrastructure dilapidating, collapsing and inflation running about 1000%, the suspension of aid by U.S., Belgium and the IMF, the Congo was on the brink of the abyss, the crisis.

In addition to pressure from internal opposition, pressure from foreign powers allied, and especially the international political change brought the regime to bow to the course of history, as President Mobutu had said in one of his speech before the hurricane, the unripe or ripe fruit falls. We can see with Professor Isango: "under pressure from his supporters, Mobutu could be deaf he knew he was invested by those same powers. But the end of the Cold War in the late 80s has completely changed the data". [55]

President Mobutu then found himself forced to bow before the hurricane. Thus ended the Second Republic by the speech of April 24, 1990 in which President Mobutu announced the end of the guiding role of MPR

---

[55]   Prof. Isango Idi Wanzila: Ibid

and consequently, of the Second Republic and Zaire entered a transitional period towards the Third Republic.

While rightly, Congolese had warmly welcome policy change, less than two weeks after his speech of April 24, 1990, President Mobutu put into question all the hope carried in the hearts of many Congolese. It was May 3, 1990 that President Mobutu announced to parliament in contrast to what had been said April 24 that the ministers would be appointed by him on the proposal of the Prime Minister as stipulated in the constitution of the Second Republic. The choice of the Prime Minister was to be done by political parties after more consultation was considered. This raised doubts about the willingness of President Mobutu to make a change. A standoff ensued, and between power and opposition around issues such as: the constitutional text that would govern the transitional period, the political family from which was to come the head of government, the nature of the conference to be held (constitutional or national, sovereign or limited?)

After internal and external pressure, President Mobutu finally signed the order convening a Sovereign National Conference. His dress was not long without clashes. The authority in power refused to challenge the constitution of the Second Republic, which were her pillar and the opposition refusing to be tricked. The authority refused to devote full sovereignty to the National Conference fearing of being excited about the new dynamic. But the opposition and other organizations, the case of the Catholic Church claimed the franchise and the full involvement of all without exception. That's how the National Conference began August 7, but had stopped, closing and reopening up the preparation of texts concerning transitional provisions for Sovereign National Conference.

In September 1991, unhappy with the situation of their pay, members of the band of paratroopers based in Kinshasa marched in the city and destroyed the stores, warehouses, ... The civilian population was not slow to join them and looting was consummated in which there was loss of human life. The situation will degenerate in other cities, it was total panic. France and Belgium sent troops to evacuate their nationals.

To return to the Sovereign National Conference on the 5th December 1992, was the creation of the High Council of the Republic (HCR), which will control the President and the Government and replace the Parliament. Bishop Mosengo is its President.

In 1993, there was conflict between President Mobutu and Prime Minister Etienne Tshisekedi. Used to autocratic power, the President allowed the circulation of 5,000,000 Z, a new bank note. It was unfortunate that the president unconstitutionally kept an important lot of the new bank notes under his responsibility. Against such method, the Prime Minister reacted by declaring illegal the use of the new bank notes.The businessman aware, took the side of the Prime minister.

But as soldiers were already paid with the unfortunate bank notes, the worse happen, as soldiers found themselves with worthless bank notes in their hands while in need of exchanging their pay with food and other needs. Then looted Kinshasa, Lubumbashi, Bukavu, etc . . . And it destroyed the already poor economic base. It then apear that the president Mobutu was not easy to accept the change that the Prime Minister Tshisekedi was determined to bring. The other side, the Prime Minister Tshisekedi was not easy to be led according to the autocratic methods that suited the President Mobutu.

This led the pro-Mobutistes to call Etienne Tshisekedi a conflictual. It is because of this (among other reasons) that Etienne Tshisekedi could not work in office as Prime Minister for more than six months during the Mobutu regime.This led many people to realize that the time Etienne Tshisekedi was in office as Prime Minister, it was against the genuine will of President Mobutu, as he could not facilitate a Prime Minister who works as an employee of the nation, the country rather than Mobutu's employee.

It is in that logic that, although in agreement with the opposition, on the 14th January, the President Mobutu announced the government's resignation and the dissolution of the High Council of the Republic to be replaced by the transitional High Council of the republic, HCR-PT (High Council of the Republic-Transitional Parliament. Later on the same year after different meetings, a consensus was reached for multipartism elections and a democratic constitution.

A question may come to mind. Could Mobutu leave real democratic elections ?, very probably not. Later Mobutu fell ill, but although his illness, Mobutu and his group did not intend to liberalize the power until the party ADFL starting from Eastern Congo engaged in the Mobutu regime's countdown up to May 17, 1997 when Kabila took power in Kinshasa. But before that in June 14, 1994 Leon Kengo wa Dondo, whose father is a Jewish-Polish and mother a Rwandan Tutsi, was named prime minister. He will not resign from office only in March 24, 1997 following a vote by the transitional parliament a motion calling for his dismissal, relying in particular on the many military failures, but also on its doubtful zaïrianity (zaïrian nationality).

Squeezed from all sides, the President Mobutu signed an order to confirm the taking of the Prime Minister by the opposition's leader Etienne Tshisekedi, proposed by the radical opposition on the 1st April 1997. But later on the 9th April the same year, president Mobutu signed to dismiss Etienne Tshisekedi who will be replaced by the General Likulia Bolongo.

At this level, let us talk a little about AFDL that was born October 18, 1996 at Lemera in South Kivu as military and political movement whose goal was to overthrow the regime in Congo by armed struggle. The ADFL was a group of four political parties below:

"–The party of the People's Revolution (PRP) of Laurent Kabila.
 –National Council of Resistance for Democracy (NCRD) to ANDRE Kisase Ngandu.
 –The Peoples Democratic Alliance (ADP) of Deogracias BUGERA head Banyamulenge.
 –And the Revolutionary Movement for the Liberation of Zaire (MRLZ) of Masasu Nendaga.

Trapped by reality on the ground (the advance of rebel troops lightning) when he refused all contact with the rebel group calling them aggressors and not rebel, Mobutu found himself forced to meet Kabila, the rebel leader, at Congolese offshore aboard the Outeniqua, a warship of South Africa, in May 4 1997. Organised by the President Nelson manila the meeting failed as the two protagonists could not meet in their views.

Continuing with Gilbert Ngijol, let say that indeed, after the faillure of May 4, 1997 and before the irresistible advance of the rebel's troops to Kinshasa, some western powers like the U.S. and France in particular had lobbied the rebel leader Kabila and Mobutu which they asked to negotiate to avoid unnecessary bloodshed in Kinshasa.

Five francophone African heads of state met at an Extra Ordinary summit on 8 May 1997 in Libreville (Gabon), they dissuaded Mobutu by asking him to step down to avoid bloodshed in Kinshasa, and urged the Zairian political forces, under the direction of the High Council of the Republic-Transitional Parliament (HCR-PT), to conduct the election of its chairman to allow smooth functioning of institutions, and thus encourage a democratic transition in accordance with the constitutional act of the transition.

Due to that recomendation and pressure from Western powers, the High Council of the Republic-Transitional Parliament met May 10, 1997, and elected as President, Archbishop of Kisangani, Lawrence Monsengo. Bishop Monsengo became "the second personality of Zaire after Mobutu and would replace him in case of a power vacuum". (1[56])

The silver lining is said to be good, although the running political situation, Zaire was having at least a basic political institution which could be counted for the transition.

But while he was often referring to non-compliance by Mobutu to what was acquired from the Sovereign National Conference to justify some of the times his strugle, came to power, Kabila put into question even the High Council of the Republic-Transitional Parliament (HCR-PT) and chooses to lead the country by the presidential decrees. Kabila justified this by citing

---

[56] GILBERT Ngijol: Ibid

an old African adage that you can not keep the water clean in a dirty gourd, thus considering the ADFL as clean water. This was an alibi because in less than one year, we realized that the ADFL was not only dirty water, but poisoned. In the following, Laurent Desire Kabila proclaimed himself President of the Republic of Congo May 17, 1997.

Faced with this situation, the country lacked a constitutional provision that could protect the country against excessive political adventure. That is how from the departure Laurent Kabila opened the door to a new political chaos that will be exploited later by the same people who brought him to power. Realizing this big mistake, as they say that better late than never, Kabila tried to cover his error, but unfortunately by appointing his close circle of friends and family members to develop a text that could fill the legal vacuum.

But far from calming the minds, this showed that the country was about to be run as a family or village. And with the experience of the past, some sons and daughters of the country had learned not to let be easily tricked.

That's like Ngijol Gilbert said: there were many Zairian opposition to both the Mobutu regime and the rebel Banyamulengue simply saying that Kabila who turned the power by force and in addition with the support of foreign troops, was not a Democrat. He might even be more dictator as Mobutu, who also took power by arms. [57]

We can still ask a question at this level: what would happen if:
–President Mobutu had met its order of April 2, 1997 confirming the appointment of Etienne Tshisekedi as Prime Minister on the proposal of the radical opposition dated April 1, 1997.
–And after May 10, 1997, after the election of the Archbishop of Kisangani, Laurent Monsengo as president of the High Council of the Republic-Transitional Parliament, President Mobutu takes historic courage to resign?

---

[57]   GILBERT Ngijol: Ibid

The legal and political consequences that migth result from, were the following: the President of the High Council of the Republic-Transitional Parliament, being the second personality in the country became President of the Republic. The Vice President of the HCR-PT became President of the HCR-PT. The country would come to a situation where Mobutu gone, the country really would have welcomed the existence of at least three branches—the President of the Republic,

−Prime Minister

−Parliament of Transition. And the transition would start on a solid foundation as at least three powers are united around a constitutional text in addition to political will.

If this were the case, what would become the rebel group and especially his supporters? Probably if the rebel group was responsible, it would be ridiculous to continue to fight with weapons such institutions. And then if the commitment of the rebel group and foreign powers behind the rebel group was referred for truly democratic assumptions they could have been happy :−to find a consensus around these institutions so that together they manage the transition.

Or after agreements to leave these institutions manage the transition and wait to win power through the ballot box.

But if the commitment of the rebel group and foreign powers behind him had not referred democratic option they were to continue with the war. As foreign powers supporting this thesis, would always find tips to guide Mobutu and Kabila in provisions that would encourage the continuation of the war to Kinshasa. After all who could pay the price of war? Who would have honored the promises made and contracts signed by the rebel group in favor of certain business circles, if the rebel group has no access to the resources of the country?

Following this logic we can understand the signing of the order confirming the appointment of Etienne Tshisekedi as prime minister April 2, 1997 and revocation on 9 April, 1997 followed by its replacement by General Likulia B.

Here we must understand that President Mobutu engulfed in international politics, could run councils that subsequently could tie him up and place him as a prey to be slaughtered at less effort.

In the event of the resignation of President Mobutu, Kabila would have been worn in memory of the Congolese people as the man who played a very important role to achieve this political situation. And perhaps, by consensus, the Congo would have agreed with his peers, a special political status. And the transitional institutions would organize elections within a reasonable time in which the people would offer to Kabila through the ballot box a gift-a massive vote-in recognition of his contribution to defuse the political situation that have long been taken hostage.

What has not been the case, and the ADFL went to Kinshasa favoured, facilitated by the current political environment: the ADFL had seized an unprecedented opportunity that the regime of Mobutu was weakened from all sides. The population was tired of Mobutu, the army demobilized had no more confidence in him and its eastern neighbors (Rwanda, Burundi, Uganda) together with Angola had decided to get rid of Mobutu, who maintained against these countries, rebel armed groups.

This is that besides, himself was ill at the time when his bosses could see no more in him future in politics and they probably sought a replacement to ensure their interests.As Mobutu was gone, people wellcomed Kabila with an open heart and rejoyced the first year of the reign of Laurent Desire Kabila: the relative decline of police harassment that characterized the Mobutu regime, some roads and bridges repaired in Kinshasa, Lubumbashi, Bukavu, etc.. .The transport within townn undergoing restoration, stabilization of exchange rates, the reduction of inflation of 8.83% in 1993 to 6% in 1997 . . .

But the wise men could not be easily tricked seeing the similarities with the beginning of the Mobutu regime and also knowing the value of legal texts on which Laurent Kabila was sitting. More than one wondered about the sincerity of the Kabila's promises: a structural program of national reconstruction of three years, but based on a two-year political transition.

Kabila's intentions were not slow to reveal itself in May 26, 1997 when he banned all demonstrations and political activities of all political parties, citing as a reason, the state security. On May 28, 1997, Kabila arrogated to itself all executive and military power. It should be noted that there was opposition demonstration against the Kabila government on May 24, 1997 in Kinshasa.

In the presence of Presidents of Angola, Tanzania, Uganda and Burundi and other personalities, Laurent Désiré Kabila sworn and made a speech where he promised democratic elections in two years to come.

The gap between Kabila and the people began to be felt gradually with what happened afterwards: July 25, 1997 in Kinshasa a violent repression of a demonstration demanding the return of Lumumba's political party activity, in which the army had opened fire on demonstrators.The brutal suppression of student demonstration 26 August 1997 at the University of Kinshasa, during which the army had again opened fire on students. [58]

This began to remind the people the sad methods of the Mobutu regime. In less than one year Kabila began to slowly but surely use methods decried during the Mobutu regime: personalization, tribalization, ethnicization etc. .., power became the rule of political management and became a source of enrichment with less effort.

Besides these enormous privileges, as stated Ngijol GILBERT, there is the "convenience of appointments to posts of the Republic called juicy ministries and agencies that are actually true sanctuaries of corruption. This is where it will make the largest embezzlement of public funds. These positions are naturally reserved only for national ethnic group or circle of friends". [59] The power was truly a family affair, not a State affair.

It here that we must understand why, the hostility of the Kabila regime to the peaceful opposition, unarmed. How can we understand that a regime with

---

[58]   GILBERT Ngijol: Ibid
[59]   GILBERT Ngijol; Ibid

democramotic set can fear of contradiction when we know that it is from the clash of ideas that light shines? Such a scheme probably feared that the opposition knowing the shenanigans, the missmanagements can not set my power strip. That's from one error Kabila opened the door to political chaos that will be operated by any sequence even those who brought him to power. It looks like they had put him at the head of the ADFL knowing it was the right person who could fall into their trap to see their diabolical plan to become reality. So the world may know by now that, ADFL did not chase Mobutu to liberate the country, but Mobutu was a pretext to gain power.

To accelerate the implementation of their plan they created so-called opposition groups, apparently to liberate the country. That is how on August 2, 1998 a rebellion began from Goma. On Sunday, August 2, i found myself by chance in Goma, as i followed as everyone to read the news release announcing the rebellion by Sylvain Bouki at radio Goma. The RCD in the way of the ADFL, imposed upon Lawrence D. Kabila a countdown up to the date of January 17, 2001, when the death of Laurent Desire Kabila was announced publicly.

During the conquest of cities by the RCD, like Mobutu, Laurent D. Kabila refused all contact with the said rebel group, calling it an aggressor, as was the case of the ADFL by Mobutu. History repeats itself they say, like Mobutu, Laurent D. Kabila found himself forced to sit at same table with his friends of yesterday but enemies of today. It may be noted that the vulnerable population, impoverished since Mobutu was liable to be corrupt as it was motivated by the search for selfish interests or by Tribality. This group was fanatical fans (blind fanatics) of Laurent D. Kabila. One may recall that this was nothing new, because at the time of Mobutu, it was even stronger than that of Lawrence D. Kabila.

But as they say in how that silver lining, it was after the death of Lawrence D. Kabila that more than one, even some fans of Lawrence D. Kabila became aware that the Congo was still ruled, managed as a village. For example, it is as if there were no legal provisions, provisions relating to the replacement of the President of the Republic in case of a power vacuum in case of death of the President of the Republic. This was not considered thinking maybe the person of the President was eternal! Yet there was a group of people forming a team called "National Assembly." This so-called National Assembly—up from scratch, without popular legitimacy, decried by any man with good sense has shown its value and maturity policies across the world. Even some of the supporters of the regime had realized that many people making up the team called the National Assembly did not know the role they should play in such periods.

This is how a group of people could decide instead of the people to impose a man parachuted to the top of the country. This was said to save the country from a bloodbath. That's how the Congo has found one day with Joseph Kabila at the head of a great and beautiful country. We remind here that Congo has suffered since Mobutu until these days so very atrocious. To help Congo is not to impose or seek to infiltrate a "Congolese" man eventually overdraw. But help Congo is helping to have institutions that guarantee peace and national harmony.

1.2   LOCATION AND MISCELLANEOUS

After these few lines on the history of the Congo, we find it necessary to do as a general overview on the location and variety of the country. That's why you find the following lines, some data on the Congo, a country that is the subject of our study.

Called Amazon of Africa [60], this vast country occupies the heart of Africa. Eleventh of the world, the Congo covers an area of 2,344,885 km2. It is bordered by Congo Brazzaville in the west, the Central African Republic in the northwest, Sudan to the north-east, Uganda to the east to the north, Rwanda, Burundi and Tanzania to the east, Zambia to the south-east and Angola to the south-west. There is a strip of 40 km which borders the Atlantic Ocean. The Congo is after Sudan and Algeria, the third

---

60.   DAVID WILLET DEANNA Swaney: Lonely Planet Africa 1995.

Giant of Africa area. As relief, this vast territory is largely covered by plains, basins, plateaus, volcanoes, mountains, . . . The Ruwenzori for example along the border with Uganda in the north-east is 5000 m altitude, altitude around Mount Kilimanjaro (5802 m) in Tanzania.

Situated between the two tropics, Congo is crossed by the equator. Thus the Congo:—equatorial climate along the equator and the surrounding area.

—The tropical wet and dry tropical climate. The system often exceeds 2,000 mm of rain in the central basin area, around 1500mm. [61]

The climate is generally potentially very suitable for agriculture and forestry. The Congo River basin dominates the appearance of the basin countries. It receives water from the north (Ubangi) east (Uele, Arruwimi) and south (Lualaba Kasaï, Kwango). The Congo has at least seven lakes Tanganyika, Mweru, Kivu, Eduard, Albert, Mai-Ndombe, Upemba etc . . . Each of these lakes has its particularities. Rivers, ponds, tidal etc . . . are many. The central basin of Congo is dominated by one of the largest equatorial forest which covers one third of the territory. Savannas and grassy woods are not the rest and that makes the flora and fauna of the Congo have the potential rich and meaningful. The fauna and flora are widely diversified. Gorillas, for example (considered as endangered in the world) are still in the mountainous regions of the east.

Congo is among the countries with large reserves or parks considered world heritage. It is also known for its basement that is extremely rich in gold, diamonds, copper, oil, cobalt, manganese, zinc, natural gas etc . . .

PIERRE GOUROU: Democratic Republic of the Congo. Physical and Social Geography. Regional Surveys of the World. Africa South of the Sahara in 2001 thirtieth edition. Europe Publishing.

---

[61]. Encyclopedia

Maize, cassava, rice, potatoes, fruits, vegetables, palm oil, tea, coffee, rubber, cotton, etc . . . are cultivate in Congo. All these possibilities can change the image of Congo, Congolese lives in a time record if exploited rationally and effectively in the political structures conducive to development.

The water is relatively abundant in Congo. The Congo River, first in Africa, is second in the world after the Amazon for the volume of water added to the Inga dam, or at least 40,000 cubic meters per second as shown in a diagram. [62]

The Congo's population is composed of more than 200 ethnic groups, some of which are found beyond national borders. And this diversity, if rationally exploited in a developmentalist political environment, is an advantage for the country. There are over 200 languages and dialects, including four (Lingala, Swahili, Tshiluba and Kikongo) that are called national spoken widely across the country in addition to French that is official. The population consists of approximately 49.41% to 50.59% of men and women.[63] The Congolese are found in many beliefs: Roman catholics 50 %, Protestant 20 %, Kimbanguiste 10%, Muslim 10 %, other (includes syncretic scts and indigenous beliefs) 10 %. The population is estimated to 71,712,867 (july 2011 estimation). [64]

In view of the foregoing in terms of natural factors of production, the potential in men, significant qualifications in different fields, the energy and electric potential, etc. . . . except developmentalist political structures that are lacking, the Congo can play an important role, not less, not only in Africa but also worldwide.

---

[62]   AFRICA ON FILE
       6.22 Africa: contemporary Regional Issues.
       Water resources: Precipitation, Lakes and Rivers.
[63]   BRITANICA . Book of the year 1996. Events of 1995
[64]   Population graphs of DRC in 2010, from google: Congo, Democratic of the–CIA –The world Fact book.

CHAPTER 2

SYSTEMATIC OF SOME AFRICAN AND WORLD SETTLEMENTS.

We believe it is important to examine the history of colonialism and political independence of any country, to understand to some extent, its evolution and the political, economic, social environment.

A. AFRICAN COLONIES

The current situation in Congo has among other reasons, the colonial action, that begun as a private company of Belgian King Leopold II, called Cabourg Saxe, and then transferred to Belgium.

Presented to the world as a philanthropic, for civilizing people found in this corner of the world, the colonial enterprise, however, mainly have nothing with the spirit of philanthropy, humanism as presented in the face of the world.

For proof, read the extract of the conversation between the Belgian minister of Colonies Jules Sharks, with the first Catholic missionaries in the Belgian Congo in 1920:

DUTIES OF MISSIONARIES IN OUR COLONY, where I quote some extract:

"Reverend fathers, dear compatriots, the main purpose of your mission is, to teach blacks to know God. They already know. They speak and submit to a Zambi or Nvidi-Mukulu, and what else. They know that killing, stealing, slander, insult . . . is bad.

Your main role is to facilitate the task of administratives and industrials. This means that you interpret the gospel in a way that best serves our interests in this part of the world.

To do this, make sure among others to: let our wild people not have interest in natural resources that filled their soil and basement because if they have interest in it, they may make us a deadly competition and dream one day to dislodge us.

The off-and to despise anything that might give them the courage to confront. refer here specifically to their many idols of war they claim make them invulnerable. Since the old to abandon them would not hear, as they will soon disappear, your action should focus on youth.

Stress-particularly on the submission and blind obedience. This virtue is best practice when there is absence of critical thinking. So avoid developing critical thinking in your schools. Teach them to believe and not to reason. Establish for them a system of confession that will make you good detectives denouncing any Black with awareness and that would claim national independence.

These are, dear compatriots, some of these principles you would apply flawless. The king attaches great importance to your mission. So, he decided to do everything to facilitate it.
So Reverend Fathers, dear compatriots, that is what, i was asked to inform you today." [65]

But as social facts are stubborn, the world got to know that the settlement was motivated by the following reasons:

---

[65]   DANIEL Mongui MBENGUE, quoted by Gilbert Ngijol: AUTOPSY OF GE-Genocide Rwanda, Burundi and the UN. Presence Africaine Paris.

"1. Economic reasons: in the eighteenth and nineteenth century, the industrial revolution took place in Europe. As the production of goods increased, European countries began to compete on markets where to supply their products.Because America and Asia, were already colonized, Africa with its wealth and its large population, became attractive.

2. Religion: as Europeans began to explore and conquer Africa, Christian missionaries came to spread their beliefs. The missionaries saw Africa as primitive and not knowing God. They came to bring the salvation they said. However during this process, they became instruments of colonization.

3. Settlement: Europe has experienced a rapid growth of its population. The stories of vast uninhabited territories in Africa, attracted Europeans.

4. The international rivalry: in the half of the nineteenth century, almost every country in Europe became involved in Africa through the activities of its businessmen, missionaries and settlers. The government would manage to have political control over African territories to ensure that their countries benefit from the exploitation of African labor, territories, minerals, and international prestige.

5. The strategy: the time that Europeans would rush to colonize Africa, they were already owners of the American colonies, the West India and Asia. The safety of these possessions overseas was important for them. There were already serious economic and military political rivalries between European nations. It was so important for each of them to protect its shipping routes and have control over those who were like strategic territories outside Europe." [66]

---

[66] UNDERSTANDING HISTORY 9. Namibian Junior Secondary text book. History of Colonial Namibia, Africa, and the World. John J. Katzao, Nangolo Mbumba, Bryn ó Callaghan, Helgard, Patemann Eddie Ivan Staden, H. Davy A Tait
Cass/Namibia Project and Longman 1993.

That's how Belgium has operated, expropriated the Congo. To mitigate the cost of the expropriation and maintain, they invented the mechanism related to the law of the falling rate of profit which is to spend little of what we earn to maintain the system. That's how to reproduce, the colonial system destroyed a small portion of his wealth to build schools, reference health centers, health clinics, social welfare . . . And in all this, the guiding principle was, primarily for the interests of the metropolis (Belgium).

In the light of historical facts, Belgium has operated almost everywhere in the Congo. But there is reason to wonder why Belgium by building schools, health centers of reference, the infrastructure of public interest . . . did so unevenly across the country? What was the reason behind this unfair distribution if we can speak in terms of distribution? In fact some provinces were more favored than others, while the productions of various provinces were replenishing the national fund (Leopoldville). It would perhaps be a fair allocation of resources to build schools, health centers, infrastructure . . . public interest. But it was not the case. By contrary Belgium favored some provinces than others. This had already creating differences, disparities, gaps between the Congolese.

At this point of view, we could perhaps understand if Congo was administered by Belgium as a federal republic where there are skills that accrue to Federal and those under the Federated States. Here one could understand that the work, the initiative in the various provinces justify the difference in infrastructure between provinces. But this was not the case because, although it has some similarities with federalism, Congo was managed as a unitary republic, characterized by unity of command, where the unit of power is exercised by the hierarchy through the State subdivision.

But we can notice shouting differences between the provinces, while no one can say without fear of contradiction that there is a province in the Congo that is so poor, to explain this difference. You'll notice that it was intended and maintained by policymakers.

Besides this, Belgium has worsened the situation by growing speech, thoughts, practices, anti-nationalist, tribalism, regionalism, hatred . . . and the Congo had gone on that strain. Certainly the problems could be missed among the tribes, villages, provinces . . . These could be perceived, considered like what happens in any society, because where there are men there is no shortage of problems and it is for men of this company to manage, minimize the emphasis on dialogue, the way the African palaver.

But the colonialists in the Congo have exploited the differences, there were some problems with emphasis on the division, misunderstanding, disputes . . . This is how Congo departured divided, weak and unprepared politically.

Faced with such a divided, weak, unprepared country, it would have had strong political structures and politicians ready and armed with a strong national consciousness that would guarantee national interests first, although international interests could not be removed completely.Because in this situation the international support is always important. But Belgium has developed structures requiring dependence and had also taken time to work on the consciousness of some political leaders, potential employees, agents pay not only for Belgium but also interested in the power lust of Congolese wealth.

Even when there was the partition of Africa, as also say Lumumba-Kasongo and Tukumbi "in the perception of those who were at the Berlin Conference, Africa was a land of opportunity for raw materials and men (labor less expensive), but a gap in the philosophical, historical and cultural." [67]

And each colonizing country has exploited this in his way. That is how for Belgium until 1960, the Congo could have less than ten university's

---

[67] Lumumba-Kasongo, Tukumbi: Towards Creating a Culture of Human Rights
      sustenance. _____
Induvidual contributors 1998 Windhoek: Gamsberg Macmillan 1998.

graduated (4[68]), with the exception of a few priests who have been graduated to major seminaries (Catholic seminaries).

In this regard, we must recognize that although almost all African countries were colonized, this settlement did not have the same effect as it was made by different countries and even though the same country but different models. Differences in infrastructure of public interest, the number of academics, kilometers of roads, paved roads, rails, health facilities . . . to independence in various countries are a reality, although the rails, roads in . . . colonized countries were first built in time to serve first the interests of the settler countries (transportation of raw materials to the mainland via the sea lanes). You can account for these differences in reading in the following tables:

A. THE AFRICAN COLONIES

I. BRITISH COLONIES

NO	COUNTRIES	AREA IN SQUARE KM	COLONISED SINCE	INDEPENDENCE IN	NUMBER OF YEARS OF COLONISATION
1	BOTSWANA	600.372	1885	1966	81
2	ZIMBABWE	390.580	1923	1980	57
3	ZAMBIA	752.614	1924	1964	40
4	UGANDA	236.036	1894	1962	68
5	KENYA	582.645	1895	1963	68
6	SUDAN	2.505.813	1899	1956	57
7	EGYPT	1.001.449	1882	1922	40
8	LIBIA	1.759.540	1912	1951	39
9	SOMALIA	637.657	1889	1960	71
10	NIGERIA	923.768	1861	1960	99
11	GHANA	238.537	1821	1957	136
12	SIERRALEONE	71.740	1787	1961	174
13	GAMBIA	11.295	1888	1965	77
14	MALAWIE	118.484	1891	1964	73

---

[68]. Lumumba-Kasongo, Tukumbi: op cit.

15	LESOTHO	30.355	1895	1963	68
16	SWAZILAND	17.363	1902	1968	66
17	SOUTH AFRICA	1.221.037	1856	1910	105
18	SEYCHELLES	445		1976	

II FORMER FRENCH COLONIES

1	CONGO BRAZZA	342.000	1910	1960	50
2	GABON	267.667	1839	1960	121
3	CENTRAL AFRICA REPUBLIC	622.984	1910	1960	50
4	TCHAD	1.284.000	1920	1960	40
5	NIGER	1.267.000	1891	1960	89
6	BURKINAFASSO	274.200	1891	1960	69
7	MALI	1.240.000	1935	1960	25
8	IVORY COAST	322.463	1882	1960	78
9	SENEGAL	196.192	1659	1960	301
10	BISSAU GUINEA	36.125	1892	1973	81
11	GUINEA	245.857	1886	1958	72
12	MAURITANIA	1.030.700	1921	1960	39
13	ALGERIA	2.381.741	1830	1962	132
14	TUNISIA	163.610	1881	1956	75
15	MOROCCO	446.550	1912	1956	44
16	BENIN	112.622	1894	1960	66
17	MADAGASCAR	594.180	1894	1960	66
18	MAURICIUS	1.865	1830	1968	138

III FORMER BELGIUM COLONIES

1	D.R.C	2.345.409	1908	1960	52

2	RWANDA	26.338	1919	1962	43
3	BURUNDI	27.834	1919	1962	43
IV	FORMER GERMAN COLONIES				
1	TOGO	56.000	1894	1960	66
2	CAMEROON	475.442	1884	1960/1961	76/75
3	TANZANIA	945.087	1884	1961	77
4	NAMIBIA	825.000	1884	1990	106
V	FORMER PORTUGESE COLONIES				
1	ANGOLA	1.246.700	1491	1975	484
2	MOZAMBIQUE	783.030	1505	1975	470
3	CAP VERDE	4.033	1492	1975	483
VI	FORMER SPANISH COLONIES				
1	EQUATO-GUINEA	28.051	16 S	1968	368
VII	FORMER ITALIAN COLONIES				
1	ERITREA	125.000	1889	1993	104
VIII	FREE FROM COLONISATION				
1	LIBERIA	111.369		1847	
2	ETSHIOPIA	1.221.900		1000 B.C	

Data on:

−the begining settlement's dates and dates of independence with the exception of dates of colonization: MOROCCO, MAURITIUS ISLANDS, SEYCHELLES, BURKINAFASSO are taken from: YESTERDAY AND TODAY THE WORLD. Social Studies c 1990. Silver Burdett Ginn Inc. and.

−Classification of countries by colonial country is from: The New Universal Family Encyclopedia. Jackt Randon House Inc. c 1985.

THE DATA AT INDEPENDENCE

I. FORMER ENGLISH COLONIES

	COUNTRIES	POPULATION	ACADEMICS	% OF ACADEMICS
1	BOTSWANA	535.000		
2	ZIMBABWE	7.126.000	8000	0,1122
3	ZAMBIA	3.596.000	536 (in 1967)	0,0149
4	UGANDA	7.313.000	888 (in 1965)	0,0121
5	KENYA	8.855.000	362	0,0040
6	SUDAN	10.404.000	802	0,0077
7	EGYPT	13.551.000	2.282 (in 1921)	0,0168
8	LIBIA	1.035.000	2.000 (in 1967)	0,1932
9	SOMALIA	2.230.000	548 (in 1969)	0,0245
10	NIGERIA	42.739.000	7.000 (in 1964)	0,0163
11	GHANA	6.034.000	960	0,0159
12	SIERRALEONNE	2.209.000	341	0,0154
13	GAMBIA	384.000		
14	MALAWI	3.794.000	487 (in 1966)	0,0128
15	LESOTHO	917.000		
16	SWAZILAND	398.000		
17	REP OF SOUTH AFRICA	5.842.000	1.171	0,0200
18	SEYCHELLES	60.000		

II. FORMER FRENCH COLONIES

1	CONGO BRAZZA	969.000	2.570 (in 1973)	0,2652
2	GABON	472.000	30 (in 1968)	0,0063
3	CENTRAL AFRICA REP	1.534.000	292 (in 1973)	0,0190
4	CHAD	3.064.000	605 (in 1973)	0,0197
5	NIGER	3.028.000	300 (in 1972)	0,0099
6	BURKINAFASSO	4.452.000	193 (in 1969)	0,0043

7	MALI	4.375.000	104 (in 1964)	0,0023
8	IVORY-COST	3.230.000	3.000 (in 1967)	0,0928
9	SENEGAL	3.187.000	1.459	0,0457
10	BISSAU-GUINEA	507.000		
11	GUINEA		12.000 (in 1975)	
12	MAURITANIA	662.000	4.526 (in 1985)	0,6836
13	ALGERIA	10.920.000	2.809	0,0257
14	TUNISIA	3.783.000	2.163	0,0571
15	MAROCCO	10.396.000	3.792	0,0364
16	BENIN	2.237.000	220 (in 1969)	0,0098
17	MALAGASY REPUBLIC		1.130	
18	MAURITIUS	787.400	178	0,0226

III. FORMER BELGIUM COLONIES

1	D.R.C	14.140.000	1.256 (in 1961) 564 (in 1959)	0,0088 0,0039
2	RWANDA	2.924.000	161 (in 1967)	0,0055
3	BURUNDI	2.996.000	397 (in 1969)	0,0132

IV. FORMER GERMAN COLONIES

1	TOGO	1.444.000	1.491 (in 1971)	0,1032
2	CAMEROON	5.681.000/5.773.000	1.986 (in 1967)	0,0349 0,0344
3	TANZANIA	10.584.000	523 (in 1965)	0,0049
4	NAMIBIA	1.339.000		

V. FORMER PORTUGUESE COLONIES

1	ANGOLA	6.117.000	1.254 (in 1978)	0,0205
2	MOZAMBIQUE	10.498.000	906 (in 1970)	0,0009
3	CAPE VERDE	299.800		

VI. FORMER SPANISH COLONY

1	EQUATORIAL GUINEA	281.000		
VII.	INDEPENDENTS			
1	LIBERIA			
2	ETSHIOPIA			

—The area is derived from Follett Student Atlas. Compiled Under the direction of Herbert H. Gross, PhD c 1975 by Follett publishing company. 1980 printing.

—The date of colonization of Morocco is from Understanding history 9. Namibian Junior Secondary text book. COLONIAL HISTORY OF NAMIBIA, AFRICA and the WORLD. John Katzao, Nangolo Mbumba, bryn Ó Callaghan, Helgard Patemann, I Eddie Van Staden, HA Tait davy c CASS/Namibia Namibia Project and Longman 1993.

—Dates of colonization: Libya, Mauritius, Somalia, Burkinafasso, Guinea, Swaziland, are taken from: Academic American Encyclopedia.

The data on:—the people at independence, with the exception of the DRC, are from HISTORICAL DATA DEMOGRAPHICAL OF THE WHOLE COUNTRY for each country to the Internet (Google)

—The population at independence (DRC) and the number of graduate students, are from: INTERNATIONAL HISTORICAL STATISTICS. AFRICA, ASIA AND OCEANIA 1750-2000. 4 ISSUE B.R MITCHELL.

LENGTH OF ROADS IN KILOMETERS IN 1962

I. FORMER ENGLISH COLONIES

	COUNTRIES	ROADS IN KILOMETERS	AREA IN KM	KILOMETERS OF ROADS BY 1000 KM	YEAR OTHER THAN 1962
1	BASUTOLAND (LESOTHO)	1.469	30.000	48	
2	BECHUANALAND (BOTSWANA)	1.600	712.249	2	

3	EGYPT	20.228	1.000.000	20	1958
4	GAMBIA	859	10.369	83	
5	GHANA	12.875	237.873	54	1958
6	KENYA	40.000	582.646	70	
7	LIBIA	* 3.831	1.759.540	2	
8	NIGERIA	60.904	878.447	69	
9	SOUTHERN RHODESIA (ZIMBABWE)	59.312	389.362	152	
10	SEYCHELLES	137	404	339	
11	RHODESIA AND NYASALAND, FEDERATION OF NORTHERN RHODESIA	31.945	746.256	43	
12	NYASALAND	9.608	117.498	82	
13	SIERRA LEONNE	4.537	72.326	63	
14	SOMALIA	14.300	637.661	22	
15	SOUTH AFRICA REPUBLIC OF	180.459	1.223.409	148	
16	SOUTH WEST AFRICA (NAMIBIA)	55.000	823.876	66	
17	SUDAN	y 30.000	2.505.823	10	
18	SWAZILAND	1.479	17.363	85	
19	UGANDA	18.833	243.410	77	
II.	FORMER FRENCH COLONIES				
1	ALGERIA	68.716	2.381.741	19	1958
2	CENTRAL AFRICAN REPUBLIC	16.000	617.000	26	
3	TCHAD	10.000	1.284.000	8	
4	CONGO BRAZZA	+ 8.400	342.000	25	
5	GABON	5.104	267.000	19	
6	IVORY COAST	28.000	322.463	87	
7	MALAGASY REPUBLIC	30.000	590.000	51	1960
8	MALI	13.000	1.204.021	11	

9	MAURITANIA	2.700	1.085.805	3	
10	MAURITIUS	1.254	2.096	598	
11	MOROCCO	46.172	443.680	104	1960
12	NIGER	15.056	1.188.794	69	
13	SENEGAL	10.000	197.161	50	
14	TUNISIA	9.145	125.180	73	
15	UPPER VOLTA (BURKINAFASO)	13.000	274.122	47	
III.	FORMER BELGIUM COLONIES				
1	D.R.C	145.213	2.344.932	62	1958
2	RWANDA-BURUNDI	12.083	54.172	223	1958
IV.	FORMER GERMAN COLONIES				
1	CAMEROON	12.000	432.500	28	
2	TANGANIKA	32.000	937.061	34	
3	ZANZIBAR AND PEMBA	907	2.643	343	
4	TOGO	4.546	57.000	80	1957
5	SOUTH WEST AFRICA (NAMIBIA)	55.000	823.876	66	
V.	FORMER PORTUGUES	COLONIES			
1	ANGOLA	35.509	1.246.700	29	1959
2	CAPE VERDE	545	4.033	135	1959
3	MOZAMBIQUE	37.564	783.000	48	1959
4	PORTUGUESE GUINEA	3.289	36.125	91	1958
VI.	FORMER SPANISH	COLONY			
1	SPANISH EQUATORIAL REGION	1.100	28.051	39	
VII	INDEPENDENTS				
1	LIBERIA	3.200	111.370	29	
2	ETSHIOPIA	6.000	1.184.320	5	

DATA OF THE RAIL WAY AT INDEPENDENCE

	COUNTRIES	KM OF RAIL WAY	PROPORTION OF RAIL WAY COMPARED TO THE AREA
1	BOTSWANA	634	0.1056
2	ZIMBABWE	3.415	0.8743
3	ZAMBIE	4.260	0.5660
4	UGANDA	1.050 (en1975)	0.4448
5	KENYA	6.872	1.1794
6	SUDAN	3.604	0.1438
7	EGYPT	4.398	0.4391
8	LIBIA	342	0.0194
9	SOMALIA	113 (1953)	0.0177
10	NIGERIA	2.864	0.3100
11	GHANA	951	0.3986
12	SIERRA LEONNE	500	0.6969
13	GAMBIA		
14	MALAWI	509	0.4295
15	LESOTHO		
16	SWAZILAND		
17	SOUTH AFRICAN REPUBLIC	12.208	0.9998
18	SEYCHELLES		
II.	**FORMER FRENCH COLONIES**		
1	CONGO BRAZZA	515	0.1505
2	GABON		
3	CENTRAL AFRICAN REPUBLIC		
4	CHAD		
5	NIGER		
6	BURKINAFASO		
7	MALI	645	0.0520

8	IVORY-COAST	1.173	0.3637
9	SENEGAL	977	0.4979
10	GUINEA BISSAU		
11	GUINEA		
12	MAURITANIA	650(en 1963)	0.0630
13	ALGERIA	3.928	0.1649
14	TUNISIA	2.106	1.2872
15	MOROCCO	1.785	0.3997
16	BENIN	579	0.5141
17	MALAGASY REPUBLICR	860	0.1447
18	MAURITIUS	132 (en 1959)	7.0777

III. FORMER BELGIUM COLONIES

1	D.R.C	5.074	0.2163
2	RWANDA		
3	BURUNDI		

IV. FORMER GERMAN COLONIES

1	TOGO	445	0.7946
2	CAMEROON	517	0.1087
3	TANZANIA	4.460 (en 1975)	0.4719
4	NAMIBIA		

v. FORMER PORTUGUESE COLONIES

1	ANGOLA	2.952	0.2367
2	MOZAMBIQUE	3.696	0.4720
3	CAPE VERDE		
IV.	FORMER ITALIAN COLONY		
1	ERITREA	306 (en 1975)	0.2448

In the table of road length in kilometers in 1962:

−+: Julliard, René (Ed.) see bibliography.

−*: Steinberg, S.h. (Ed.) see bibliography.

—Y Europa Ltd publication. cf. bibliography.

Data on road length in kilometers in and around 1962 (1957-60) are from:
AFRIKA-INSTITUTE ATLAS. AFRICA MAPS AND STATISTICS No 1 July 1962.

Data on the miles of rail to independence are from:
INTERNATIONAL HISTORICAL STATISTICS—AFRICA, ASIA AND OCEANIA 1750-2000
4 Edition. B.R MITCELL.

HEALTH INFRASTRUCTURE IN 1958 AND AROUND

I. FORMER BRITISH COLONIES

No	COUNTRIES	YEAR	STATE HOSPITAL (GENERAL HOSPITAL)		SPECIALISED HOSPITAL		MEDICAL CLINIC		TOTAL		POPULATION PAR LIT DANS LES HOPITAUX ET CENTRES MEDICAUX
			NUMBER	BEDS	NUMBER	BEDS	NUMBER	BEDS	NUMBER	BEDS	
1	BOTSWANA	1958	...	741	1	30	-	-	...	741	430
2	ZIMBABWE (SOUTHERN RHODESIA)	1958	189	109.955	25	1.589	-	-	214	112.544	220
3	ZAMBIA (RHODESIA AND NYASALAND FED OF NORTHERN RHODESIA)	1958	91	7.043	5	1.056	196	965	292	9.064	250
4	UGANDA	1958	...	5.000	2	470	...	3.710	...	9.180	700
5	KENYA	1958	...	7.150	...	2.021	...	...	...	9.171	700
6	SUDAN	1958	50	8.078	-	-	...	2.094	...	10.172	1.100
7	EGYPT	1956	261	20.479	329	20.578	358	5.396	948	46.453	510

8	LIBIA	1958	13	2.826	5	690	11	80	29	3.606	320
9	SOMALIA	1958	16	2.280	3	260	26	247	45	2.787	705
10	NIGERIA	1958	182	13.697	31	1.850	-	-	213	15.547	2.100
11	GHANA	1955	...	2.582	-	-	-	-	-	2.582	1.800
12	SIERRA LEONNE	1958	29	1.753	-	-	4	25	33	1.778	1.300
13	GAMBIA	1957	2	220	1	24	6	30	9	274	1.000
14	MALAWI (NYASALAND)	1958	79	3.235	1	280	...	77	...	3.515	750
15	LESOTHO (BASUTOLAND)	1958	13	774	-	-	-	-	13	774	850
16	SWAZILAND	1958	9	539	...	...	...	...	9	539	500
17	SOUTH AFRICAN REP	1960	450	58.142	98	4.050	67	3.581	615	65.773	240
18	SEYCHELLES	1958	4	208	1	60	1	2	6	270	160

II. FORMER FRENCH COLONIES

1	CONGO BRAZZA	1958	60	2.930	-	-	20	886	80	3.816	200
2	GABON	1959	4	...	5	...	30	...	39	3.680	110
3	CENTRAL AFRICAN REP	1958	7	814	-	-	74	327	81	1.141	1.020

№	Country	Year									
4	CHAD	1958	22	1.765	-	-	64	320	86	2.085	1.250
5	NIGER	1959	30	1.044	...	...	19	25	49	1.069	2.300
6	BURKINAFASO	1958	2	...	...	...	67	...	...	1.965	1.700
7	MALI	1958	3	592	7	420	32	2.537	42	3.549	1.000
8	IVORY COAST	1958	3	543	-	-	326	4.554	329	5.097	610
9	SENEGAL	1958	37	1.736	-	-	4	50	41	1.786	1.300
10	BISSAU GUINEA										
11	GUINEA		...								
12	MAURITANIA	1959	3	...	7	...	13	...	23	...	...
13	ALGERIA	1958	150	28.566	...	...	...	...	150	28.566	330
14	TUNISIA	1957	66	6.373	1	605	32	841	99	7.819	490
15	MOROCCO	1959	127	12.574	23	5.425	-	-	150	17.999	580
16	BENIN (DAHOMEY)	1958	...	...	...	...	...	...	439	...	...
17	MALAGASY REP	1959	200	10.127	...	...	247	2.866	447	12.993	410
18	MAURITIUS	1958	34	1.791	5	964	-	-	39	2.755	220

III. FORMER BELGIUM COLONIES

№	Country	Year									
1	D.R.C	1958	459	52.255	99	14.293	2.483	20.051	3.041	86.599	160

2	RWANDA BURUNDI	1958	35	3.823	23	1.360	96	1.086	154	6.269	750
IV. FORMER GERMAN COLONIES											
1	TOGO	1956	11	1.490	18	450	4	54	33	1.994	550
2	CAMEROON	1958	85	10.215	11	60	315	1.048	400	11.263	1.570
3	TANZANIA	1958	172	12.010	14	1.691	52	1.827	238	15.528	1.010
4	NAMIBIA	1958	20	1.350	...	...	...	....	20	1.350	390
V. FORMER PORTUGUESE COLONIES											
1	ANGOLA	1957	15	...	46	...	158	...	219	...	...
2	MOZAMBIQUE	1958	80	...	2	...	....	....	82	...	...
3	CAPE VERDE	1957	3	...	5	...	....	....	8	...	...
VI. INDEPENDENTS											
1	LIBERIA	1956	20	742	1	50	-	-	21	792	1.600
2	ETSHIOPIA	1956	61	6.489	3	390	-	-	64	6.879	3.000

−1. ...: means data not available.−2.: means nil or magnitude negligible.

MEDICAL PERSONEL IN 195

1. FORMER BRITISH COLONIES

NO	COUNTRIES	YEAR	DOCTORS	OTHER MEDICAL PERSONEL	TOTAL	PEOPLE BY DOCTOR AND OTHER MEDICAL PERSONNEL
1	BOTSWANA	1958	20	-	20	17.000
2	ZIMBABWE	1959	688	-	688	4.400
3	ZAMBIA	1959	299	8	307	7.800
4	UGANDA	1958	377	373	750	7.700
5	KENYA	19558	607	88	695	9.100
6	SUDAN	1958	250	501	751	150.000
7	EGYPT	1958	8.854	. . .	8.854	2.800
8	LIBIA	1958	149	-	149	7.800
9	SOMALIA	1958	80	30	110	27.500
10	NIGERIA	1959	958	-	958	35.000
11	GHANA	1955	182	43	225	21.000
12	SIERRA LEONNE	1958	36	. . .	36	66.670
13	GAMBIA	1958	15	-	15	19.000
14	MALAWI	1959	80	7	87	32.000
15	LESOTHO	1958	32	3	35	19.000
16	SWAZILAND	1958	23	8	31	7.870
17	SOUTH AFRICA AND (S.W.A)	1960	7.939	-	7.939	2.060
18	SEYCHELLES	1058	7	-	7	6.000

II. FORMER FRENCH COLONIES

1	CONGO BRAZZA	1958	49	15	64	12.000
2	GABON	1959	51	. . .	51	8.200
3	CENTRAL AFRICAN REP	1958	32	9	41	28.000
4	CHAD	1958	34	4	38	68.000

5	NIGER	1958	26	14	40	62.000
6	BURKINAFASO	1959	64	. . .	64	5.520
7	MALI	1959	53	45	98	44.000
8	IVORY COAST	1958	100	75	175	18.000
9	SENEGAL	1959	55	59	114	22.000
10	BISSAU GUINEA					
11	GUINEA	. . .	. . .	. . .	. . .	. . .
12	MAURITANIA	1954	7	. . .	7	81.000
13	ALGERIA	1958	2.070	-	2.070	4.700
14	TUNISIA	1956	548	-	548	6.900
15	MOROCCO	1959	1.093	-	1.093	10.000
16	BENIN	1960	63	. . .	63	30.000
17	MALAGASY REPUBLIC	1959	195	449	644	8.000
18	MAURITIUS	1958	132	-	132	4.600

III. FORMER BELGIUM COLONIES

1	D.R.C	1958	703	128	831	16.000
2	RWANDA BURUNDI	1958	89	92	181	26.000

IV. FORMER GERMAN COLONIES

1	TOGO	1956	22	14	36	30.000
2	CAMEROON	1958/1959	139	49	188	73.000
3	TANZANIA	1959	547	265	812	19.100
4	NAMIBIA					

V. FORMER PORTUGUESE COLONIES

1	ANGOLA	1958	217	-	217	20.770
2	MOZAMBIQUE	1959	187	-	187	33.750
3	CAPE VERDE	1959	17	-	17	11.500

VI. INDEPENDENTS

1	LIBERIA	1956	62	-	62	20.000
2	ETSHIOPIA	1956	207	. . .	207	105.000

Data:

−Health facilities in and around 1958.

−Medical staff in 1958 are from: AFRIKA-INSTITUTE ATLAS. MAPS AND STATISTICS JULY 1962 N0.

In the following tables are arranged in order of size, proportion of data that are in the tables above.

THE PERCENTAGE OF GRADUATE STUDENTS AT INDEPENDENCE IN ORDER OF LARGEST TO SMALLEST

	COUNTRIES	%	NUMBER OF COLONIZATION	FORMER COLONY
1	MAURITANIA	0,6836	39	FRENCH
2	CONGO BRAZZA	0,2652	50	FRENCH
3	LIBIA	0,1932	39	BRITISH
4	ZIMBABWE	0,1122	57	BRITISH
5	TOGO	0,1032	66	GERMAN
6	IVORY COAST	0,0928	78	FRENCH
7	TUNISIA	0,0571	75	FRENCH
8	SENEGAL	0,0457	301	FRENCH
9	MOROCCO	0,0364	44	FRENCH
10	CAMEROON	0,0349 0,0344	76/75	GERMAN
11	ALGERIA	0,0257	132	FRENCH
12	SOMALIA	0,0245	71	BRITISH
13	MAURITIUS	0,0226	138	FRENCH
14	ANGOLA	0,0205	484	PORTUGUESE
15	SOUTH AFRICAN REP	0,0200	105	BRITISH
16	CHAD	0,0197	40	FRENCH
17	CENTRAL AFRICAN REP	0,0190	50	FRENCH
18	EGYPT	0,0168	40	BRITISH
19	NIGERIA	0,0163	99	BRITISH
20	GHANA	0,0159	136	BRITISH

21	SIERRA LEONNE	0,0154	174	BRITISH
22	ZAMBIA	0,0149	40	BRITISH
23	BURUNDI	0,0132	43	BELGIUM
24	MALAWI	0,0128	73	BRITISH
25	UGANDA	0,0121	68	BRITISH
26	NIGER	0,0099	89	FRENCH
27	BENIN	0,0098	66	FRENCH
28	D.R.C	0,0088 0,0039	52	BELGIUM
29	SUDAN	0,0077	57	BRITISH
30	GABON	0,0063	121	FRENCH
31	RWANDA	0,055	43	BELGIUM
32	TANZANIA	0,0049	77	GERMAN
33	BURKINAFASO	0,0043	69	FRENCH
34	KENYA	0,0040	68	BRITISH
35	MALI	0,0023	25	FRENCH
36	MOZAMBIQUE	0,0009	470	PORTUGUESE

PROPORTION OF ROADS (km of road per 1000 km2 in 1962) AND AROUND IN ORDER, LARGEST TO SMALLEST

	COUNTRIES	KM OF ROAD BY 1000KM2	NUMBER OF COLONIZATION	FORMER COLONY
1	MAURITIUS	598	138	FRENCH
2	SEYCHELLES	339		BRITISH
3	TANZANIA (ZANZIBAR, PEMBA ET TANGANIKA	377	77	GERMAN
4	RWANDA-BURUNDI	223	43	BELGIUM
5	SOUTHERN RHODESIA (ZIMBABWE)	152	57	BRITISH
6	SOUTH AFRICAN REP	148	105	BRITISH
7	CAPE VERDE	135	483	PORTUGUESE
8	MOROCCO	104	44	FRENCH
9	PORTUGUESE GUINEA	91		PORTUGUESE
10	IVORY COAST	87	78	FRENCH
11	SWAZILAND	85	66	BRITISH
12	GAMBIA	83	77	BRITISH
13	NYASALAND (MALAWI)	82	73	BRITISH
14	TOGO	80	66	GERMAN
15	UGANDA	77	68	BRITISH
16	TUNISIA	73	75	FRENCH
17	KENYA	70	68	BRITISH
18	NIGERIA	69	99	BRITISH
18	NIGER	69	89	FRENCH
19	NAMIBIA (S.W.A)	66	106	GERMAN
20	SIERRA LEONNE	63	174	BRITISH
21	D.R.C	62	52	BELGIUM
22	GHANA	54	136	BRITISH
23	MALAGASY REP	51	66	FRENCH
24	SENEGAL	50	301	FRENCH
25	BASUTOLAND (LESOTHO)	48	68	BRITISH
26	BURKINAFASO (UPPER VOLTA)	47	+−160	FRENCH

27	RHODESIA AND NYASALAND OF NORTHERN RHODESIA	43	40	BRITISH
28	SPANISH EQUATORIAL REGION	39		SPANISH
29	ANGOLA	29	484	PORTUGUESE
29	LIBERIA	29		
30	CAMEROON	28	76/75	GERMAN
31	CENTRAL AFRICAN REP	26	50	FRENCH
32	CONGO BRAZZA	25	50	FRENCH
33	SOMALIA	22	71	BRITISH
34	EGYPT	20	40	BRITISH
35	ALGERIA	19	132	FRENCH
35	GABON	19	121	FRENCH
36	MALI	11	25	FRENCH
37	SUDAN	10	57	BRITISH
38	CHAD	8	40	FRENCH
39	ETSHIOPIA	5		
40	MAURITANIA	3	39	FRENCH

PROPORTION OF RAIL IN KM AT INDEPENDENCE IN ORDER OF MAGNITUDE. THE BIGGEST TO SMALLEST

	COUNTRIES	PROPORTION OF RAIL COMPARED TO THE AREA	NUMBER OF THE YEARS OF COLONIZATION	FORMER COLONY
1	MAURITIUS	7.0777	138	FRENCH
2	TUNISIA	1.2872	75	FRENCH
3	KENYA	1.1794	68	BRITISH
4	SOUTH AFRICAN REP	0.9998	105	BRITISH
5	ZIMBABWE	0.8743	57	BRITISH
6	TOGO	0.7946	66	GERMAN
7	SIERRA LEONNE	0.6969	174	BRITISH
8	ZAMBIA	0.5660	40	BRITISH
9	BENIN	0.5141	66	FRENCH
10	SENEGAL	0.4979	301	FRENCH
11	MOZAMBIQUE	0.4720	470	PORTUGUESE
12	TANZANIA	0.4719	77	GERMAN
13	UGANDA	0.4448	68	BRITISH
14	EGYPT	0.4391	40	BRITISH
15	MALAWI	0.4295	73	BRITISH
16	MOROCCO	0.3997	44	FRENCH
17	GHANA	0.3986	136	BRITISH
18	IVORY COAST	0.3637	78	FRENCH
19	NIGERIA	0.3100	99	BRITISH
20	ERITREA	0.2448	104	ITALIAN
21	ANGOLA	0.2367	484	PORTUGUESE
22	D.R.C	0.2163	52	BELGIUM
23	ALGERIA	0.1649	132	FRENCH
24	CONGO BRAZZA	0.1505	50	FRENCH
25	MALAGASY REP	0.1447	66	FRENCH
26	SUDAN	0.1438	57	BRITISH
27	CAMEROON	0.1087	76/75	GERMAN
28	BOTSWANA	0.1056	81	BRITISH

29	MAURITANIA	0.0630	39	FRENCH
30	MALI	0.0520	25	FRENCH
31	LIBIA	0.0194	39	BRITISH
32	SOMALIA	0.0177	71	BRITISH

NUMBER OF PEOPLE BY BED IN HOSPITALS AND MEDICAL CENTERS AROUND 1958, IN ORDER (FROM THE SMALLEST TO THE BIGGEST.

	COUNTRIES	YEARS	POPULATION BY BED	NUMBER OF COLONIZATION	FORMER COLONIE
1	GABON	1959	110	121	FRENCH
2	D.R.C	1958	160	52	BELGIUM
2	SEYCHELLES	1958	160		BRITISH
3	CONGO BRAZZA	1958	200	50	FRENCH
4	ZIMBABWE	1958	220	57	BRITISH
4	MAURITIU	1958	220	138	FRENCH
5	SOUTH AFRICAN REP	1960	240	105	BRITISH
6	ZAMBIA	1958	250	40	BRITISH
7	LIBIA	1958	320	39	BRITISH
8	ALGERIA	1958	330	132	FRENCH
9	NAMIBIA	1958	390	106	GERMAN
10	MALAGASY REP	1959	410	66	FRENCH
11	BOTSWANA	1958	430	81	BRITISH
12	TUNISIA	1957	490	75	FRENCH
13	SWAZILAND	1958	500	66	BRITISH
14	EGYPT	1956	510	40	BRITISH
15	TOGO	1956	550	66	GERMAN
16	MOROCCO	1959	580	44	FRENCH
17	IVORY COAST	1958	610	78	FRENCH
18	UGANDA	1958	700	68	BRITISH
18	KENYA	1958	700	68	BRITISH

19	SOMALIA	1958	705	71	BRITISH
20	RWANDA-BURUNDI	1958	750	43	BELGIUM
20	MALAWI	1958	750	73	BRITISH
21	LESOTHO	1958	850	68	BRITISH
22	MALI	1958	1.000	25	FRENCH
22	GAMBIA	1957	1.000	77	BRITISH
23	TANZANIA	1958	1.010	77	GERMAN
24	CENTRAL AFRICAN REP	1958	1.020	50	FRENCH
25	SUDAN	1958	1.100	57	BRITISH
26	CHAD	1958	1.250	40	FRENCH
27	SIERRA LEONNE	1958	1.300	174	BRITISH
27	SENEGAL	1958	1.300	301	FRENCH
28	CAMEROON	1958	1.570	76/75	GERMAN
29	LIBERIA	1956	1.600		INDEPENDENT
30	BURKINAFASO	1958	1.700	69	FRENCH
31	GHANA	1955	1.800	136	BRITISH
32	NIGERIA	1958	2.100	99	BRITISH
33	NIGER	1959	2.300	89	FRENCH
34	ETSHIOPIA	1956	3.000		

NUMBER OF PEOPLE BY DOCTOR AND OTHER MEDICAL PERSONNEL IN 1958 IN ORDER

NO	COUNTRIES	INHABITANT BY DOCTOR AND OTHER MEDICAL PERSONNEL	NUMBER OF YEARS OF COLONIZATION	FORMER COLONY
1	SOUTH AFRICAN REP	2.060	105	BRITISH
2	EGYPT	2.800	40	BRITISH
3	ZIMBABWE	4.400	57	BRITISH
4	MAURITIUS	4.600	138	FRENCH
5	ALGERIA	4.700	132	FRENCH
6	BURKINAFASO	5.520	69	FRENCH
7	SEYCHELLES	6.000		BRITISH
8	TUNISIA	6.900	75	FRENCH
9	UGANDA	7.700	68	BRITISH
10	ZAMBIA	7.800	40	BRITISH
10	LIBIA	7.800	39	BRITISH
11	SWAZILAND	7.870	66	BRITISH
12	MALAGASY REP	8.000	66	FRENCH
13	GABON	8.200	121	FRENCH
14	KENYA	9.100	68	BRITISH
15	MOROCCO	10.000	44	FRENCH
16	CAPE VERDE	11.500	483	PORTUGUESE
17	CONGO BRAZZA	12.000	50	FRENCH
18	D.R.C	16.000	52	BELGIUM
19	BOTSWANA	17.000	81	BRITISH
20	IVORY COAST	18.000	78	FRENCH
21	LESOTHO	19.000	68	BRITISH
21	GAMBIA	19.000	77	BRITISH
22	TANZANIA	19.100	77	GERMAN
23	LIBERIA	20.000		INDEPENDENT
24	ANGOLA	20.770	484	PORTUGUESE
25	GHANA	21.000	136	BRITISH
26	SENEGAL	22.000	301	FRENCH

27	RWANDA-BURUNDI	26.000	43	BELGIUM
28	SOMALIA	27.500	71	BRITISH
29	CENTRAL AFRICAN REP	28.000	50	FRENCH
30	TOGO	30.000	66	GERMAN
31	BENIN	30.700	66	FRENCH
32	MALAWI	32.000	73	BRITISH
33	MOZAMBIQUE	33.750	470	PORTUGUESE
34	NIGERIA	35.000	99	BRITISH
35	MALI	44.000	25	FRENCH
36	NIGER	62.000	89	FRENCH
37	SIERRA LEONNE	66.670	174	BRITISH
38	CHAD	68.000	40	FRENCH
39	CAMEROON	73.000	76/75	GERMAN
40	MAURITANIA	81.000	72	FRENCH
41	ETSHIOPIA	105.300		INDEPENDENT
42	SUDAN	150.000	57	BRITISH

NUMBER OF YEARS OF SETTLEMENT IN ORDER

	COUNTRIES	NUMBER OF COLONIZATION'S YEARS	FORMER COLONY
1	ANGOLA	484	PORTUGUESE
2	CAPE VERDE	483	PORTUGUESE
3	MOZAMBIQUE	470	PORTUGUESE
4	EQUATORIAL GUINEA	368	SPANISH
5	SENEGAL	301	FRENCH
6	SIERRA LEONNE	174	BRITISH
7	MAURITIUS	138	FRENCH
8	GHANA	136	BRITISH
9	ALGERIA	132	FRENCH
10	GABON	121	FRENCH
11	NAMIBIA	106	GERMAN

12	SOUTH AFRICAN REP	105	BRITISH
13	NIGERIA	99	BRITISH
14	NIGER	89	FRENCH
15	BOTSWANA	81	BRITISH
15	BISSAU GUINEA	81	FRENCH
16	IVORY COAST	78	FRENCH
17	GAMBIA	77	BRITISH
17	TANZANIA	77	GERMAN
18	CAMEROON	76	GERMAN
19	TUNISIA	75	FRENCH
20	MALAWI	73	BRITISH
21	GUINEA	72	FRENCH
22	SOMALIA	71	BRITISH
23	BURKINAFASO	69	FRENCH
24	LESOTHO	68	BRITISH
24	UGANDA	68	BRITISH
24	KENYA	68	BRITISH
25	BENIN	66	FRENCH
25	TOGO	66	GERMAN
25	SWAZILAND	66	BRITISH
25	MALAGASY REP	66	FRENCH
26	SUDAN	57	BRITISH
26	ZIMBABWE	57	BRITISH
27	D.R.C	52	BELGIUM
28	CENTRAL AFRICAN REP	50	FRENCH
28	CONGO BRAZZA	50	FRENCH
29	MAROC	44	FRENCH
30	BURUNDI	43	BELGIUM
30	RWANDA	43	BELGIUM
31	EGYPT	40	BRITISH
31	ZAMBIA	40	BRITISH
31	CHAD	40	FRENCH
32	MAURITANIA	39	FRENCH
33	MALI	25	FRENCH

The data in the tables above, are related to data independence. But for those whose data independence is not available, we took around the dates of independence.

And here we advise the reader that these data around the dates of independence should be considered as illustrative (to give us an idea of the facts) and not exhaustive.

GDP/cap IN RAND (SOUTH AFRICAN REP CURRENCY) IN 1961 IN ORDE

NO	COUNTRIES	G.D.P/Cap IN RAND	FORMER COLONY
1	SOUTH AFRICA,NAMIBIA,BOTSWANA, LESOTHO, SWAZILAND	343e	BRITISH
2	ALGERIA	200	FRENCH
3	LIBIA	148	BRITISH
4	GHANA	142	BRITISH
5	IVORY COAST	129	FRENCH
6	SENEGAL	125	FRENCH
7	ZIMBABWE, ZAMBIA, MALAWI	116m	BRITISH
8	TUNISIA	114	FRENCH
9	MOROCCO	107	FRENCH
10	GABON	95	FRENCH
11	EGYPT	86	BRITISH
12	SUDAN	67	BRITISH
13	D.R.C	60c	BELGIUM
14	NIGERIA	58	BRITISH
15	KENYA	57	BRITISH
16	MALAGASY REP	54	FRENCH
17	SIERRA LEONNE	50	BRITISH
17	TOGO	50	GERMAN
17	CAMEROON	50b	GERMAN
18	UGANDA	49	BRITISH

19	GUINEA	43	FRENCH
20	MALI	42	FRENCH
20	BURUNDI	42	BELGIUM
20	TANZANIA	42	GERMAN
21	ETSHIOPIA	32	INDEPENDENT
22	CONGO BRAZZA	31	FRENCH
23	RWANDA	28	BELGIUM
23	CHAD	28	FRENCH
23	NIGER	28	FRENCH
23	BURKINAFASO	28	FRENCH
24	SOMALIA	20d	

Around 1960 when the Congo through the Congolese leaders, the case of Lumumba, demanded immediate independence, the Belgian had felt it was very early and had to wait on the plan Van Bill Sen until 1985.

From this point of view we want to exploit the variable time, the variable number of years between colonization and independence, and its impact on the future life of the colonized countries. The number of years would be an important determinant in the development of the colonized countries?

Data on the GDP/Cap in 1961, one year after the independence of Congo, are from: AFRIKA-INSTITUTE ATLAS. AFRICA MAPS AND STATISTICS N 1 JULY 1962.

In the column G.D.P/Cap in 1961, there are:
−B. GDP/Cap data refers only to East CAMEROON with a population of 3.3 million.
−C. Refers to1959 total GNP per capita,figure expressed in terms of 1959 population of 13.8 million.
−D. Refers to Southern Region with population of only 1.4 million.
−E. Including South West Africa, Basutoland, Bechuanaland and Swaziland.
−M. These three countries were in a federation (Rhodesia, Nyasaland, Fed of).

Based on this assumption, greater was the number of years of colonization, the greater the colony had probably the time to prepare ready for true independence.

But you could realize in the preceding pages that the colonial powers in Africa did not come to prepare the colonies to self-management, since before the colonial powers came, African countries had their management, which could have developed more positively over time.

If it is true that the settlers, colonized countries in good faith and wanted to prepare the colony for the benefit of the colony, it would be seen through the preparations for this philanthropy, charity. The colonizing country would do its best to let:

−A sufficient basic infrastructure: roads, railways (linking the country to help integrate economic and social and political), and also connecting to other countries.
−A production relatively proportional to the wealth of the country.
−Health infrastructure, educational infrastructure and academic proportionate to the population and the economy.
−A body of ideas to promote unity, social cohesion, national harmony.

Now let's see the facts, taking the examples of:

I. THE FORMER FRENCH COLONIES

1. Senegal with 301 years of colonization, had:
−1459 graduated at university or colleges to independence, is 0.0457% as the proportion of graduated from the population at independence.
−977 km of rail to independence, or 0.4979 share of rail compared to the size of the country.
−10,000 km of road is 50 km per 1000 km2 in 1962, two years after independence.
−22,000 people per doctor and other medical staff in 1959, one year before independence.

−1,300 people per bed in hospitals and medical centers in 1958, two years before independence.

−And a GDP/Cap 125-R (rand) in 1961, one year after independence.

2. The islands of Mauritius with 138 years of colonization, had :

−178 graduate students (universities or colleges) to independence, or 0.0226% of the population at independence.

−132 km of rail in 1959 (nine years before independence), or 7.0777 of proportion to the area.

−1254 Km of road is 598 Km per 1000 Km2 in 1962, six years before independence.

−4,600 people per doctor and other medical staff in 1958, ten years before independence.

−220 persons per bed in hospitals and health centers in 1958.

−But the GDP/Cap en1961 is not available.

3. ALGERIA with 132 years of colonization, had:

−2809 graduate students to independence, or 0.0257% of the population at independence.

−3,928 km of rail at independence or 0.1649 as the proportion to the area.

−68,716 km of road, 19 Km per 1000 Km2 in 1958 four years before independence.

−4,700 people per doctor and other medical staff in 1958.

−330 persons per bed in hospitals and medical centers in 1958.

−And a GDP/Cap of 200 Rand in 1961, one year before independence.

4. THE GABON with 121 years of colonization, had :

−30 graduate students in 1968, eight years after independence, 0.0063% as the proportion to the population at independence.

−5,104 km of road, 19 km per 1000 km2 in 1962, two years after independence.

−8,200 persons per physician and other medical staff in 1959, one year before independence.

−110 persons per bed in hospitals and medical centers in 1959.

−And a GDP/Cap of 95 Rand in 1961, one year after independence.

5. THE NIGER with 89 years of colonization, had :

−300 graduate students in 1972, twelve years after independence, 0.0099 as the proportion relative to the population at independence.

−15,056 km of road, 69 km per 1000 km2 in 1962, two years after independence.

−69 persons per physician and other medical staff in 1958, two years before independence.

2300 persons per bed in hospitals and medical centers in 1959, a year before independence.

−And a GDP/Cap of 28 Rand in 1961 one year after independence.

6. GUINEA BISSAU with 81 years of colonization has no data available.

7. IVORY COAST, with 78 years of colonization had:

−3000 graduate students in 1967, seven years after independence, is 0.0928% as the proportion to the population at independence.

−1,173 km of rail to independence, or 0.3637 as the proportion to the area.

−28,000 km of road, 87 km per 1000 km2 in 1962, two years after independence.

−18,000 people per doctor and other medical staff in 1958, two years before independence.

−610 persons per bed in hospitals and medical centers in 1958.

−And a GDP/Cap of 129 Rand in1961, a year after independence.

8. TUNISIA with 75 years of colonization, had :

−2163 graduate students to independence, the proportion is 0.0571 compared to the population at independence.

−2,106 km of rail to independence, the proportion is 1.2872 compared to the area.

−9,145 km of road, 73 km per 1000 km2 in 1962, six years after independence.

−6,900 persons per physician and other medical staff in 1956, the year of independence.

−490 persons per bed in hospitals and other medical centers in 1957, a year after independence.

−And a GDP/Cap of 114 Rand in 1961, five years after independence.

9. Guinea with 72 years of colonization, had:
−1200 graduate students in 1975, seventeen years after independence. But data on the population for independence are not available. This is also the case of the data on rail, roads, the number of people per doctor, per bed in hospitals and medical centers.
−GDP/Cap of 43 Rand in 1961, three years after independence.

10. The BurkinaFaso with 69 years of colonization, had :
−193 graduate students in 1969, nine years after independence, as 0.0043 proportion to the population at independence.
−13,000 km of road, 47 km per 1000 km2 in 1962, two years after independence.
−5,520 persons per physician and other medical staff in 1959, a year before independence.
−1,700 people per bed in hospitals and medical centers in 1958, two years before independence.
−And a GDP/Cap of 28 Rand in1961, a year after independence.

11. Benin with 66 years of colonization, had:
−220 graduate students in 1969, nine years after independence, 0.0098% as a proportion to the population at independence.
−579 km of rail to independence, or 0.5141 as a proportion relative to the area.
−30,700 people per doctor and other medical staff in 1960, the year of independence.
−However, data on GDP in 1961 are not available.

12. THE MADAGASCAR with 66 years of colonization, had :
−1130 graduate students to independence.
−860 km of rail to independence, or 0.1447 as a proportion relative to the area.
−30,000 km of road, 51 Km by 1000 Km2en 1960, the year of independence.
−8,000 people per doctor and other medical staff in 1959, a year before independence.

−410 persons per bed in hospitals and medical centers in 1959.

−And a GDP/Cap of 54 Rand in 1961, a year after independence.

13. CENTRAL AFRICAN REPUBLIC with 50 years of colonization, had:

−292 graduate students in 1973, thirteen years after independence, 0.0190% as a proportion to the population at independence.

−16,000 km of road, 26 km per 1000 km2 in 1962, two years after independence.

−28,000 people per doctor and other medical staff in 1958, two years before independence.

−1020 persons per bed in hospitals and medical centers in 1958.

−However, data on GDP/Cap in 1961 are not available.

14. CONGO BRAZZA with 50 years of colonization, had:

−2570 graduate students in 1973, thirteen years after independence, 0.2652% as a proportion to the population at independence.

−515 km of rail to independence, or 0.1505 as a proportion relative to the area.

−8,400 km of road, 25 km per 1000 km2 in 1962, two years after independence.

−12,000 people per doctor and other medical staff in 1958, two years before independence.

−200 persons per bed in hospitals and medical centers in 1958.

−And a GDP/Cap of 31 Rand in 1961, a year after independence.

15. THE MOROCCO with 44 years of colonization, had :

−3792 graduate students to independence, 0.0364% of proportion to the population at independence.

−1,785 km of rail to independence, the .3997 proportion to the area.

−46,172 km of road, 104 Km by 1000 Km2 in 1960, four years after independence.

−10,000 people per doctor and other medical staff in 1959, three years after independence.

−580 persons per bed in hospitals and medical centers in 1959.

−And a GDP/Cap of 107 Rand in 1961, five years after independence.

14. THE CHAD with 40 years of colonization, had :

–605 graduate students in 1973, thirteen years after independence, 0.0197% as a proportion to the population at independence.

–10,000 km of road, 8 km per 1000 km2 in 1962, two years after independence.

–68,000 people per doctor and other medical staff in 1958, two years before independence.

–1250 persons per bed in hospitals and medical centers in 1958.

–And a GDP/Cap of 28 Rand in 1961, a year after independence.

15. MAURITANIA with 39 years of colonization, had :

–4526 graduate students in 1985, twenty-five years after independence, 0.6836% as a proportion to the population at independence.

–650 km of rail in 1963, three years after independence, as 0.0630 proportion to the area.

–2,700 km of road, 3 km per 1000 km2 in 1962, two years after independence.

–81,900 people per doctor and other medical staff in 1954, six years before independence.

–But the data in GDP/Cap in 1961 are not available.

16. THE MALI with 25 years of colonization, had :

–104 graduate students in 1964, four years after independence, 0.0023% as a proportion to the population at independence.

–645 km of rail to independence, the proportion is 0.0520 compared to the area.

–13,000 km of road, 11 km per 1000 km2 in 1962, two years after independence.

–44,000 people per doctor and other medical staff in 1959, a year before independence.

–1,000 people per bed in hospitals and medical centers in 1958, two years before independence.

–And a GDP/Cap of 42 Rand in 1961, a year after independence.

II. FORMER ENGLISH COLONIES

1. The Sierra Leonne with 174 years of colonization, had:
−341 graduate students to independence, 0.0154% the proportion of students from the population at independence.
−500 km of rail to independence, the proportion is 0.6969 compared to the area.
−4,537 km of road, 63 km per 1000 km2 in 1962, a year after independence.
−66,670 people per doctor and other medical staff in 1958, three years before independence.
−1,300 people per bed in hospitals and medical centers in 1958.
−And a GDP/Cap of 50 Rand in 1961, the year of independence.

2. Ghana with 136 years of colonization, had:
−960 graduate students to independence, the proportion of 0.0159% compared to the population at independence.
−951 km of rail to independence, or 0.3986 share of the rail over the area.
−12,875 km of road is 54 km per 1000 km2 in 1958, a year after independence.
−21,000 people per doctor and other medical staff in 1955, two years before independence.
−1,800 people per bed in hospitals and medical centers in 1955.
−And a GDP/Cap of 142 Rand in1961, four years after independence.

3. SOUTH AFRICA with 105 years of colonization, had :
−1171 graduate students to independence, the proportion is 0.0200 compared to the population at independence.
−12,208 km of rail to independence, the proportion is 0.9998 compared to the area.
−180,459 km of road is 148 Km per 1000 Km2 in 1962, fifty-two years after independence.
−2,060 persons per physician and other medical staff in 1960, fifty years after independence.
−240 persons per bed in hospitals and medical centers in 1960.
−And a GDP/Cap to 343rd in 1961, fifty-one years after independence.

4. Nigeria with 99 years of colonization, had :

−7000 graduate students in 1964, four years after independence, 0.0163 as the proportion relative to the population at independence.

−2,864 km of rail to independence, the proportion is 0.3100 compared to the area.

−60,904 km of road, 69 km per 1000 km2 in 1962, two years after independence.

−35,000 people per doctor and other medical staff in 1959, a year before independence.

−21,000 people per bed in hospitals and medical centers in 1958, two years before independence.

−And a GDP/Cap of 58 Rand in 1961, a year before independence.

5. Botswana with 81 years of colonization, had :

−No data on the students.

−634 Km of rail to independence, the proportion is 0.1056 compared to the area.

−1,600 km of road, 48 km per 1000 km2 in 1962, four years before independence.

−17,000 people per doctor and other medical staff in 1958, eight years before independence.

−430 persons per bed in hospitals and medical centers in 1958.

−And a GDP/Cap 343rd of Rand in 1961, five years before independence.

6. GAMBIA with 77 years of colonization, had :

−859 km of road, 83 km per 1000 km2 in 1962, three years before independence.

−19,000 people per doctor and other medical staff in 1958, seven years before independence.

−1,000 people per bed in hospitals and medical centers in 1957.

−However, data on GDP/Cap in 1961 are not available.

7. Malawi, with 73 years of colonization, had:

−487 graduate students in 1966, two years after independence, 0.0128% as the proportion to the population at independence.

−509 km of rail to independence, the proportion is 0.4295 compared to the area.

−9608 Km of road is 82 km per 1000 km2 in 1962, two years before independence.

−32,000 people per doctor and other medical staff in 1959, five years before independence.

−750 persons per bed in hospitals and medical centers in 1958, six years before independence.

−And a GDP/Cap of 116m Rand in 1961, three years before independence.

8.   SOMALIA with 71 years of colonization, had :

−548 graduate students in 1969, nine years after independence, 0.0245% as a proportion to the population at independence.

−113 km of rail in 1953, seven years before independence, as 0.0177 proportion to the area.

−14,300 km of road, 22 km per 1000 km2 in 1962, two years after independence.

−27,500 people per doctor and other medical staff in 1958, two years before independence.

−705 persons per bed in hospitals and medical centers in 1958.

−And a GDP/Cap de 20d Rand in 1961, a year after independence.

9.   THE LESOTHO with 68 years of colonization, had:

−1,469 km of road, 48 km per 1000 km in 1962, a year before independence.

−19,000 people per doctor and other medical staff in 1958, five years before independence.

−850 persons per bed in hospitals and medical centers in 1958.

−And a GDP/Cap 343rd of Rand in 1961, two years before independence.

−E: Means Including South West Africa, Basutoland, Bechuanaland and Swaziland.

−M: Means that the three Countries were in a federation (Rhodesia, Nyasaland, Fed of).

9.   UGANDA with 68 years of colonization, had:
−888 graduate students in 1965, three years after independence, 0.0121% as a proportion to the population at independence.
−1,050 km of rail in 1975, thirteen years after independence, as 0.4448 proportion to the area.
−18,833 km of road, 77 km per 1000 km2 in 1962, the year of independence.
−7,700 persons per physician and other medical staff in 1958, four years before independence.
−700 persons per bed in hospitals and medical centers in 1958.
−And a GDP/cap of 49 Rand in 1961, a year before independence.

9.   Kenya with 68 years of colonization, had :
−362 graduate students to independence, 0.0040% the proportion of students from the population at independence.
−6,872 km of rail independence, 1.1794 is the proportion of rail over the area.
−40,000 km of road, 70 km per 1000 km2 in 1962, a year before independence.
−9,100 persons per physician and other medical staff in 1958, five years before independence.
−700 persons per bed in hospitals and medical centers in 1958.
−And a GDP/Cap of 57 Rand in 1961, two years before independence.

10. THE SWAZILAND with 66 years of colonization, had:
−1,479 km of road, 85 km per 1000 km2 in 1962, six years before independence.
−7,870 persons per physician and other medical staff in 1958, ten years before independence.
−500 persons per bed in hospitals and medical centers in 1958.
−And a GDP/Cap 343rd of Rand in 1961, seven years before independence.

11. SUDAN with 57 years of colonization, had:

−802 graduate students to independence, or 0.0077% the proportion of students from the population at independence.

−3,604 km of rail to the independence or the proportion of rail 0.1438 compared to the area.

−30.000(y) km of road, 10 km per 1000 km2 in 1962, six years after independence.

−150,000 people per doctor and other medical staff in 1958, two years after independence.

  1100 persons per bed in hospitals and medical centers in 1958.

−And a GDP/Cap of 67 Rand in 1961, five years after independence.

−D: refers only to Southern region with population of 1.4 million.

−E: Means Including South West Africa, Basutoland, Bechuanaland and Swaziland.

−(Y): Europa Publications Ltd bibliography cf.

11. Zimbabwe with 57 years of colonization, had:

−8000 graduate students to independence, the proportion of 0.1122% compared to the population at independence.

−3,415 km of rail to independence, or 0.8743 of proportion to the area.

−Route 59 312, or 152 km per 1000 km2 in 1962, eighteen years before independence.

−4,400 persons per physician and other medical staff in 1959, twenty-one year before independence.

−220 persons per bed in hospitals and medical centers in 1958, twenty-two years before independence.

−And a GDP/Cap of 116 (m) Rand in 1961, ten new-years before independence.

12. EGYPT with 40 years of colonization, had:

  2282 graduate students in 1921, a year before independence, the proportion of 0.0168% compared to the population at independence.

−4,398 km of rail to independence, the proportion is 0.4391 compared to the area.

−20,228 km of road, 20 km per 1000 km2 in 1958, thirty-six years after independence.

−2,800 people per doctor and other medical staff in 1958, thirty-six years after independence.

−510 persons per bed in hospitals and medical centers in 1956, thirty-four years after independence.

−And a GDP/Cap of 86 Rand in 1961, thirty-nine years after independence.

12. ZAMBIA with 40 years of colonization, had :

−536 graduate students in 1967, three years after independence, 0.0149% as the proportion to the population at independence.

−4,260 km of rail to independence, the proportion is 0.5660 compared to the area.

−31,945 km of road, 43 km per 1000 km2 in 1962, two years before independence.

−7,800 persons per physician and other medical staff in 1959, five years before independence.

−250 persons per bed in hospitals and medical centers in 1958, six years before independence.

−And a GDP/Cap Rand 116 (m) in 1961, three years before independence.

III. FORMER PORTUGUESE COLONIES

1. Angola with 484 years of colonization, had :

−1254 graduate students in 1978, three years after independence, 0.0205 as the proportion relative to the population at independence.

−2,952 km of rail to independence, the proportion is 0.2367 compared to the area.

−35,509 km of road, 29 km per 1000 km2 in 1959, sixteen years before independence.

−20,770 people per doctor and other medical staff in 1958, seventeen years before independence.

−But the data in GDP/Cap in 1961 are not available.

2.   Cape Verde with 483 years of colonization, had :

−545 km of road is 135 Km per 1000 Km2 in 1959, sixteen years before independence.

   11,500 persons per physician and other medical staff in 1959.

−But the data in GDP/Cap in 1961 are not available.

3.   Mozambique with 473 years of colonization, had :

−906 graduate students in 1970, five years before independence, 0.0009% as the proportion to the population at independence.

−3,696 km of rail to independence, the proportion is 0.4720 compared to the area.

−37,564 km of road, 48 Km per 1000 Km2 1959en in 1959, sixteen years before independence.

−33,750 people per doctor and other medical staff in 1959.

−But the data in GDP/Cap in 1961 are not available.

IV. FORMER BELGIAN COLONIES

1.   THE R.D.C with 52 years of colonization, had:

−1256 graduate students in 1961 one year after independence, 0.0088% as the proportion to the population at independence.

−5,074 km of rail to independence, the proportion is 0.2163 compared to the area.

−145,213 km of road, 62 km per 1000 km2 in 1958, two years before independence.

−16,000 people per doctor and other medical staff in 1958, two years before independence.

−160 persons per bed in hospitals and medical centers in 1958.

−And a GDP/Cap 60c of Rand in 1961, a year after independence.

2.   THE RWANDA with 43 years of colonization, had :

−161 graduate students in 1967, five years after independence, 0.0055% as a proportion to the population at independence.

−12,083 km of road is 223 km per 1000 km2 for the Rwanda-Burundi in 1958, four years before independence.

- 26,000 people per doctor and other medical personnel in Rwanda-Burundi in 1958, four years before independence.
- 750 persons per bed in hospitals and medical centers for the Rwanda-Burundi in 1958, four years before independence.
- And a GDP/Cap of 38 Rand for Rwanda in 1961, a year before independence.

———————————◄———————————

- e: means including South West Africa, Basutoland, Swaziland and Bechuanaland.
- b: G.D.P data refer to East Cameroon only with a population of 3.3 million.

3. THE BURUNDI with 43 years of colonization, had :−397 graduate students in 1969, seven years after independence, 0.0132% as a proportion to the population at independence.
- 12,083 km of road is 223 km per 1000 km2 for the Rwanda-Burundi in 1958, four years before independence.
- 26,000 people per doctor and other medical personnel to Rwanda and Burundi in 1958.
- 750 persons per bed in hospitals and medical centers for Rwanda and Burundi in 1958.
- And a GDP/Cap of 42 Rand in 1961, a year before independence.

V. FORMER GERMAN COLONIES

1. NAMIBIA with 106 years of colonization, had :
- 55,000 km of road, 66 km per 1000 km2 in 1962, twenty-eight years before independence.
- 390 persons per bed in hospitals and medical centers in 1958, thirty-two years before independence.
- And a GDP/Cap 343rd of Rand in 1961, twenty-nine years before independence.

2. TANZANIA with 77 years of colonization, had :

−523 graduate students in 1965, four years after independence, 0.0049% as the proportion to the population at independence.

−4,460 km of rail in 1975, fourteen years after independence, 0.4719 as the proportion relative to the area.

−32,907 km of road is 423 Km per 1000 Km2 in 1962, a year after independence.

−19,100 people per doctor and other medical staff in 1959, two years before independence.

−1010 persons per bed in hospitals and medical centers in 1958, three years before independence.

−And a GDP/Cap of 42 Rand in 1961, the year of independence.

3. THE CAMEROON with 76 years of colonization, had :

−1986 graduate students in 1967 six or seven years after independence, 0.0349% as the proportion to the population at independence.

−517 km of rail to independence, the proportion is 0.1087 compared to the area.

−12,000 km of road per 1000 km soit28 Km2 in 1962, a year or two years after independence.

−73,000 people per doctor and other medical staff in 1958/59.

−1570 persons per bed in hospitals and medical centers in 1958.

−And a GDP/Cap 50b of Rand in 1961.

4. THE TOGO with 66 years of colonization, had :

−1491 graduate students in 1971, eleven years after independence, 0.1032% as the proportion to the population at independence.

−445 km of rail to independence, or 0.7946 as the proportion to the area.

−4,546 km of road, 80 Km per 1000 Km2 en1957, three years before independence.

−30,000 people in medical and other medical staff in 1956, four years before independence.

−550 persons per bed in hospitals and medical centers in 1956.

−And a GDP/cap of 50 Rand in 1961, a year after independence.

VI. FORMER ITALIAN COLONIES

1. L ERITREA avec 109 years of colonization, had:
−306 km of rail in 1975, eighteen years before independence

VII. THE INDEPENDENTS (FREE FROM COLONIZATION)

1. LIBERIA independent since 1847, had :
−20,000 people per doctor and other medical staff in 1956.
−1,600 people per bed in hospitals and medical centers in 1956.
−However, data on GDP/Cap in 1961 are not available.
2. ETSHIOPIA, independent since 1000 before Christ, had:
−105,500 people per doctor and other medical staff in 1956.
−3,000 people per bed in hospitals and medical centers in 1956.
−However, data on GDP/Cap in 1961 are not available.

−(m) Rand is the currency of South Africa.
You can realize that:
−Proportions of students are calculated based on data from different years. For example in the case of Gabon: the student data are from 1968, while those of the population in 1960. This proportion is taken for illustrative purposes because the data on students to independence were not available in the statistics at hand. That's why we made the data available about the independence.
−Some of the proportions km of rail, are not calculated based on data independence because they were not available in the statistics at hand. These proportions are illustrative.
−Data on miles of road do not correspond to a year. This is because of the unavailability of data. This is also true of data on the number of people per doctor and also the number of persons per bed in hospitals and medical centers.

After these data on the different colonies, we give in order of magnitude the gross national product/capita of the different colonies to allow us to test the applicability of the variables: number of years, number of academics, infrastructures and their probable involvement in gross national product.

In light of the dates of "political independence" of African countries, we can notice that most of African countries, with the exception of a few such as Namibia, had their "politicalitical independence" between 1950 and 1985.

To test the applicability of the correlation between the number of years of colonization and the economic and social progress, which is a reflection of relatively good/bad governance, we have the GDP/Cap of:
−1961, one year after independence of DRC.
−1980, A few years before perestroika.
−1993, 1994, 1995, several years after Mobutu's speech announcing Chairing the democratization of political institutions in Zaire. It's also a few years after perestroika.
−2001, the end of the late Laurent Kabila regime and the beginning of the regime of Joseph Kabila.
−2006, 2007, 2009, during the regime of Joseph Kabila.

GDP /CAPITA IN RAND (AFRICAN COUNTRIES IN 1961) IN ORDER

NO	COUNTRIES	GDP/CAP IN RAND	NUMBER OF COLONIZATION'S YEARS	FORMER COLONY
1	SOUTH AFRICA,NAMIBIA, BOTSWANA, LESOTHO, SWAZILAND	343e	105, 106, 81, 68, 66	BRITISH, GERMAN (NAMIBIA)
2	ALGERIA	200	132	FRENCH
3	LIBIA	148	39	BRITISH
4	GHANA	142	136	BRITISH
5	IVORY COAST	129	78	FRENCH
6	SENEGAL	125	301	FRENCH

7	ZIMBABWE, ZAMBIA, MALAWI	116m	57, 40, 73	BRITISH
8	TUNISIA	114	75	FRENCH
9	MOROCCO	107	44	FRENCH
10	GABON	95	121	FRENCH
11	EGYPT	86	40	BRITISH
12	SUDAN	67	57	BRITISH
13	D.R.C	60c	52	BELGIUM
14	NIGERIA	58	99	BRITISH
15	KENYA	57	68	BRITISH
16	MALAGASY REP	54	66	FRENCH
17	SIERRA LEONE	50	174	BRITISH
17	TOGO	50	66	GERMAN
17	CAMEROON	50b	76/75	GERMAN
18	UGANDA	49	68	BRITISH
19	GUINEA	43	72	FRENCH
20	MALI	42	25	FRENCH
20	TANZANIA	42	77	GERMAN
20	BURUNDI	42	43	BELGIUM
21	ETSHIOPIA	32		
22	CONGO BRAZZA	31	50	FRENCH
23	RWANDA	28	43	BELGIUM
23	CHAD	28	40	FRENCH
23	NIGER	28	89	FRENCH
23	BURKINAFASO	28	69	FRENCH
24	SOMALIA	20d 71		BRITISH

The informations on GDP/Cap in 1961 (one year after the independance of DRC) are taken from: AFRIKA-INSTIUTE ATLAS.

AFRIKA MAPS AND STATISTICS n0 July 1962.
In this column of GDP/Cap, there is :

b.   G.D.P data refer to East Cameroon only with a population of 3.3 million.

c.   Total G.D.P refers to 1959 and per capita figure is expressed in terms of 1959 population of 13.8 million.

d.   Refers to Southern Region only with population of 1.4 million.

e.   Including South West Africa, Basutoland, Swaziland and Bechuanaland.

m.   These three countries were in a federation (Rhodesia, Nyasaland, Fed of).

GDP /CAPITA IN U.S. DOLLAR IN 1980 IN ORDER OF MAGNITUDE AND THE PERCENTAGES OF UNIVERSITY IN 1980

NO	COUNTRIES	GDP/CAP IN U.S $	NUMBER OF COLONIZATION'S YEARS	% OF GRADUATE STUDENTS IN 1980	FORMER COLONY
1	LIBIA	8.640	39	0.861	BRITISH
2	GABON	3.680	121	0.122*	FRENCH
3	SOUTH AFRICAN REP	2.290	105	0.403	BRITISH
4	ALGERIA	1.920	132	0.424	FRENCH
5	SEYCHELLES	1.770	102		BRITISH
6	NAMIBIA	1.410	106	_	GERMAN
7	TUNISIA	1.310	75	0.502	FRENCH
8	IVORY COAST	1.150	78	0.242	FRENCH
9	MAURITIUS	1.060	138		MAURITIUS
10	NIGERIA	1010	99	0.194	BRITISH
11	BOTSWANA	910	81	_	BRITISH
12	MOROCCO	860	44	0.553	FRENCH
13	CONGO BRAZZA	730	50	0.472	FRENCH
14	SWAZILAND	680	66		BRITISH
15	CAMEROON	670	76/75	0.142	GERMAN
16	ZIMBABWE	630	57	0.108	BRITISH
17	EGYPT	580	40		BRITISH
18	ZAMBIA	560	40	0.129	BRITISH
19	LIBERIA	520		0.202*	INDEPENDENT
20	ANGOLA	470	484	0.021	PORTUGUESE

20	SUDAN	470	57	1.789	BRITISH
21	SENEGAL	450	301	0.247	FRENCH
22	KENYA	420	68	0.054	BRITISH
22	GHANA	420	136	0.068	BRITISH
23	TOGO	410	66	0.173	GERMAN
24	LESOTHO	390	68		BRITISH
25	MALAGASY REP	350	66	_	FRENCH
26	NIGER	330	89	0.027	FRENCH
27	MAURITANIA	320	39	0.276	FRENCH
28	BENIN	300	66	0.135	FRENCH
28	CAPE VERDE	300	483	_	PORTUGUESE
28	CENTRAL AFRICAN REP	300	50	0.072	FRENCH
29	UGANDA	280	68	0.046	BRITISH
29	SOMALIA	280	71	0.062	BRITISH
30	SIERRA LEONNE	270	174	0.052	BRITISH
30	MOZAMBIQUE	270	470	0.008	PORTUGUESE
31	TANZANIA	260	77	0.021	GERMAN
32	GAMBIA	250	77	_	BRITISH
33	MALAWI	230	73	0.058	BRITISH
34	D.R.C	220	52	0.098	BELGIUM
35	RWANDA	200	43	0.024	BELGIUM
35	BURUNDI	200	43	0.041	BELGIUM
36	BURKINAFASO	190	100	0.699	FRENCH
36	MALI	190	25	0.024	FRENCH
37	BISSAU GUINEA	160	81	_	FRENCH
38	ETSHIOPIA	140		0.005	INDEPENDENT
39	CHAD	120	40	0.036	FRENCH

Source data on GDP/Cap in 1980: protein deficiency and malnutrition. Published in 1990 by The United Nations Educational, Scientific and Cultural Organization.

7. Place de Fontenoy, 75700 Paris, Typeset by Coupé, Sautron. Printed by Imprimerie des Presses Universitaires de France, Vendôme.
   ISBN 92-3-102083-8 c UNESCO 1990 Printed in France.

–Asterix The column percentages of university in 1980 in the table above, mean that these percentages (these proportions are illustrative), as data on students to independence were not available we took the data about independence.

GDP/CAPITA IN U.S DOLLAR IN 1993 AFRICAN IN ORDER OF SIZE

NO	COUNTRIES	GDP/CAP IN U.S $	NUMBER OF COLONIZATION'S YEARS	FORMER COLONY
1	LIBIA	6.510	39	BRITISH
2	SEYCHELLES	5.450	102	BRITISH
3	SOUTH AFRICAN REP	2.930	105	BRITISH
4	BOTSWANA	2.590	81	BRITISH
5	MAURITIUS	2.270	138	FRENCH
6	NAMIBIA	1.660	106	GERMAN
7	ALGERIA	1650	132	FRENCH
8	SWAZILAND	1.080	66	BRITISH
9	MOROCCO	1.030	44	FRENCH
10	CONGO BRAZZA	920	50	FRENCH
11	CAP VERDE	870	483	PORTUGUESE
12	TUNISIA	780	75	FRENCH
13	CAMEROON	770	76/75	GERMAN
14	SENEGAL	740	301	FRENCH
15	EGYPT	660	40	BRITISH
15	LESOTHO	660	68	BRITISH
16	IVORY COAST	630	78	FRENCH
17	ANGOLA	620	484	PORTUGUESE
18	ZIMBABWE	540	57	BRITISH
19	LIBERIA	450		FRENCH

20	MAURITANIA	438	39	FRENCH
21	GHANA	430	136	BRITISH
22	SUDAN	420	57	BRITISH
23	BENIN	420	66	FRENCH
23	CENTRAL AFRICAN REP	390	50	FRENCH
24	ZAMBIA	370	40	BRITISH
25	GAMBIA	360	77	BRITISH
26	EQUATORIAL GUINEA	360	368	SPANISH
26	TOGO	330	66	GERMAN
27	NIGERIA	310	99	BRITISH
28	BURKINAFASSO	300	69	FRENCH
29	MALI	300	25	FRENCH
29	NIGER	270	89	FRENCH
30	KENYA	270	68	BRITISH
30	MALAGASY REP	240	66	FRENCH
31	BISSAU GUINEA	233	81	FRENCH
32	MALAWI	230	73	BRITISH
33	D.R.C	220	52	BELGIUM
34	RWANDA	200	43	BELGIUM
35	CHAD	200	40	FRENCH
35	UGANDA	190	68	BRITISH
36	BURUNDI	180	43	BELGIUM
37	SOMALIA	150	71	BRITISH
38	SIERRA LEONNE	140	174	BRITISH
39	TANZANIA	100	77	GERMAN
40	ETSHIOPIA	100		BRITISH
41	MOZAMBIQUE	70	470	PORTUGUESE

In the table of GDP/Cap in 1993 above, data on: Seychelles, Mauritius, Swaziland are from: Britannica Book of the Year. Events of 1993. Britannica Book of the Year 1994.

But for the rest of countries: Encyclopaedia Britannica Book for the year 1996. Events of 1995. Encyclopaedia Britannica 1996 c, Inc.

GDP/CAPITA IN U.S. $ OF AFRICAN COUNTRIES IN ORDER OF MAGNITUDE EN1994

NO	COUNTRIES	GDP/Cap IN U.S $	NUMBER OF COLONISATION'S YEARS	FORMER COLONY
1	LIBIA	6.000	39	BRITISH
2	SEYCHELLES	5.400	102	BRITISH
3	GABON	4.500	121	FRENCH
4	BOTSWANA	2.800	81	BRITISH
5	MAURITIUS	2.750	138	FRENCH
6	SOUTH AFRICAN REP	2.650	105	BRITISH
7	TUNISIA	1.700	75	FRENCH
8	NAMIBIA	1.650	106	GERMAN
9	MOROCCO	1.000	44	FRENCH
10	CONGO BRAZZA	970	50	FRENCH
11	SWAZILAND	870	66	BRITISH
12	CAMEROON	840	76/75	GERMAN
13	CAP VERDE	810	483	PORTUGUESE
14	ALGERIA	800	132	FRENCH
15	SENEGAL	760	301	FRENCH
16	ANGOLA	730	484	PORTUGUESE
17	IVORY COAST	720	78	FRENCH
18	EGYPT	650	40	BRITISH
18	ZIMBABWE	650	57	BRITISH
19	LESOTHO	600	68	BRITISH
20	MAURITANIA	500	39	FRENCH
21	GHANA	420	136	BRITISH
22	CENTRAL AFRICAN REP	400	50	FRENCH
23	EQUATORIAL GUINEA	390	368	SPANISH

24	BENIN	370	66	FRENCH
25	TOGO	360	66	GERMAN
26	KENYA	350	68	BRITISH
27	BURKINAFASO	320	69	FRENCH
28	NIGERIA	310	99	BRITISH
29	SUDAN	290	57	BRITISH
30	ZAMBIA	280	40	BRITISH
31	RWANDA	240	43	BELGIUM
31	GAMBIA	240	77	BRITISH
32	CHAD	230	40	FRENCH
33	MALAGASY REP	210	66	FRENCH
34	BURUNDI	190	43	BELGIUM
34	SIERRALEONNE	190	174	BRITISH
35	BISSAU GUINEA	180	81	FRENCH
35	UGANDA	180	68	BRITISH
36	MALAWI	170	73	BRITISH
37	SOMALIA	160	71	BRITISH
38	D.R.C	140	52	BELGIUM
39	TANZANIA	120	77	GERMAN
40	ETSHIOPIA	110		

The data on GDP/Cap in 1994 in the table above are from: A LONELY PLANET AFRICA 1995. Climate Charts compiled from information Supplied by Patrick J. Tyson, 1995.

GDP/CAP IN U.S. $ OF AFRICAN COUNTRIES IN 1995 IN ORDER OF MAGNITUDE

NO	COUNTRIES	GDP/Cap IN U.S $	NUMBER OF COLONIZATION'S YEARS	FORMER COLONY
1	LIBIA	6.510	39	BRITISH
2	SEYCHELLES	6.370	102	BRITISH
3	GABON	4.050	121	FRENCH
4	MAURITIUS	2.980	138	FRENCH
5	SOUTH AFRICAN REP	2.930	105	BRITISH
6	BOTSWANA	2.590	81	BRITISH
7	NAMIBIA	1.660	106	GERMAN
8	ALGERIA	1.650	132	FRENCH
9	SWAZILAND	1.210	66	BRITISH
10	MOROCCO	1.030	44	FRENCH
11	CONGO BRAZZA	920	50	FRENCH
12	CAP VERDE	870	483	PORTUGUESE
13	SENEGAL	740	301	FRENCH
14	LESOTHO	660	68	BRITISH
15	IVORY COAST	630	78	FRENCH
16	ANGOLA	620	484	PORTUGUESE
17	ZIMBABWE	540	57	BRITISH
18	MAURITANIA	438	39	FRENCH
19	GHANA	430	136	BRITISH
20	BENIN	420	66	FRENCH
21	CENTRAL AFRICAN REP	390	50	FRENCH
22	EQUATORIAL GUINEA	373	368	SPANISH
23	ZAMBIA	370	40	BRITISH
24	GAMBIA	360	77	BRITISH
25	TOGO	330	66	GERMAN
26	NIGERIA	310	99	BRITISH
27	BURKINAFASO	300	69	FRENCH

27	SUDAN	300	57	BRITISH
28	KENYA	270	68	BRITISH
28	NIGER	270	89	FRENCH
29	MALAGASY REP	240	66	FRENCH
30	BISSAU GUINEA	233	81	FRENCH
31	MALAWI	230	73	BRITISH
32	D.R.C	220	52	BELGIUM
33	CHAD	200	40	FRENCH
33	RWANDA	200	43	BELGIUM
34	UGANDA	190	68	BRITISH
35	BURUNDI	180	43	BELGIUM
36	SOMALIA	150	71	BRITISH
37	SIERRA LEONNE	140	174	BRITISH
38	TANZANIA	100	77	GERMAN
38	ETSHIOPIA	100		

The data on GDP/Cap in 1995 in the table above are from: Encyclopaedia Britannica Book of the Year 1997.Events of 1996.

After the data on GDP/Cap, now let see the data on the number of years of colonization, arranged in order of magnitude, from largest to smallest number.

NUMBER OF YEARS OF SETTLEMENT ARRANGED IN ORDER OF SIZE FROM LARGEST TO SMALLEST.

NO	COUNTRIES	NUMBER OF COLONIZATION'S YEARS	FORMER COLONY
1	ANGOLA	484	PORTUGUESE
2	CAP VERDE	483	PORTUGUESE
3	MOZAMBIQUE	470	PORTUGUESE
4	EQUATORIAL GUINEA	368	SPANISH
5	SENEGAL	301	FRENCH
6	SIERRA LEONNE	174	BRITISH
7	MAURITIUS	138	FRENCH
8	GHANA	136	BRITISH
9	ALGERIA	132	FRENCH
10	GABON	121	FRENCH
11	NAMIBIA	106	GERMAN
12	SOUTH AFRICAN REP	105	BRITISH
13	ERITHREA	104	ITALIAN
14	SEYCHELLES	102	BRITISH
15	NIGERIA	99	BRITISH
16	NIGER	89	FRENCH
17	BOTSWANA	81	BRITISH
17	BISSAU GUINEA	81	FRENCH
18	IVORY COAST	78	FRENCH
19	GAMBIA	77	BRITISH
19	TANZANIA	77	GERMAN
20	CAMEROON	76	GERMAN
21	TUNISIA	75	FRENCH
22	MALAWI	73	BRITISH
23	GUINEA	72	FRENCH
24	SOMALIA	71	BRITISH
25	BURKINAFASO	69	FRENCH
26	LESOTHO	68	BRITISH
26	UGANDA	68	BRITISH

26	KENYA	68	BRITISH
27	BENIN	66	FRENCH
27	TOGO	66	GERMAN
27	SWAZILAND	66	BRITISH
27	MALAGASY REP	66	FRENCH
28	SUDAN	57	BRITISH
28	ZIMBABWE	57	BRITISH
29	D.R.C	52	BELGIUM
30	CENTRAL AFRICAN REP	50	FRENCH
30	CONGO BRAZZA	50	FRENCH
31	MOROCCO	44	FRENCH
32	BURUNDI	43	BELGIUM
32	RWANDA	43	BELGIUM
33	EGYPT	40	BRITISH
33	ZAMBIA	40	BRITISH
33	CHAD	40	FRENCH
34	MAURITANIA	39	FRENCH
34	LIBIA	39	BRITISH
35	MALI	25	FRENCH

Using data on GDP/Cap in the tables above, we can realize that:
1. The Libya, a former French colony and English with 39 years of colonization (the second to have fewer years of colonization), was third in GDP/Cap in 1961, first in 1980, 1993, 1994, 1995.
2. The Seychelles, a former British colony with 102 years of colonization has no data on GDP/Cap in 1961, was fifth in GDP/Cap in 1980, second in 1993, 1994, 1995.
3. Gabon, former French colony with 121 years of colonization, was tenth in GDP/cap in 1980, third in 1993, 1994, 1995.
4. The South Africa, former British colony with 105 years of colonization, was the first in GDP/Cap in 1961 (but the GDP/Cap was for all countries including South Africa, Namibia, Botswana, Lesotho and Swaziland), third in 1980, fourth in 1993, sixth in 1994, fifth in 1995.

5. The Mauritius, a former French colony with 138 years of colonization, were ninth in 1980, sixth in 1993, fifth in 1994, fourth in 1995, but the data in 1961 are not available.

6. Botswana, former British colony with 81 years of colonization, was the first in GDP/Cap in 1961 (but the GDP/Cap was for all countries including South Africa, Namibia, Botswana, Lesotho, Swaziland), eleventh in 1980, in 1993 fifth, fourth in 1994 and sixth in 1995.

7. Namibia, a former German colony and protectorate South African with 106 years of colonial protectorate included, was the first in GDP/Cap in 1961 (but the GDP/Cap was for all countries including South Africa, Namibia, Botswana, Lesotho and Swaziland), sixth in 1980, seventh in 1993 and 1995, eighth in 1994.

8. Algeria, former French colony with 132 years of colonization, was second in GDP/cap in 1961, fourth in 1980, eighth in 1993 and 1995, the fourteenth in 1994.

9. Tunisia, former French colony with 75 years of colonization, was eighth in GDP/Cap in 1961, seventh in 1980 and 1994, the thirteenth in 1993, but data for 1995 are not available.

10. Morocco, former French colony with 44 years of colonization, was ninth in GDP/Cap in 1961, 1994, 1995, in 1980 twelfth, tenth in 1993.

11. Swaziland, former British colony with 66 years of colonization, was the first in GDP/Cap in 1961 (but the GDP/Cap was for all countries including South Africa, Namibia, Botswana, Lesotho, Swaziland), fourth 1980, 1993.1995 ninth, eleventh in 1994.

12. Congo Brazza, a former French colony with 50 years of colonization, was twenty-second in GDP/cap in 1961, thirteenth in 1980, the eleventh in 1993, 1995, the tenth in 1994.

13. The Ivory Coast, a former French colony with 78 years of colonization, was fifth in GDP/Cap in 1961, eighth in 1980, the seventeenth in 1993, 1994, the fifteenth in 1995.

14. Cameroon, former German colony with 75 or 76 years of colonization, was seventeenth in GDP/Cap in 1961, the fifteenth in 1980, the fourteenth in 1993, twelfth in 1994, but data on GDP/Cap in 1995 are not available.

15. Egypt, the former British colony with 40 years of colonization, was the eleventh in GDP/Cap in 1961, the seventeenth in 1980, in 1993

sixteenth, eighteenth in 1994, but data on GDP/Cap in 1995 are not available.

16. Cape Verde, a former Portuguese colony with 483 years of colonization, was twenty-eighth in GDP/Cap in 1980, twelfth in 1993, 1995, the thirteenth in 1994, but data for 1961 are not available.

17. Lesotho, former British colony with 68 years of colonization, was the first in GDP/Cap in 1961 (but it was GDP for all countries including South Africa, Namibia, Botswana, Lesotho, Swaziland), twenty-fourth in 1980, the sixteenth in 1993, nineteenth in 1994, the fourteenth in 1995.

18. Senegal, former French colony with 301 years of colonization, was sixth in 1961, the twenty-first en1980, fifteenth in 1993, 1994, the thirteenth in 1995.

19. Liberia without having been colonized, was the nineteenth in GDP/Cap in 1980, the twenty-first in 1993, but data on GDP/Cap in 1961, 1994, 1995 are not available.

20. Angola, former Portuguese colony with 484 years of colonization, was the twentieth in GDP/Cap in 1980, eighteenth in 1993, the sixteenth in 1995, GDP/Cap for 1961 is not available.

21. Zimbabwe, former British colony with 57 years of colonization, was seventh in GDP/cap in 1961 (but the GDP/Cap was for all countries including Zimbabwe, Zambia and Malawi), the sixteenth in 1980, in the twentieth 1994, eighteenth in 1994, the seventeenth in 1995.

22. Nigeria, former British colony with 99 years of colonization, was the fourteenth in GDP/Cap in 1961, tenth in 1980, twenty-ninth in 1993, twenty-eighth in 1994, twenty-sixth in 1995.

23. Ghana, former British colony with 136 years of colonization, was fourth in GDP/cap in 1961, twenty-second in 1980, twenty-third in 1993, the twenty-first in 1994, nineteenth in 1995.

24. Mauritania, a former French colony with 39 years of colonization, was twenty-seventh in GDP/cap in 1980, twenty-second in 1993, the twentieth in 1994, eighteenth in 1995, but data on GDP/Cap in 1961 only are not available.

25. Benin, former French colony with 66 years of colonization, was twenty-eighth in GDP/Cap in 1980, twenty-fourth in 1993, 1994, the twentieth in 1995, GDP/Cap for 1961 is not available.

26. Equatorial Guinea, a former Spanish colony with 368 years of colonization, was twenty-seventh in GDP/cap in 1993, twenty-third in 1994, twenty-second in 1995.

27. Zambia, a former British colony with 40 years of colonization, was seventh in GDP/cap in 1961 (but the GDP/Cap was for all countries including Zimbabwe, Zambia and Malawi), eighteenth in 1980 twenty-sixth in 1993, thirty in 1994, twenty-third in 1995.

28. Central African Republic, a former French colony with 50 years of colonization, was twenty-eighth in GDP/Cap in 1980, twenty-fifth in 1993, twenty-second in 1994 and twenty-first in 1995, GDP/Cap in 1961 is not available.

28. Sudan, the former British colony with 57 years of colonization, was twelfth in GDP/Cap in 1961, the twentieth in 1980, twenty-fourth in 1993, twenty-ninth in 1994, twenty-seventh in 1995.

29. Togo, former German colony with 66 years of colonization, was seventeenth in GDP/Cap in 1961, twenty-third in 1980, twenty-eighth in 1993, twenty-fifth in 1994, 1995.

30. The Niger, a former French colony with 89 years of colonization, was twenty-third in GDP/Cap in1961, twenty-sixth in 1980, thirty-first in 1993, twenty eighth in 1995, GDP/Cap 1994 is not available.

31. Gambia former British colony with 77 years of colonization, was thirty-second in GDP/cap in 1961, twenty-seventh in 1993, thirty-first in 1994, and twenty-fourth in 1995, GDP/Cap in 1980 is not available.

32. Kenya, former British colony with 68 years of colonization, was twenty-second in 1980, thirty-first in 1993, twenty-sixth in 1994, twenty-eighth in 1995.

33. The Burkinafaso, former French colony with 69 years of colonization, was twenty-third in GDP/Cap in 1961, thirty-sixth in 1980, thirty in 1993, twenty-seventh in 1994.1995.

34. Malagasy Republic, a former French colony with 66 years of colonization, was sixteenth in GDP/Cap in 1961, twenty-fifth in 1980, thirty-second in 1993, thirty-third in 1994, twenty-ninth in 1995.

35. Mali, former French colony with 25 years of colonization, was the twentieth in GDP/Cap in 1961, thirty-sixth in 1980, thirty in 1993, but data on GDP/Cap in 1994, 1995 are not available.

36. Malawi, former British colony with 73 years of colonization, was seventh in GDP/cap in 1961 (but the GDP/Cap was for all countries including Zimbabwe, Zambia and Malawi), thirty-third in 1980 thirty-fourth in 1993, thirty-sixth in 1994, thirty-first in 1995.

37. Uganda, a former British colony with 68 years of colonization, was the eighteenth in GDP/Cap in 1961, twenty-ninth in 1980, thirty-eighth in 1993, thirty-fifth in 1994 and thirty in 1995.

37. Rwanda, former Belgian colony with 43 years of colonization, was twenty-third in GDP/Cap in 1961, thirty-fifth in 1980, thirty-sixth in 1993, thirty-first in 1994, thirty-third in 1995.

38. Guinea Bissau, a former French colony with 81 years of colonization, was thirty-seventh in GDP/cap in 1980, thirty-third in 1993, thirty-fifth in 1994, thirty in 1995, but data on GDP/Cap in 1961 are not available.

39. DRC, former Belgian colony with 52 years of colonization, was the thirteenth in GDP/Cap in 1961, thirty-fourth in 1980, thirty-fifth in 1993, thirty-eighth in 1994, thirty-second in 1995.

40. Mozambique, former Portuguese colony with 470 years of colonization, was thirtieth in GDP/Cap en1980, forty-third, or last in GDP/cap in 1993, but data on GDP/Cap in 1994, 1995 are not available.

41. Burundi, former Belgian colony with 43 years of colonization, was the twentieth in GDP/Cap in 1961, thirty-fifth in 1980, 1994, 1995, thirty-ninth in 1993.

41. Chad, former French colony with 40 years of colonization, was twenty-third in GDP/Cap in 1961, thirty-ninth or last in 1980, thirty-seventh in 1993, thirty-second in 1994, thirty-third in 1995.

42. Somalia, a former British colony with 71 years of colonization, was twenty-fourth, or last in GDP/cap in 1961, twenty-ninth in 1980, fortieth in 1993, thirty-seventh in 1994 and thirty-sixth in 1995.

42. Sierra Leone, a former British colony with 174 years of colonization, was seventeenth in GDP/Cap in 1961, thirty in 1980, forty-first in 1993, thirty-fourth in 1994, thirty-seventh in 1995.

43. Tanzania, a former German colony with 77 years of colonization, was the twentieth in GDP/Cap in 1961, thirty-first in 1980, forty-second in 1993, thirty-ninth (second last) in 1994, thirty-eighth (before last) in 1995.

44. The Etshiopie without having been colonized, was the twenty-first in GDP/Cap in 1961, thirty-eighth or before last in 1980, forty-second or second last in 1993, last in 1994 is forty and thirty-eighth or last 1995.

After this, let continue with the GDP/Cap in 2006 (year in which there was the so-called elections that have extended the "term" of Joseph Kabila, eleven years after 1995), and GDP/Cap in 2009.

GDP/CAP IN U.S. $ OF AFRICAN COUNTRIES IN 2006 IN ORDER

NO	COUNTRIES	GDP/CAP IN U.S $	NUMBER OF COLONIZATION'S YEARS	FORMER COLONY
1	EQUATORIAL GUINEA	16.630.43	368	SPANISH
2	SEYCHELLES	8.743.98	102	BRITISH
3	LIBIA	8.435.53	39	BRITISH
4	GABON	6.790.59	121	FRENCH
5	BOTSWANA	5.875.09	81	BRITISH
6	SOUTH AFRICA	5.380.60	105	BRITISH
7	MAURITIUS	5.144.63	138	FRENCH
8	ALGERIA	3.440.30	132	FRENCH
9	NAMIBIA	3.106.82	106	GERMAN
10	TUNISIA	2.990.30	75	FRENCH
11	ANGOLA	2.686.36	484	PORTUGUESE
12	SWAZILAND	2.351.35	66	BRITISH
13	CAP VERDE	2.207.15	483	PORTUGUESE
14	MOROCCO	1.879.12	44	FRENCH
15	CONGO BRAZZA	1.799.01	50	FRENCH
16	EGYPT	1.425.58	40	BRITISH
17	CAMEROON	1.098.31	76	GERMAN
18	SUDAN	1.015.17	57	BRITISH
19	IVORY COAST	946.73	78	FRENCH
20	ZAMBIA	919.50	40	BRITISH
21	MAURITANIA	844.26	39	FRENCH
22	LESOTHO	825.11	68	BRITISH
23	NIGERIA	792.31	99	BRITISH
24	SENEGAL	749.17	301	FRENCH
25	KENYA	602.85	68	BRITISH
26	CHAD	654.99	40	FRENCH
27	GHANA	572.77	136	BRITISH
28	SOMALIA	565.78	71	BRITISH

29	BENIN	549.25	66	FRENCH
30	BURKINAFASO	456.73	69	FRENCH
31	MALI	426.24	25	FRENCH
32	ZIMBABWE	382.88	57	BRITISH
33	MOZAMBIQUE	377.69	470	PORTUGUESE
34	CENTRAFRICAN REP	362.86	50	FRENCH
35	GUINEA	360.60	72	FRENCH
36	TOGO	350.06	66	GERMAN
37	GAMBIA	328.89	77	BRITISH
38	TANZANIA	323.83	77	GERMAN
39	UGANDA	312.04	68	BRITISH
40	MALAGASY REP	288.12	66	FRENCH
41	RWANDA	269.74	43	BELGIUM
42	SIERRA LEONE	255.80	174	BRITISH
43	NIGER	245.84	89	FRENCH
44	ERITHREA	239.07	104	ITALIAN
45	LIBERIA	186.68	-	LIBRE
46	BISSAU GUINEA	186.46	81	FRENCH
47	ETSHIOPIA	183.13	-	FREE
48	MALAWI	169.53	73	BRITISH
49	D.R.C	143.28	52	BELGIUM
50	BURUNDI	102.97	43	BELGIUM

Source: HISTORICAL COUNTRIES, UNIONS OR OTHER REGIONS.
G.D.P/CAP STATISTICS-COUNTRIES COMPARED NATION MASTER.
AT INTERNET (GOOGLE

GDP/CAP OF AFRICAN COUNTRIES IN US $ IN 2009 IN ORDER

NO	COUNTRIES	GDP/CAP IN U.S $	NUMBER OF COLONIZATION'S YEARS	FORMER COLONY
1	SEYCHELLES	19.274.43	102	BRITISH
2	EQUATORIAL GUINEA	16.852.81	368	SPANISH
3	GABON	14.420.69	121	FRENCH
4	LIBIA	14.380.85	39	BRITISH
5	BOTSWANA	13.416.66	81	BRITISH
6	MAURITIUS	12.356.23	138	FRENCH
7	SOUTH AFRICA	9.961.02	105	BRITISH
8	TUNISIA	8.284.82	75	FRENCH
9	ALGERIA	6.854.93	132	FRENCH
10	NAMIBIA	6.610.35	106	GERMAN
11	ANGOLA	6.179.24	484	PORTUGUESE
12	EGYPT	6.147.12	40	BRITISH
13	SWAZILAND	5.839.31	66	BRITISH
14	MOROCCO	4.587.11	44	FRENCH
15	CONGO BRAZZA	4.155.91	50	FRENCH
16	CAP VERDE	3.579.73	483	PORTUGUESE
17	SUDAN	2.376.43	57	BRITISH
18	NIGERIA	2.199.08	99	BRITISH
19	CAMEROON	2.147.15	76	GERMAN
20	MAURITANIA	2.086.09	39	FRENCH
21	SENEGAL	1.751.62	301	FRENCH
22	KENYA	1.750.82	68	BRITISH
23	IVORY COAST	1.679.58	78	FRENCH
24	CHAD	1.674.00	40	FRENCH
25	BENIN	1.643.14	66	FRENCH
26	GHANA	1.571.83	136	BRITISH
27	ZAMBIA	1.544.01	40	BRITISH
28	GAMBIA	1.430.05	77	BRITISH

29	TANZANIA	1.414.36	77	GERMAN
30	BURKINAFASO	1.303.08	69	FRENCH
31	LESOTHO	1.288.21	68	BRITISH
32	UGANDA	1.202.69	68	BRITISH
33	MALI	1.166.84	25	FRENCH
34	RWANDA	1.092.42	43	BELGIUM
35	GUINEA	997.566	72	FRENCH
36	MALAGASY REP	981.148	66	FRENCH
37	ETSHIOPIA	955.286	–	LIBRE
38	MOZAMBIQUE	938.018	470	PORTUGUESE
39	MALAWI	880.083	73	BRITISH
40	TOGO	822.946	66	GERMAN
41	CENTRAFRICAN REP	754.367	50	FRENCH
42	SIERRA LEONE	746.587	174	BRITISH
43	ERITHREA	738.618	104	ITALIAN
44	NIGER	736.055	89	FRENCH
45	BISSAU GUINEA	788.915	81	FRENCH
46	BURUNDI	400.75	43	BELGIUM
47	D.R.C	333.839	52	BELGIUM
48	LIBERIA	378.921	–	FREE
49	ZIMBABWE	8.542	57	BRITISH

Source : ECONOMY WATCH. ECONOMIC STATISTICS DATABASE (GDP per cap (PPP), US DOLLARS DATA FOR ALL COUNTRIES. INTERNET (GOOGLE).

Based on data in the tables above we can realize that:

1. With 39 years of colonization, Libya was the first in GDP/Cap in 1980, was 3rd /50 2006, 4th /49 in 2009.

2. With 121 years of colonization, Gabon, who was second in GDP/cap in 1980, was 4th /50 in 2006 3rd /49 in 2009.

3. With 105 years of colonization, South Africa was third in GDP/Cap in 1980, was 6th /50 in 2006 7th /49 in 2009.

4. With 132 years of colonization, Algeria was the fourth in GDP/cap in 1980, was 8th /50 in 2006 9th /49 in 2009.
5. With 102 years of colonization, Seychelles, who were fifth in GDP/Cap in 1980, was 2nd /50 in 2006 1st /49 in 2009.
6. With 106 years of colonization, Namibia was sixth in GDP/cap in 1980, was 9th /50 in 2006 10th /49 in 2009.
7. With 75 years of colonialism, Tunisia was the seventh in GDP/cap in 1980, was 10th /50 in 2006 8th /49 in 2009.
8. With 78 years of colonization, the Ivory Coast who was eighth in GDP/Cap in 1980, was 10th /50 in 2006 23rd /49 in 2009.
9. With 138 years of colonization, Mauritius who were ninth in GDP/Cap in 1980, was 7th /50 in 2006 6th /49 in 2009.
10. With 99 years of colonialism, Nigeria was the tenth in GDP/cap in 1980, was 23rd /50 in 2006 18th /49 in 2009.
11. With 81 years of colonization, Botswana was the eleventh in GDP/Cap in 1980, was 5th /50 in 2006 5th /49 in 2009.
12. With 44 years of colonization, Morocco was the twelfth in GDP/Cap 14th /50 was in 2006, 14th /49 in 2009.
13. With 50 years of colonization, Congo Brazza, who was thirteenth in GDP/Cap in 1980, was 15th /50 in 2006 15th /49 in 2009.
14. With 66 years of colonization, Swaziland was the fourteenth in GDP/Cap in 1980, was 12th /50 in 2006 13th /49 in 2009.
15. With 76 years of colonization, Cameroon was the fifteenth in GDP/Cap in 1980, was 17th /50 in 2006 19th /49 in 2009.
16. With 57 years of colonization, Zimbabwe was the sixteenth in GDP/Cap in 1980, was 32nd /50 in 2006 49th /49 in 2009.
17. With 40 years of colonialism, Egypt was the seventeenth in GDP/Cap in 1980, was 16th /50 in 2006 12th /49 in 2009.
18. With 40 years of colonization, Zambia was the eighteenth in GDP/Cap in 1980, was 20th /50 in 2006, 27th /49 in 2009.
19. Without having been colonized, Liberia was in the nineteenth GDP/Cap in 1980, was 45th /50 in 2006, 47th /49 in 2009.
20. With 484 years of colonization, Angola was the twentieth in GDP/Cap in 1980, was 11th /50 in 2006, 11th /49 in 2009.
20. With 57 years of colonization, Sudan was in the twentieth GDP/Cap in 1980, was 18th /50 in 2006, 17th /49 in 2009.

21. With 301 years of colonization, Senegal was twenty-first was in GDP/ Cap in 1980, was 24th /50 in 2006 21st /49 in 2009.

22. With 68 years of colonization, Kenya was second in twenty-GDP/Cap in 1980, was 26th /50 in 2006, 22nd /49 in 2009.

23. With 66 years of colonization, Togo was twenty-third in 1980, was 36th /50 in 2006 40th /49 in 2009.

24. With 68 years of colonization, Lesotho was twenty-fourth in GDP/cap in 1980, was 22nd/50 in 2006, 31st /49 in 2009.

25. With 66 years of colonization, Madagascar was twenty-fifth in GDP/ Cap in 1980, was 40th /50 in 2006 36th /49 in 2009.

26. With 89 years of colonization, Niger was twenty-sixth in GDP/cap in 1980, was 43rd /50 in 2006, 44th /49 in 2009.

27. With 39 years of colonization, Mauritania, who was twenty-seventh in GDP/cap in 1980, was 21st/50 in 2006, 20th /49 in 2009.

28. With 66 years of colonization, Benin was twenty-eighth in GDP/Cap in 1980, was 29th /50 in 2006, 25th /49 in 2009.

28. With 483 years of colonization, Cape Verde, which was twenty-eighth in GDP/Cap in 1980, 13th /50 in 2006, 16th /49 in 2009.

28. With 50 years of colonization, the Central African Republic who was twenty-eighth in GDP/Cap in 1980, was 34th /50 in 2006, 41st/49 in 2009.

29. With 68 years of colonization, Uganda was twenty-ninth in GDP/Cap in 1980, was 39th /50 in 2006, 32nd /49 in 2009.

30. With 174 years of colonization, Sierra Leone was thirtieth in GDP/Cap in 1980, was 42nd /50 in 2006, 42nd /49 in 2009.

30. With 470 years of colonization in Mozambique which was thirtieth in GDP/Cap in 1980, was 35th /50 in 2006, 38th /49 in 2009.

31. With 77 years of colonization, Tanzania was the thirty-first in GDP/Cap in 1980, was 38th /50 in 2006, 29th /49 in 2009.

32. With 77 years of colonization, the Gambia who was thirty-second in GDP/cap in 1980, was 37th /50 in 2006 28th /49 in 2009.

33. With 73 years of colonization, Malawi that was thirty-third in GDP/Cap in 1980, was 48th /50 in 2006, 39th /49 in 2009.

34.   With 52 years of colonization, the DRC was thirty-fourth in GDP/ cap in 1980, 49th /50 in 2006, 48th /49 in 2009.

35. With 43 years of colonization, Rwanda was thirty-fifth in GDP/Cap in 1980, was 41st/50 in 2006, 34th /49 in 2009.

35. With 43 years of colonization, Burundi, who was thirty-fifth in GDP/Cap in 1980, was 50th /50 in 2006, 46th /49 in 2009.

36. With 69 years of colonization, Burkina Faso, who was thirty-sixth in GDP/cap in 1980, was 30th /50 in 2006, 30th /49 in 2009.

36. With 25 years of colonization, Mali, who was thirty-sixth in GDP/cap in 1980, was 31st/50 in 2006, 33rd /49 in 2009.

37. With 81 years of colonization, Guinea Bissau, which was thirty-seventh in GDP/cap in 1980, was 46th /50 in 2006, 45th /49 in 2009.

38. No history of colonization, which was Etshiopie thirty-eighth in GDP/Cap in 1980, was 47th /50 in 2006, 37th /49 in 2009.

39. With 40 years of colonization, Chad, who was thirty-ninth in GDP/Cap in 1980, was 25th /50 in 2006, 24th /49 in 2009.

In interpreting the above data, we can observe—with the exception of Libya (which has a number of years of colonization relatively lower compared to the other, or second to have fewer years of colonization), the Morocco (which also has a relatively lesser number of years of colonization, the fifth to have fewer years of colonization)—a correlation between a number of years of colonization and a GDP/Cap relatively strong in 1961, 1993, 1994, 1995, 2006, 2009. This is how countries like:

1. The Seychelles with 102 years thirteenth among countries with a large number of years, was among the top ten in GDP/Cap in 1980, 1993, 1994, 1995, 2006, 2009, with the exception of 1961 where the data are not available.

2. Gabon, with 121 years, the tenth among the countries with a large number of years, was among the top ten in GDP/Cap in 1961, 1980, 1993, 1994, 1995, 2006, 2009.

3. South Africa with 105, twelfth among countries with a large number of years, was among the top ten in GDP/Cap in 1961, 1980, 1993, 1994, 1995, 2006, 2009.

4. The Mauritius with 138 years, seventh among the countries with a large number of years, was among the top ten in GDP/Cap in 1980, 1993, 1994, 1995, 2006, 2009, except 1961 for which data are not available.

5. Botswana with 81 year seventeenth among the countries with a large number of years, was among the top ten in GDP/Cap in 1961, 1980, 1993, 1994, 1995, 2006, 2009.
6. Namibia with 106 years eleventh among countries with a large number of years, was among the top ten in GDP/Cap in 1961, 1980, 1993, 1994, 1995, 2006, 2009.
7. Algeria, with 132 years, ninth among the countries with a large number of years, was among the top ten in GDP/Cap in 1961, 1980, 1993, 1994, 1995, 2006, 2009.
8. Tanzania, with 75 years, twenty-second among the countries with a large number of years, was among the top ten in and around GDP/Cap in 1961, 1980, 1993, 1994, 1995, 2006, 2009.

However, this correlation is not absolute since, as can be seen on the one hand all countries with many years of colonization are not at the top ten. This applies to:

1. The Angola with 484, is first among the countries with many years of colonization, but is not among the top ten in GDP/Cap in 1961, 1980, 1993, 1994, 1995, 2006, 2009.
2. Cape Verde with 483, is second among the countries with many years of colonization, but is not among the top ten in GDP/Cap in 1961, 1980, 1993, 1994, 1995, 2006, 2009.
3. Mozambique with 470, is third among the countries with many years of colonization, but is not among the top ten in GDP/Cap en1961, 1980, 1993, 1994, 1995, 2006, 2009.
4. Equatorial Guinea with 368, is fourth among the countries with a large number of years, but is not among the top ten in GDP/Cap in 1993, 1994, 1995. The data in GDP/Cap in 1961, 1980 are not available.
5. Senegal with 301, is fifth among the countries with a large number of years, but not with the exception of 1961, the top ten in GDP/Cap in 1980, 1993, 1994, 1995, 2006, 2009.
6. Sierra Leone 174 years, sixth among the countries with a large number of years, but is not among the top ten in GDP/Cap in 1961, 1980, 1993, 1994, 1995, 2006, 2009.

7. Ghana with 136-year-old, eighth among the countries with a large number of years, but are not with the exception of 1961, the top ten in GDP/Cap in 1980, 1993, 1994, 1995, 2006, 2009 .

8. Nigeria with 99 years fifteenth among the countries with a large number of years, but not with the exception of 1980, the top ten in GDP/Cap in 1961, 1993, 1994, 1995, 2006, 2009 .

9. Nigeria with 89 years, sixteenth among the countries with a large number of years, is not among the top ten in GDP/Cap in 1961, 1980, 1993, 1994, 1995, 2006, 2009.

10. Guinea Bissau with 81 year eighteenth among the countries with a large number of years, is not among the top ten in GDP/Cap in 1961, 1980, 1993, 1994, 2006, 2009.

On the other hand countries with fewer years of colonization, are among the top ten in GDP/Cap. This applies to countries such as:

1. The Libya with 39, second among the countries with fewer years of colonization, not only among the top ten, but the top four in GDP/Cap in 1961, 1980, 1993, 1994, 1995, 2006, 2009.

2. Morocco with 44, fifth among the countries with fewer years of colonization, is among the top ten in and around GDP/Cap in 1961, 1980, 1993, 1994, 1995, 2006, 2009.

That aside, there are countries such as: Somalia, Malawi, Tanzania, Gambia, Burkina Faso, Lesotho, Uganda, Kenya, Togo, Guinea, Malagasy Rep, with the number of years between 66 and 78, have GDP/Cap lower than those of Tunisia, the Ivory Coast, Cameroon, which also have the number of years of colonization between 66 and 78.

This is also true of countries such as: Sudan, Zimbabwe, DRC, Burundi, Rwanda, Chad, Zambia, Central African Republic with the number of years between 40 and 57, have GDP/Cap lower than those of countries such as Egypt, Congo Brazza, which also have a number of years of colonization between 40 and 57.

Given all this, it appears that the factor of years of colonization is not sufficient to determine the propensity of a strong GDP/Cap. Besides this factor there are many other factors, such as natural resources, production tools, the labor force, the percentage of academics, the proportion of roads, rail, access to many waters (ocean) that promote international trade, the political system, political instability for countries such as Angola, Sudan, Somalia . . . which have experienced many years of war.

It should be said that the factor of years of colonization is not very decisive or absolute to promote a real independence of colonized countries, since this factor must be associated on the one hand to the will of the colonizers 'prepare the colony forming a responsible elite, building a consistent infrastructure, . . . , and other factors associated with the production, the conscience of peoples for the development of their country . . . .

Speaking of the factor number of years and the amount of infrastructure (roads, rail, hospitals . . .) and the proportion of academics produced at independence or around—in light of the data tables for these variables, it can be observed a weak correlation between the number of years and the realization of these variables. For example, the proportion of roads in 1962 and around, in one hand not all countries that have many years of settlement are among the top ten. This applies to:—Gabon with 121 years of colonization is one of the last six as a proportion of roads.
—Algeria with 132 years of colonization, is among the last six as a proportion of roads.
—Angola with 484 years of colonization is one of the last twelve as a proportion of roads.

On the other hand countries such as:—the Rwanda-Burundi with 43 years of colonization is the top four in the proportion of roads.
—Zimbabwe with 57 years of colonization is among the top 5 in the proportion of roads.
—Tanzania with 77 years of colonization is one of the first two as a proportion of roads.
-Morocco with 44 years of colonization is the top eight in the proportion of roads.
—The Ivory Coast with 78 years of colonization is among the top ten in the proportion of roads.

However there is one hand countries such as:

–The Mauritius with a great number of years of colonization, or 138 years, are first in proportion of roads.

–The Seychelles with 102 years, are among the top two in proportion of roads.

–South Africa with 105, are among the top six in the proportion of roads.

–Cape Verde with 483 years, are among the top seven in the proportion of roads.

On the other hand countries such as:

–Mauritania with fewer years of colonization, 39 years, the second to have fewer years, is last in percentage of roads.

–Chad with 40 years, third among the countries with fewer years is among the last three as a proportion of roads.

–Sudan for 57 years, eighth among the countries with fewer years of colonization is the last in percentage of roads.

By the same exercise for the Km of rail, medical facilities, the percentage of academics, we arrive at similar conclusions regarding the number of years of colonization and correlation with these variables.

Now let us see in what follows, the factor share of academics and GDP/Cap. And here is the hypothesis: education would positively affect the management of the country, GDP/Cap.

based on:

–The percentage of academics at or around Independence on page 49-51,

–The GDP/Cap Rand in 1961 on page 76-77,

–The GDP/Cap $ U.S in 1980 on page 78-80,

–The GDP/Cap $ U.S in 1993 on page 81-83,

–The GDP/Cap $ U.S in 1994 on page 83-85,

–The GDP/Cap $ U.S in 1995 on page 85-87,

–The number of years of colonization on page 87-90,

–The GDP/Cap U.S dollars in 2006 on page 93-95,

–GDP/Cap in U.S. $ in 2009 on page 95-97, we can see a part that:

1. Mauritania, first as a percentage of academics, is not among the top ten in GDP/Cap in 1961, 1993, 1994, 1995, 2006, 2009, except 1961 for which data are not available.
2. Congo Brazza, second in percentage of academics, is not among the top ten in GDP/Cap in 1961, 1980, 1993, 1995, 2006, 2009, with the exception of 1994 where he was tenth.
3. Zimbabwe, fourth in percentage of academics, is not among the top ten in GDP/Cap in 1980, 1993, 1994, 1995, 2006, 2009, with the exception of 1961.
4. Togo, fifth in percentage of academics, is not among the top ten in GDP/Cap in 1961, 1980, 1993, 1994, 1995, 2006, 2009.
5. The Ivory Coast, the sixth in percentage of academics, is not among the top ten in GDP/Cap in 1993, 1994, 1995, 2006, 2009, except 1961 and 1980.
6. Senegal, eighth in percentage of academics, is not among the top ten in GDP/Cap in 1980, 1993, 1994, 1995, 2006, 2009, with the exception of 1961.
7. Cameroon, the tenth in percentage of academics, is not among the top ten in GDP/Cap in 1961, 1980, 1993, 1994, 1995, 2006, 2009.
8. Somalia, twelfth percentage of academics, is not among the top ten in GDP/Cap in 1961, 1980, 1993, 1994, 1995, 2006, 2009.

On the other hand:
1. Libya's third in percent of academics, is among the top ten in GDP/ Cap in 1961, 1980, 1993, 1994, 1995, 2006, 2009.
2. Tunisia, seventh in percentage of academics, is among the top ten in GDP/Cap in 1961, 1980, 1994, 2006, 2009, with the exception of 1993 where it is the thirteenth and 1995 whose data available.

For cons:
1. Algeria, the eleventh in the percentage of academics, is among the top ten in GDP/Cap in 1961, 1993, 1995, 2006, 2009, with the exception of 1994 where it is the fourteenth.
2. The Mauritius, the thirteenth percentage of academics, is among the top ten in GDP/Cap in 1980, 1993, 1994, 1995, 2006, 2009, except 1961 for which data are not available.

3. South Africa, the fifteenth in the percentage of academics, is among the top ten in GDP/Cap in 1961, 1980, 1993, 1994, 1995, 2006, 2009.
4. Gabon, thirty percent of academics, is among the top ten in GDP/Cap in 1961, 1980, 1993, 1994, 1995, 2006, 2009.

From the above we can observe a correlation between the percentage of academics at independence and around, and a good GDP/Cap. However, this correlation is not absolute. Factor and the percentage of university to be effective, must be linked with other factors such as political, the political will of governments, natural resources, infrastructure, access to many waters (ocean), the religious affiliation, the area . . . .

Therefore in the following pages you will find the data in these variables. And we will classify the data according to the colonizing countries.

AREA, NATURAL RESOURCES, TYPE OF GOVERNMENT, ACCESS TO WATER, MAIN RELIGIOUS AFFILIATION.

I. THE AFRICAN CONTINENT

I. FORMER BRITISH COLONIES

NO	COUNTRIES	AREA IN Km2	NATURAL RESOURCES
1	BOTSWANA	600.372	Diamonds, copper, nickel, coal.
2	ZIMBABWE	390.580	Gold, copper, chrome, coal, asbestos, emeralds, nickel.
3	ZAMBIA	752.614	Copper, cobalt, coal, zinc, lead, emeralds.
4	UGANDA	236.036	Copper
5	KENYA	582.645	Coffee, tea, . . . , petroleum products, cement, hides.
6	SUDAN	2.505.813	Iron ore, manganese, chrome ore, gold, copper ore, oil.
7	EGYPT	1.001.449	Oil, phosphates, iron ore, salt
8	LIBIA	1.759.540	Oil, natural gas.
9	SOMALIA	637.657	Uranium, shale, iron core, quartz.
10	NIGERIA	923.768	Oil, tin, doves, iron core, plomb, zinc, coal, . . . , uranium core.
11	GHANA	238.537	Or, diamond, manganese, bauxite.
12	SIERRA LEONE	71.740	Diamond, iron core, bauxite, rutile.
13	GAMBIA	11.295	Main exports: Peanuts, peanut oil, fish and fish box, cons
14	MALAWI	118.484	Asbestos, bauxite, graphite.
15	LESOTHO	30.355	Diamonds.
16	SOIUTH AFRICA	1.221.037	Gold, diamonds, textiles, wines and fruits.

II.   FORMER FRENCH COLONIES

NO	COUNTRIES	AREA IN Km2	NATURAL RESOURCES
1	MALAGASY REP	594.180	Chrome, graphite, mica, bauxite, copper, nickel.
2	CONGO BRAZZA	342.000	Oil, silicone, zinc, copper, iron ore, diamonds, potash.
3	GABON	267.667	Oil, manganese, uranium, gold, iron ore.
4	CENTRAFRICAN REP	622.984	Diamonds and uranium.

5	CHAD	1.284.000	Oil, natron, uranium
6	NIGER	1.267.000	Uranium, cassiterite, iron ore, calcium, phosphate, coal.
7	BURKINAFASSO	274.200	Manganese
8	MALI	1.240.000	Phosphates, gold.
9	IVORY COAST	322.463	Oil, iron, gold, diamond.
10	SENEGAL	196.192	Phosphate, minerai de fer, tourbe.
11	BISSAU GUINEA	36.125	Main exports: peanuts, palm kernels.
12	MAURITANIA	1.030.700	Iron ore, copper, gypsum.
13	ALGERIA	2.381.741	Oil, iron ore, zinc, phosphates, lead, mercury, gold, uranium.
14	TUNISIA	163.610	Iron, lead, zinc, calcium, phosphate, oil.
15	MOROCCO	446.550	Phosphate, coal, lead, manganese, petroleum, iron ore.
16	BENIN	112.622	Oil, iron ore, gold, phosphates, gypsum

III. FORMER BELGIUM COLONIES

1	D.R.C	2.345.409	Copper, silver, coal, zinc, cobalt, diamonds, oil, uranium, cadmium, gold.
2	RWANDA	26.338	Tin, tungstène, colombo-tantalite, gold, zinc, uranium.
3	BURUNDI	27.834	Bastnasitte, uranium, nickel.

IV. FORMER SPANISH COLONY

1	EQUATORIAL GUINEA	28.051	Main exports: coca, timber, coffee

V. FORMER GERMAN COLONIES

1	TOGO	56.000	Phosphates.
2	CAMEROON	475.442	Oll, bauxite, cassiterite.
3	TANZANIA	945.087	Diamonds, gold, tin.
4	NAMIBIA	825.000	Uranium, diamonds, tin, vanadium, lead, zinc, copper, silver.

VI.	FORMER PORTUGUESE COLONIES		
1	ANGOLA	1.246.700	Oil, diamonds, iron, salt, gypsum, gold, silver, manganese.
2	MOZAMBIQUE	783.030	Coal, colombo-tantalum, iron ore, bauxite
3	CAP VERDE	4.033	Main exports: vegetables, food, beverages, animals and animal products.
VII.	FORMER ITALIAN COLONY		
1	ERITHREA	125.000	Natural gas, gold, copper, iron ore.
VIII.	INDEPENDNTS		
1	ETSHIOPIA	1.221.900	Or, tungstène, plomb, lignite.
2	LIBERIA	111.369	Iron ore, diamonds, gold.

ACCESS TO WATER, TYPE OF GOVERNMENT, EXECUTIVE BRANCH, OFFICIAL RELIGION

I. EX BRITISH COLONIES

No	COUNTRIES	ACCES TO GREAT WATER	TYPE OF GOVERNMENT	EXECUTIVE BRANCH		OFICIAL RELIGION
				HEAD OF STATE	HEAD OF GOVERNMENT	
1	BOTSWANA	No	REPUBLIC	PRESIDENT		NONE
2	ZIMBABWE	No	REPUBLIC	PRESIDENT NONE		
3	ZAMBIA	No	REPUBLIC	PRESIDENT		NONE
4	UGANDA	No	REPUBLIC	PRESIDENT		NONE
5	KENYA	YES	REPUBLIC	PRESIDENT		NONE
6	SUDAN	YES	ISLAMIC MILITARY REGIME	PRESIDENT		ISLAM WAS IMPOSED IN 1995
7	EGYPT	YES	REPUBLIC	PRESIDENT	PRIME MINISTER	ISLAM
8	LIBIA	YES	SOCIALIST STATE	REV LEADER	SEC G.P.C	ISLAM
9	SOMALIA	YES	REPUBLIC	NO EFFECTIVE CENTRAL GOVERNMENT		ISLAM
10	NIGERIA	YES	FEDERAL REPUBLIC	PRESIDENT P.C NONE		
11	GHANA	YES	REPUBLIC	PRESIDENT NONE		
12	SIERRA LEONE	YES	REPUBLIC	(CHAIRMAN) S.C.S		NONE

#	Country		Type	Head of State	Prime Minister	Religion
13	GAMBIA	YES	REPUBLIC	CHAIRMAN A.F.P.R.C		NONE
14	MALAWI	No	REPUBLIC	PRESIDENT		NONE
15	LESOTHO	No	CONSTITUTIONAL MONARCHY	ROI	PRIME MINISTER	CHRISTIANITY
16	SOUTH AFRICA	YES	REPUBLIC	PRESIDENT		NONE
II.	FORMER FRENCH COLONIES					
1	MALAGASY REP	YES	REPUBLIC	PRESIDENT	PRIME MINISTER	NONE
2	CONGO BRAZZA	YES	REPUBLIC	PRESIDENT	PRIME MINISTER	NONE
3	GABON	YES	REPUBLIC	PRESIDENT	PRIME MINISTER	NONE
4	CENTRAFRICAN REP	No	REPUBLIC	PRESIDENT	PRIME MINISTER	NONE
5	CHAD	No	REPUBLIC	PRESIDENT	PRIME MINISTER	NONE
6	NIGER	No	REPUBLIC	PRESIDENT	PRIME MINISTER	NONE
7	BURKINAFASSO	No	REPUBLIC	PRESIDENT	PRIME MINISTER	NONE
8	MALI	No	REPUBLIC	PRESIDENT	PRIME MINISTER	NONE
9	IVORY COAST	YES	REPUBLIC	PRESIDENT	PRIME MINISTER	NONE

10	SENEGAL	YES	REPUBLIC	PRESIDENT	PRIME MINISTER	NONE
11	BISSAU GUINEA	YES	REPUBLIC	PRESIDENT	PRIME MINISTER	NONE
12	MAURITANIA	YES	REPUBLIC	PRESIDENT		ISLAM
13	ALGERIA	YES	REPUBLIC	PRESIDENT	PRIME MINISTER	ISLAM
14	TUNISIA	YES	REPUBLIC	PRESIDENT	PRIME MINISTER	ISLAM
15	MOROCCO	YES	CONSTITUTIONAL MONARCHY	KING		ISLAM
16	BENIN	YES	REPUBLIC	PRESIDENT		NONE
III.	FORMER BELGIUM COLONIES					
1	D.R.C	YES	REPUBLIC	PRESIDENT	PRIME MINISTER	NONE
2	RWANDA	No	REPUBLIC	PRESIDENT	PRIME MINISTER	NONE
3	BURUNDI	No	REPUBLIC	PRESIDENT	PRIME MINISTER	NONE
IV.	FORMER GERMAN COLONIES					
1	TOGO	YES	REPUBLIC	PRESIDENT	PRIME MINISTER	NONE
2	CAMEROON	YES	REPUBLIC	PRESIDENT	PRIME MINISTER	NONE
3	TANZANIA	YES	REPUBLIC	PRESIDENT		NONE
4	NAMIBIA	YES	REPUBLIC	PRESIDENT		

V.	**FORMER SPANISH COLONY**					
1	EQUATORIAL GUINEA	YES	REPUBLIC	PRESIDENT	PRIME MINISTER	NONE
VI.	**FORMER PORTUGUESE COLONIES**					
1	ANGOLA	YES	REPUBLIC	PRESIDENT		NONE
2	MOZAMBIQUE	YES	REPUBLIC	PRESIDENT		NONE
3	CAP VERDE	YES	REPUBLIC	PRESIDENT	PRIME MINISTER	NONE
VII.	**FORMER ITALIAN COLONY**					
1	ERTHREA	YES	REPUBLIC	PRESIDENT		
VIII.	**INDEPENDENTS**					
1	ETSHIOPIA	YES	REPUBLIC	PRESIDENT	PRIME MINISTER	NONE
2	LIBERIA	YES	REPUBLIC	(CHAIRMAN) C.S		NONE

RELIGIOUS AFFILIATION

I. FORMER BRITISH COLONIES

NO	COUNTRIES	RELIGIOUS AFFILIATION
1	BOTSWANA	1980: Traditional 49.2%, Protestant 29.0%, 11.8% African Christians, Roman Catholic 9.4, and others 0,6.
2	ZIMBABWE	1980: Indigenous African 13.6%, Roman Catholic 11.7%, animist 40.4%, other 14.8%.
3	ZAMBIA	1980: Christian 72.6% 34.2% which Protestant, Roman Catholic 26.2%, Christians in Africa, 8 3%, indigenous beliefs 27%, Muslim 0.3%, other 0.7%.
4	UGANDA	1980: Roman Catholic 49.6%, Protestant 28.7%, Muslim 6.6%, other 15.1%.
5	KENYA	1987: Christian 73.0% of which Roman Catholic 27%, Protestant 19%, other Christian (mainly indigenous Africans), Anglican and Eastern Orthodox 27%, traditional beliefs 19.0%, Muslim 6.0%, other 2%.
6	SUDAN	1992: Sunni Muslim 74.7%, traditional beliefs 17.1%, Christian 8.2%
7	EGYPT	1990: Sunni Muslim c. 90%, Christian c. 10%

8	LIBIA	1992: Sunni Muslim 97.7%, other 3.0%.
9	SOMALIA	1980: Sunni Muslim 99.8%, chrétiiens 0.1%, other 0.1%.
10	NIGERIA	1980: Christian 49% of which 26.3% Protestant, Roman Catholic 12.1%, 10.6% indigenous African, muslim 45 % and others 6 %
11	GHANA	1980: Christian 62.6% 27.9% which Protestant, Roman Catholic 18.7%, indigenous African 16%, traditional beliefs 21.4%, Muslim 15.7%.
12	SIERRA LEONE	1993: Sunni Muslim 60%, indigenous beliefs 30%, Christian 10%.
13	GAMBIA	1993: Muslim 95%, Christian 4%, indigenous beliefs and other 1%.
14	MALAWI	1980: Christian 64.5% of which 33.7% Protestant, Roman Catholic 27.6%, indigenous beliefs 19%, Muslim 16.2%, other 0.3%.
15	LESOTHO	1992: Christian 93% of which 42.8% Roman Catholic, Protestant, mainly Evangelical Lesotho 29.1%, other Christian 21.1%, other mostly traditional beliefs 7%.
16	SOUTH AFRICA	1990: Christian 67.8% of which 22.2% black independent churches, reformed Afrikaans 11.8%, Roman Catholic 7.6%, Methodist 5.9%, Anglican 3.8%, Lutheran 2.5%, Hindu 1 , 3%, Muslim 1.1%, Jewish 0.4% other 29.4% traditional beliefs.

II.	FORMER FRENCH COLONIES	
1	MALAGASY REP	
2	CONGO BRAZZA	1980: Roman Catholic 53.9%, Protestant 24.9%, African Christian 14.2%, traditional beliefs 4.8%, other 2.2%.
3	GABON	1980: Christian 96.2% of which 65.2% Roman Catholic, Protestant 18.8% 12.1% indigenous African, traditional 2.9%, Muslim 0.8%, other 0.1%, 7.99% Amadiyah.
4	CENTRAFRICAN REP	1985: Protestant 40%, Roman Catholic 28%, traditional 24%, Muslim 8%
5	CHAD	1993: Muslim 53.9%, Christian 34.7% of which Roman Catholic 20.3%, Protestant 14.4%, 11.4% traditional beliefs.
6	NIGER	1988: mostly Sunni Muslims 98.7% Christians 0.4%, other mostly traditional animistic beliefs 0.9%.
7	BURKINAFASSO	1980: Traditional 44.8%, Muslim 43%, Christian 12.2% of which Roman Catholic 9.8%, Protestant 2.4%.
8	MALI	1983: Muslim 90%, indigenous beliefs 9%, Christian 1%.
9	IVORY COAST	1988: Muslim 38.7%, Catholic 20.8%, animist 17%, atheist 13.4%, Protestant 5.3%, excluding Harrism 1.4%, other 3.4%.
10	SENEGAL	1988: 94% Sunni Muslims, Christians prédominanment Roman Catholic 4.9%, indigenous beliefs and other 1.1%
11	BISSAU GUINEA	1992: Indigenous beliefs 54%, Muslim 38%, Christian 8%.
12	MAURITANIA	1980: Muslims 99.4% Christians 0.4%, other 0.2%.
13	ALGERIA	1990: Muslim 99.9%, Catholic 0.1%.
14	TUNISIA	1980: Sunni 99.4%, Christian 0.3%, Jewish 0.1%, other 0.2%.

15	MOROCCO	1993: mostly Sunni Muslims 98.7% Christians 1.1%
16	BENIN	Indigenous beliefs 62%, Christian 23.3% Roman Catholic which 21%, Protestant 2.3%, Muslim 12%, other 2.7%.

III. FORMER BELGIUM COLONIES

1	D.R.C	1980: Roman Catholic 48.4%, Protestant 29%, Christian 17.1%, indigenous, traditional beliefs 3.4%, Muslim 1.4%, other 0.7%.
2	RWANDA	1991: The largest Roman Catholic religious organization was representing 44%, Muslim 8-9%, the remaining Protestant churches or traditional animist beliefs.
3	BURUNDI	1990: Roman Catholic 65.1%, non-religious 18.6%, Protestant 13.8%, Muslim 1.6%, indigenous beliefs 0.3%, consisting of other indigenous African 0.6%.

IV. FORMER GERMAN COLONIES

1	TOGO	1981: Traditional beliefs 58.9%, Roman Catholic 21.5%, Muslim 12.1%, Protestant 6.8%, other 0.7%.
2	CAMEROON	1990: Roman Catholic 34.7%, animist 26.0%, Muslim 21.8%, Protestant 17.5%.
3	TANZANIA	1984: Muslim 35%, animist 35%, Christian 30%.
4	NAMIBIA	1981: Lutheran 51.2%, 19.8% Roman Catholic, Dutch reformed 6.1%, Anglican 5%, other 17.9%.

V. FORMER SPANISH COLONY

1	EQUATORIAL GUINEA	1980: Christians mainly Roman Catholic 88.8%, indigenous beliefs 4.6%, atheist 1.4%, Muslim 0.5%, other 0.2%, none 4.5%.

VI.	FORMER PORTUGUESE COLONIES	
1	ANGOLA	Christians 90% of which Roman Catholic 68.7%, Protestant 19.8%, indigenous beliefs 9.5%, other 0.5%.
2	MOZAMBIQUE	Christians 90% of which Roman Catholic 68.7%, Protestant 19.8%, indigenous beliefs 9.5%, other 0.5%.
3	CAPE VERDE	1991: 93.2% Roman Catholic, Protestant and other 6.8%.
VII.	FORMER ITALIAN COLONY	
1	ERITHREA	
VIII.	INDEPENDENTS	
1	ETSHIOPIA	1980: Orthodox Etshiopiens 52.5%, Muslim 31.4%, 11.4% traditional beliefs.
2	LIBERIA	1984: Christian 67.7%, Muslim 13.8%, indigenous beliefs and other 18.5%.

The data that is on page 105 to 116:

–The area and access to many waters, are: FOLLET STUDENT ATLAS. Compiled Under the leadership of Herbert H. Gross.Ph.D.Follet Publishing Company c 1975 Chicago. But the areas of Madagascar, Burundi, DRC, Mozambique, Namibia, Eritrea, Tanzania, Gambia, Burkinafasso, Mali, Etshiopie, Cape Verde, Tunisia, Somalia, are taken from: A Lonely Planet Africa 1995.

–The official religion, religious affiliation, natural resources, the type of government and executive branch, are from: Encyclopaedia Britannica Book of the Year 1996.Events of 1995.Encyclopaedia Britannica c 1996.

–Religious affiliation, the type of government for the years indicated. However they can change over time depending on the decisions of the country. This can also be the case of the official religion.

–The abbreviations are in the column, the executive branch, pages 94 to 96 are:

1.　AFPRC: Armed Forces Provisional Ruling Council (Armed Forces Provisional Ruling Council of.
2.　C.S: Council of State (Conseil d'Etat)
3.　F.C: Federal Council (Federal Council)
4.　GPC: General People's Committee (General of people)
5.　P.C: Provisional Council (Provisionel)
6.　S.C: State Council (State Council)
7.　SCS: Supreme Council of State (Supreme Council of State)

Encyclopaedia Britannica from the Book of the Year 1996.Events of 1995.

After that, given that until 1980, most African countries had "political independence," we give in the pages that follow, the percentages of academics in 1994, several years after "political independence." This will allow us to see the progress that African countries have made in education to universities or colleges.

PERCENTAGE OF ACADEMICS AT INDEPENDENCE AND 1994 IN ORDER.

NO	COUNTRIES	PERCENTAGE AT INDEPENDENCE	PERCENTAGE IN 1994	PROGRESSION
1	MAURITANIA	0.6836	0.3534	-0.3302
2	CONGO BRAZZA	0.2652	0.5522	0.287
3	LIBIA	0.1932	1.4038	1.4038
4	ZIMBABWE	0.1122	0.0372	-0.075
5	TOGO	0.1032	0.2793	0.1761
6	IVORY COAST	0.0928	0.3768	0.284
7	TUNISIA	0.0571	0.0011	-0.056
8	SENEGAL	0.0457	0.2716	0.2259
9	MOROCCO	0.0364	0.0007	-0.0357
10	CAMEROON	0.0349 0.0344	0.0002	-0.0347-0.0342
11	ALGERIA	0.0257	0.0010	-0.0247
12	SOMALIA	0.0245	-	-
13	MAURITIUS	0.0226	-	-
14	ANGOLA	0.0205	0.0597	0.0392
15	SOUTH AFRICA	0.0200	0.5447	0.5247
16	CHAD	0.0197	0.0541	0.0344
17	CENTRAFRICAN REP	0.0190	0.1122	0.0932
18	EGYPT	0.0168	-	-
19	NIGERIA	0.0163	0.378	0.3617
20	GHANA	0.0159	0.0568	0.0409
21	SIERRA LEONE	0.0154	0.0558	0.0404
22	ZAMBIA	0.0149	0.1686	0.1537
23	BURUNDI	0.0132	0.0697	0.0565
24	MALAWI	0.0128	0.0487	0.0359
25	UGANDA	0.0121	0.1393	0.1272
26	NIGER	0.0099	0.0795	0.0696
27	BENIN	0.0098	-	-
28	D.R.C	0.0088 0.0039	0.00021	-0.00859-0.00369
29	SUDAN	0.0077	0.00023	-0.00747
30	GABON	0.0063	0.3923	-0.0063

31	RWANDA	0.0055	0.0437	0.0382
32	TANZANIA	0.0049	0.040	0.0351
33	BURKINAFASSO	0.0043	0.0945	0.0902
34	KENYA	0.0040	0.0817	0.0777
35	MALI	0.0023	0.0793	0.077
36	MOZAMBIQUE	0.0009	0.0387	0.0378

PERCENTAGE PROGRESSION OF GRADUATED STUDENTS FROM INDEPENDANCE UP TO 1994 IN ORDER

NO	COUNTRIES	PROGRESSION OF PERCENTAGE IN ORDER	NUMBER OF YEARS FROM INDEPENDNCE TO 1994	NUMBER OF COLONIZATION'S YEARS
1	LIBIA	1.2106	43	39
2	SOUTH AFRICA	0.5247	84	105
3	NIGERIA	0.3617	34	99
4	CONGO BRAZZA	0.287	44	50
5	IVORY COAST	0.284	34	78
6	SENEGAL	0.2259	34	301
7	TOGO	0.1761	34	66
8	ZAMBIA	0.1537	30	40
9	UGANDA	0.1272	32	68
10	CENTRAFRICAN REP	0.0932	34	50
11	BURKINAFASSO	0.0902	34	69
12	KENYA	0.0777	31	68
13	MALI	0.077	34	25
14	NIGER	0.0696	34	89
15	BURUNDI	0.0565	32	43
16	GHANA	0.0409	37	136
17	SIERRA LEONE	0.0404	33	174
18	ANGOLA	0.0392	19	484
19	RWANDA	0.0382	32	43

20	MOZAMBIQUE	0.0378	19	470
21	MALAWI	0.0359	30	73
22	TANZANIA	0.0351	33	77
23	CHAD	0.0344	34	40
24	GABON	-0.0063	34	121
25	SUDAN	-0.00747	38	57
26	D.R.C	-0.00859	34	52
27	ALGERIA	-0.0247	32	132
28	CAMEROON	-0.0347	34/33	76/75
29	MOROCCO	-0.0357	38	44
30	TUNISIA	-0.056	38	75
31	ZIMBABWE	-0.075	14	57
32	MAURITANIA	-0.3302	34	39

From the above data, we can classify in one hand, the top ten and second in the last ten GDP/Cap in 1980, 1993, 1994, 1995, 2006, 2009. This will allow us to see:

–Former colonial power which country whose former colony has a frequent (mode) among the top ten countries in GDP/Cap in different years.

–What former colonizer countries including the former colony has a frequent (mode) from the last ten in GDP/Cap in different years.

-What political system which the country shows a high incidence among the top ten in GDP/Cap.

-What political system which the country shows a high incidence in the last ten GNP/Cap.

–How dominant religious affiliation with the country shows a high incidence among the top ten in GDP/Cap.

–How dominant religious affiliation with the country shows a high incidence in the last ten GDP/Cap.

–What political system which the country has experienced a high incidence among the top ten countries recorded a large increase in percentage of academic independence in 1994.

–What political system which the country has experienced a high incidence among the ten countries, an increase of percentage of academic independence in 1994.

Let's start with the top ten countries in GDP/cap in 1980.

TOP TEN AFRICAN COUNTRIES GDP/Cap IN 1980.

NO	COUNTRIES	GDP/Cap IN U.S $	AREA IN Km2	NATURAL RESOURCES	ACCES TO WATER ?	TYPE OF GOVERNMENT	EXECUTIVE BRANCH	
							HEAD OF STATE	CHIEF OF GOVERNMENT
1	LIBIA	8.640	1.759.540	Oil, natural gas.	YES	Socialist STATE	Rev. leader	Sec G.P.C
2	GABON	3.680	267.667	Oil, manganese, uranium, gold, iron ore.	YES	Republic	President	Prime minister
3	SOUTH AFRICA	2.290	1.221.037	Gold, diamonds, textiles, wines and fruits.	YES	Republic	President	
4	ALGERIA	1.920	2.381.741	Oil, iron ore, zinc, phosphates, lead, mercury, gold, uranium.	YES	Republic	President	Primeminister

5	NAMIBIA	1.410	825.000	Uranium, diamonds, tin, vanadium, lead, zinc, copper, silver.	YES	Republic	President	
6	TUNISIA	1.310	163.610	Iron, lead, zinc, calcium, phosphate, oil.	YES	Republic	President	Prime minister
7	IVORY COAST	1.150	322.463	Oil, iron, gold, diamond.	YES	Republic	President	Primeminister
8	NIGERIA	1.010	923.768	Oil, tin, doves, iron core, plomb, zinc, coal, . . . , uranium core.	YES	Federal Republic	President P.C	
9	BOTWANA	910	600.372	Diamonds, copper, nickel, coal.	No	Republic	President	
10	MOROCCO	860	446.550	Phosphate, coal, lead, manganese, petroleum, iron ore.	YES	Constitutional Monarchy	King	

After the first ten, now see the last ten in GDP/Cap in 1980.

LAST TEN COUNTRIES IN AFIRCAINS GDP/Cap IN 1980

No	COUNTRIES	GDP/Cap IN U.S $	AREA IN Km2	NATURAL RESOURCES	ACCES TO WATER ?	TYPE OF GOVERNMENT	EXECUTIVE BRANCH	
							HEAD OF STATE	CHIEF OF GOVERNMENT
1	MOZAMBIQUE	270	783.030	Coal, colombo-tantalum, iron ore, bauxite	YES	Republic	President	
2	TANZANIA	260	945.087	Diamonds, gold, tin.	YES	Republic	President	
3	GAMBIA	250	11.295	Main exports: Peanuts, peanut oil, fish and fish box, cons	YES	Republic	Chairman S.C.S	
4	MALAWI	230	118.484	Asbestos, bauxite, graphite.	No	Republic	President	
5	D.R.C	220	2.345.409	Copper, silver, coal, zinc, cobalt, diamonds, oil, uranium, cadmium, gold.	YES	Republic	President	Prime minister

6	RWANDA	200	26.338	Tin, tungstène, colombo-tantalite, gold, zinc, uranium.	No	Republic	President	Prime minister
6	BURUNDI	200	27.834	Uranium, Bastnasite, nickel.	No	Republic	President	Prime minister
7	BURKINAFASSO	190	274.200	Manganese	No	Republic	President	Prime minister
7	MALI	190	1.240.000	Phosphates	No	Republic	President	Prime minister
8	BISSAU GUINEA	160	36.125	Main exports: peanuts, palm kernels.	YES	Republic	President	Prime minister
9	ETSHIOPIA	140	1.221.900	Gold, tungsten lead, lignite.	YES	Republic	President	Prime minister
10	CHAD	120	1.284.000	Oil, natron, uranium	No	Republic	President	Prime minister

TOP TEN AFRICAN COUNTRIES GDP/Cap IN 1993

No	COUNTRIES	GDP/Cap IN U.S $	AREA IN Km2	NATURAL RESOURCES	ACCES TO WATER?	TYPE OF GOVERNMENT	HEAD OF STATE	CHIEF OF GOVERNMENT
1	LIBIA	6.510	1.759.540	Oil, natural gas.	YES	Socialist State	Rev. Leader	Sec G.P.C
2	GABON	4.050	267.667	Oil, manganese, uranium, gold, iron ore.	YES	Republic	President	Prime minister
3	SOUTH AFRICA	2.930	1.221.037	Gold, diamonds, textiles, wines and fruits.	YES	Republic	President	
4	BOTSWANA	2.590	600.372	Diamonds, copper, nickel, coal.	No	Republic	President	
5	NAMIBIA	1.660	825.000	Uranium, diamonds, tin, vanadium, lead, zinc, copper, silver.	YES	Republic	President	
6	ALGERIA	1.650	2.381.741	Oil, iron ore, zinc, phosphates, lead, mercury, gold, uranium.	YES	Republic	President	Prime minister

7	MOROCCO	1.030	Phosphate, coal, lead, manganese, petroleum, iron ore.	YES	Constitutional Monarchy	King	Prime minister
8	CONGO BRAZZA	920	Oil, silicone, zinc, copper, iron ore, diamonds, potash.	YES	Republic	President	Prime minister
9	CAP VERDE	870	Main exports: vegetables, food, beverages, animals and animal products.	YES	Republic	President	
10	TUNISIA	780	Iron, lead, zinc, calcium, phosphate, oil.	YES	Republic	President	Prime minister

After the first ten, now see the last ten in GDP/Cap in 1993.

LAST TEN AFRICAN COUNTRIES GDP/Cap IN 1993

No	COUNTRIES	GDP/Cap IN U.S $	AREA IN Km2	NATURAL RESOURCES	ACCES TO WATER?	TYPE OF GOVERNMENT	EXECUTIVE BRANCH	
							HEAD OF STATE	CHIEF OF GOVERNMENT
1	BISSAU GUINEA	233	36.125	Main exports: peanuts, palm kernels.	YES	Republic	President	Prime minister
2	MALAWI	230	118.484	Asbestos, bauxite, graphite.	No	Republic	President	
3	D.R.C	220	2.345.409	Copper, silver, coal, zinc, cobalt, diamonds, oil, uranium, cadmium, gold.	YES	Republic	President	Prime minister
4	RWANDA	200	26.338	Tin, tungsten, Colombo-tantalite, gold, zinc, uranium.	No	Republic	President	Prime minister
4	CHAD	200	1.284.000	Oil, natron, uranium.	No	Republic	President	Prime minster
5	UGANDA	190	236.036	Copper	No	Republic	President	

6	BURUNDI	180	27.834	Uranium, bastnasite, nickel.	No	Republic		Prime minister
7	SOMALIA	150	637.657	Uranium, shale, iron ore, quartz.	YES	Republic	No effective central government	
8	SIERRA LEONE	140	71.740	Diamonds, iron ore, bauxite, rutile.	YES	Republic	Chairman A.F.P.R.C	
9	TANZANIA	100	945.087	Diamonds, gold, tin.	YES	Republic	President	
9	ETSHIOPIA	100	1.221.900	Gold, tungsten, lead, lignite.	YES	Republic	President	Prime minister
10	MOZAMBIQUE	70	783.030	Coal, colombo-tantalum, iron ore, bauxite	YES	Republic	President	

TOP TEN AFRICAN COUNTRIES GDP/Cap IN 1994

NO	COUNTRIES	GDP/Cap IN U.S $	AREA IN Km2	NATURAL RESOURCES	ACCES TO WATER?	TYPE OF GOVERNMENT	EXECUTIVE BRANCH	
							CHEF D'ETAT	CHEF DE GOUVERNEMENT
1	LIBIA	6.000	1.759.540	Oil, natural gas.	YES	Socialist State	Rev leader	Sec g.p.c
2	GABON	4.500	267.667	Oil, manganese, uranium, gold, iron ore.	YES	Republic	President	Prime minister
3	BOTSWANA	2.800	600.372	Diamonds, copper, nickel, coal.	No	Republic	President	
4	SOUTH AFRICA	2.650	1.221.037	Gold, diamonds, textiles, wines and fruits.	YES	Republic	President	
5	TUNISIA	1.700	163.610	Iron, lead, zinc, calcium, phosphate, oil.	YES	Republic	President	Prime minister
6	NAMIBIA	1.650	825.000	Uranium, diamonds, tin, vanadium, lead, zinc, copper, silver.	YES	Republic	President	

PROPOSAL OF SOLUTION ON THE CHAOTIC POLITICAL SITUATION IN DRC   151

7	MOROCCO	1.000	446.550	Phosphate, coal, lead, manganese, petroleum, iron ore.	YES	Constitutional Monarchy	King	
8	CONGO BRAZZA	970	342.000	Oil, silicone, zinc, copper, iron ore, diamonds, potash.	YES	Republic	President	Prime minister
9	CAMEROON	840	475.442	Oil, bauxite, cassiterite.	YES	Republic	President	Prime minister
10	CAP VERDE	810	4.033	Main exports: vegetables, food, beverages, animals and animal products.	YES	Republic	President	Prime minister

After the first ten, now see the last ten in GDP/Cap in 1994.

LAST TEN AFRICAN COUNTRIES GDP/Cap IN 1994

No	COUNTRIES	GDP/Cap IN U.S $	AREA IN Km2	NATURAL RESOURCES	ACCES TO WATER?	TYPE OF GOVERNMENT	EXECUTIVE BRANCH	
							HEAD OF STATE	CHIEF OF GOVERNMENT
1	GAMBIA	240	11.295	Main exports: Peanuts, peanut oil, fish and fish box cons	YES	Republic	Chairman A.F.P.R.C	
2	CHAD	230	1.284.000	Oil, natron, uranium	No	Republic	President	Prime minister
3	MALAGASY REP	210	594.180	Chrome, graphite, mica, bauxite, copper, nickel.	YES	Republic	President	Prime minister
4	BURUNDI	190	27.834	Uranium, bastnasite, nickel.	No	Republic	President	Prime minister
5	SIERRA LEONE	190	71.740	Diamonds, iron ore, bauxite, rutile.	YES	Republic	Chairman S.C.S	

#	Country			Main exports			President	Prime minister
6	BISSAU GUINEA	180	36.125	Main exports: peanuts, palm kernels.	YES	Republic		Prime minister
7	UGANDA	180	236.036	Copper	No	Republic	President	
8	MALAWI	170	118.484	Asbestos, bauxite, graphite.	No	Republic	President	
9	SOMALIA	160	637.657	Uranium, shale, iron ore, quartz.	YES	Republic	No effective central government	
10	D.R.C	140	2.345.409	Copper, silver, coal, zinc, cobalt, diamonds, oil, uranium, cadmium, gold.	YES	Republic	President	Prime minister
11	TANZANIA	120	945.087	Diamonds, gold, tin.	YES	Republic	President	
12	ETSHIOPIA	110	1.221.900	Gold, tungsten, lead, lignite.	YES	Republic	President	Prime minister

TOP TEN AFRICAN COUNTRIES GDP/Cap IN 1995

No	COUNTRIES	GDP/Cap IN U.S $	AREA IN Km2	NATURAL RESOURCES	ACCES TO WATER?	TYPE OF GOVERNMENT	EXECUTIVE BRANCH	
							HEAD OF STATE	HEAD OF GOVERNMENT
1	LIBIA	6.510	1.759.540	Oil, natural gas.	YES	Socialist State	Rev leader	Sec G.P.C
2	GABON	4.050	267.667	Oil, manganese, uranium, gold, iron ore.	YES	Republic	President	Prime minister
3	SOUTH AFRICA	2.930	1.221.037	Gold, diamonds, textiles, wines and fruits.	YES	Republic	President	
4	BOTSWANA	2.590	600.372	Diamonds, copper, nickel, coal.	No	Republic	President	
5	NAMIBIA	1.660	825.000	Uranium, diamonds, tin, vanadium, lead, zinc, copper, silver.	YES	Republic	President	
6	ALGERIA	1.650	2.381.741	Oil, iron ore, zinc, phosphates, lead, mercury, gold, uranium.	YES	Republic	President	Prime minister
7	MOROCCO	1.030	446.550	Phosphate, coal, lead, manganese, petroleum, iron ore.	YES	Constitutional Monarchy	King	

8	CONGO BRAZZA	920	342.000	Oil, silicone, zinc, copper, iron ore, diamonds, potash.	YES	Republic	President	Prime minister
9	CAPE VERDE	870	4.033	Main exports: vegetables, food, beverages, animals and animal products.	YES	Republic	President	Prime minister
10	SENEGAL	740	196.192	Phosphates, iron ore, peat.	YES	Republic	President	Prime minister

After the first ten, now see the last ten in GDP/Cap in 1995.

LAST TEN AFRICAN COUNTRIES GDP/Cap IN 1995

NO	COUNTRIES	GDP/Cap IN U.S $	AREA IN Km2	NATURAL RESOURCES	ACCES TO WATER?	TYPE OF GOVERNMENT	EXECUTIVE BRANCH	
							HEAD OF STATE	HEAD OF GOVERNMENT
1	MALAGASY REP	240	594.180	Chrome, graphite, mica, bauxite, copper, nickel.	YES	Republic	President	Prime minister

#	Country			Main exports		Republic	President	Prime minister
2	BISSAU GUINEA	233	36.125	Main exports: peanuts, palm kernels.	YES	Republic	President	Prime minister
3	MALAWI	230	118.484	Asbestos, bauxite, graphite.	No	Republic	President	
4	D.R.C	220	2.345.409	Copper, silver, coal, zinc, cobalt, diamonds, oil, uranium, cadmium, gold.	YES	Republic	President	Prime minister
5	CHAD	200	1.284.000	Oil, natron, uranium	No	Republic	President	Prime minister
5	RWANDA	200	26.338	Tin, tungsten, Colombo-tantalite, gold, zinc, uranium.	No	Republic	President	Prime minister
6	UGANDA	190	236.036	Cuivre.	No	Republic	President	
7	BURUNDI	180	27.834	Uranium, bastnasite, nickel.	No	Republic	President	Prime minister
8	SOMALIA	150	637.657	Uranium, shale, iron ore, quartz.	YES	Republic	No effective central government	
9	SIERRA LEONE	140	71.740	Diamonds, iron ore, bauxite, rutile.	YES	Republic	Chairman S.C.S	
10	TANZANIA	100	945.087	Diamonds, gold, tin.	YES	Republic	President	
10	ETSHIOPIA	100	1.221.900	Gold, tungsten, lead, lignite.	YES	Republic	President	Prime minister

TOP TEN AFRICAN COUNTRIES GDP/Cap In2006

No	COUNTRIES	GDP/Cap IN U.S $	AREA IN Km2	NATURAL RESOURCES	ACCES TO WATER?	TYPE OF GOVERNMENT	EXECUTIVE BRANCH	
							HEAD OF STATE	HEAD OF GOVERNMENT
1	EQUATORIAL GUINEA	16.630.43	28.051	Main exports: coca, timber, coffee	YES	Republic	President	Prime minister
2	SEYCHELLES	8.743.98	445	Main exports: fish and preparation of fish , beverages and tobacco, oil seeds, spices	YES	Republic	President	
3	LIBIA	8.435.53	1.759.540	Oil, natural gas.		Socialist State	Rev leader	Sec G.P.C
4	GABON	6.790.59	267.667	Oil, manganese, uranium, gold, iron ore.	YES	Republic	President	Prime minister
5	BOTSWANA	5.875.09	600.372	Diamonds, copper, nickel, coal.	No	Republic	President	
6	SOUTH AFRICA	5.380.60	1.221.037	Gold, diamonds, textiles, wines and fruits.	YES	Republic	President	

No	COUNTRIES	GDP/Cap IN U.S $	AREA IN Km2	NATURAL RESOURCES	ACCES TO WATER?	TYPE OF GOVERNMENT	President	Prime minister
7	MAURITIUS	5.144.63	1.865	Main exports: sugar, electronic components, knitwear, textiles and clothing	YES	Republic	President	Prime minister
8	ALGERIA	3.440.30	2.381.741	Oil, iron ore, zinc, phosphates, lead, mercury, gold, uranium.	YES		President	Prime minister
9	NAMIBIA	3.106.82	825.000	Uranium, diamonds, tin, vanadium, lead, zinc, copper, silver.	YES		President	
10	TUNISIA	2.990.30	163.610	Iron, lead, zinc, calcium, phosphate, oil.	YES		President	Prime minister

LAST TEN AFRICAN COUNTRIES GDP/Cap IN 2006

No	COUNTRIES	GDP/Cap I IN U.S $	AREA IN Km2	NATURAL RESOURCES	ACCES TO WATER?	TYPE OF GOVERNMENT	EXECUTIVE BRANCH	
							HEAD OF STATE	HEAD OF GOVERNMENT
1	RWANDA	269.74	26.338	Tin, tungsten, Colombo-tantalite, gold, zinc, uranium.	YES	Republic	President	Prime minster

No.	Country			Exports	Independent	Type		
2	SIERRA LEONE	255.80	71.740	Diamants, minerai de fer, bauxite, rutile.	YES	Republic		Chairman S.C.S
3	NIGER	245.84	1.267.000	Uranium, cassiterite, iron ore, calcium, phosphate, coal.	No	Republic	President	Prime minister
4	ERITHREA	239.07	125.000	Natural gas, gold, copper, iron ore.	YES	Republic	President	
5	LIBERIA	186.68	111.369	Iron ore, diamonds, gold.	YES	Republic		Chairman C.S
6	BISSAU GUINEA	186.46	36.125	Main exports: peanuts, palm kernels.	YES	Republic	President	Prime minister
7	ETSHIOPIA	183.13	1.221.900	Gold, tungsten, lead, lignite.	YES	Republic	President	Primeminister
8	MALAWI	169.53	118.484	Asbestos, bauxite, graphite.	No	Republic	President	
9	D.R.C	143.28	2.345.409	Copper, silver, coal, zinc, cobalt, diamonds, oil, uranium, cadmium, gold.	YES	Republic	President	Prime minister
10	BURUNDI	102.97	27.834	Uranium, bastnasite, nickel.	No	Republic	President	Prime minister

TOP TEN AFRICAN COUNTRIES GDP/Cap IN 2009 IN U.S. $

No	COUNTRIES	GDP/Cap IN U.S $	AREA	NATURAL RESOURCES	ACCES TO WATER?	TYPE OF GOVERNMENT	EXECUTIVE BRANCH HEAD OF STATE	HEAD OF GOVERNMENT
						Republic		
1	SEYCHELLES	19.274.43	445	Main exports: fish and preparation of fish , beverages and tobacco, oil seeds, spices	YES	Republic	President	
2	EQUATORIAL GUINEA	16.852.81	28.051	Main exports: coca, timber, coffee	YES	Republic	President	Prime minister
3	GABON	14.420.69	267.667	Oil, manganese, uranium, gold, iron ore.	YES	Republic	President	Prime minister
4	LIBIA	14.380.85	1.759.540	Oil, natural gas.	YES	Socialist State	Rev leader	Sec G.P.C
5	BOTSWANA	13.416.66	600.372	Diamonds, copper, nickel, coal.	No	Republic	President	
6	MAURITIUS	12.356.23	1.865	Main exports: sugar, electronics, fabrics, textiles and clothing.	YES	Republic	President	Prime minister
7	SOUTH AFRICA	9.961.02	1.221.037	Gold, diamonds, textiles, wines and fruits.	YES	Republic	President	

8	TUNISIA	8.284.82	163.610	Iron, lead, zinc, calcium, phosphate, oil.	YES	Republic	President	Prime minister
9	ALGERIA	6.854.93	2.381.741	Oil, iron ore, zinc, phosphates, lead, mercury, gold, uranium.	YES	Republic	President	Prime minister
10	NAMIBIA	6.610.35	825.000	Uranium, diamonds, tin, vanadium, lead, zinc, copper, silver.	YES	Republic	President	

LAST TEN AFRICAN COUNTRIES GNP/Cap IN 2009

NO	COUNTRIES	GDP/Cap IN U.S $	AREA	NATURAL RESOURCES	ACCES TO WATER?	TYPE DE GOUVERNEMENT	BRANCHE EXECUTIVE	
							HEAD OF STATE	HEAD OF GOVERNMENT
1	TOGO	822.946	56.000	Phosphates	YES	Republic	President	Prime minister
2	CENTRAL AFRICA REP	754.367	622.984	Diamonds and uranium.	No	Republic	President	Prime minister
3	SIERRA LEONE	746.587	71.740	Diamonds, iron ore, bauxite, rutile.	YES	Republic	Chairman S.C.S	

#	Country			Resources				
4	ERITHREA	738.618	125.000	Natural gas, gold, copper, iron ore.	YES	Republic	President	
5	NIGER	736.055	1.267.000	Uranium, cassiterite, iron ore, calcium, phosphate, coal.	No	Republic	President	Prime minister
6	BISSAU GUINEA	488.915	36.125	Main exports: peanuts, palm kernels.	YES	Republic	President	Prime minister
7	BURUNDI	400.75	27.834	Uranium, bastnasite, nickel.	No	Republic	President	Prime minister
8	LIBERIA	378.921	111.369	Iron ore, diamonds, gold.	YES	Republic	Chairman C.S	
9	D.R.C	333.839	2.345.409	Copper, silver, coal, zinc, cobalt, diamonds, oil, uranium, cadmium, gold.	YES	Republic	President	Prime minister
10	ZIMBABWE	8.542	390.580	Gold, copper, chrome, coal, asbestos, emerald nickel.	No	Republic	President	

TOP TEN COUNTRIES INCREASE% OF ACADEMICS

FROM INDEPENDENCE TO 1994.

NO	COUNTRIES	% OF PROGRESSION	AREA	NATURAL RESOURCES	ACCES TO WATER?	TYPE OF GOVERNMENT	EXECUTIVE BRANCH	
							HEAD OF STATE	HEAD OF GOVERNMENT
1	LIBIA	1,2106	1.759.540	Oil	YES	Socialist State	Rev leader	Sec. G.P.C
2	SOUTH AFRICA	0,5247	1.221.037	Gold, diamonds, textiles, wines and fruits.	YES	Republic	President	
3	NIGERIA	0,3617	923.768	Petroleum, tin, columbite, iron ore, lead, zinc, coal, uranium ore.	YES	Federal Republic	President P.C	
4	CONGO BRAZZA	0,287	342.000	Oil, silicone, zinc, copper, iron ore, diamonds, potash.	YES	Republic	President	Prime minister
5	IVORY COAST	0,284	322.463	Oil, iron, gold, diamond.	YES	Republic	President	Prime minister

6	SENEGAL	0,2259	196.192	Phosphates, iron ore, peat.	YES	Republic	President	Prime minister
7	TOGO	0,1761	56.000	Phosphates.		Republic	President	Prime minister
8	ZAMBIA	0,1537	752.614	Copper, cobalt, coal, zinc, lead, emeralds.	No	Republic	President	
9	UGANDA	0,1272	236.036	Copper	No	Republic	President	
10	CENTRAL AFRICA REP	0,0932	622.984	Diamonds and uranium.	No	Republic	President	Prime minister

LAST TEN COUNTRIES INCREASE% OF UNIVERSITY

INDEPENDENCE TO 1994

NO	COUNTRIES	% OF PROGRESSION	AREA	NATURAL RESOURCES	ACCES TO WATER?	TYPE OF GOVERNMENT	EXECUTIVE BRANCH	
							HEAD OF STATE	HEAD OF GOVERNMENT
						Republic		

#	Country			Resources				
1	CHAD	-0,0344	1.284.000	Oil, natron, uranium.	No	Republic	President	Prime minister
2	GABON	-0,0063	267.667	Oil, manganese, uranium, gold, iron ore.	YES	Republic	President	Prime minister
3	SUDAN	-0,00747	2.505.813	Copper	YES	Islamique military regime	President	
4	D.R.C	-0,00859	2.345.409	Copper, silver, coal, zinc, cobalt, diamonds, oil, uranium, cadmium, gold.	YES	Republic	President	Prime minister
5	ALGERIA	-0,0247	2.381.741	Oil, iron ore, zinc, phosphates, lead, mercury, gold, uranium.	YES	Republic	President	Prime minister
6	CAMEROON	-0,0347	475.442	Petroleum, bauxite, cassiterite.	YES	Republic	President	Pirme minister
7	MOROCCO	-0,0357	446.550	Phosphate, coal, lead, manganese, petroleum, iron ore.	YES	Constitutional Monarchy	King	

HONORE MATAMBA

#	Country						President	Prime minister
8	TUNISIA	-0,056	163.610	Iron, lead, zinc, calcium, phosphate, oil.	YES	Republic	President	Prime minister
9	ZIMBABWE	-0,075	390.580	Gold, copper, chrome, coal, asbestos, emerald nickel.	No	Republic	President	
10	MAURITANIA	-0,3302	1.030.700	Iron ore, copper, gypsum.	YES	Republic	President	

At this level, we can arrange the data in search of mode (the variable that has the high frequency). We want to know first, how often have:

–Former colonial countries such as English, French, German, Portuguese, Belgian . . . , top ten countries in GDP/cap in 1980, 1993, 1994, 1995, 2006, 2009;

–Such executive branch, the top ten countries in GDP/cap in 1980, 1993, 1994, 1995, 2006, 2009;

Such main-religious affiliation, the top ten countries in GDP/cap in 1980, 1993, 1994, 1995, 2006, 2009;

–Such natural wealth, the top ten countries in GDP/cap in 1980, 1993, 1994, 1995, 2006, 2009.

Ex-colonial countries such as English, French, German, Portuguese, Belgian . . . The top ten percent increase of academic independence in 1994.

On the other hand, how often have:

Ex-colonial countries such as English, French, German, Portuguese, Belgian, . . . among the ten countries with GDP/Cap in 1980, 1993, 1994, 1995, 2006, 2009;

Executive branch, as among the ten countries in GDP/cap in 1980, 1993, 1994, 1995, 2006, 2009;

Such main-religious affiliation, among the ten countries in GDP/cap in 1980, 1993, 1994, 1 1995, 2006, 2009;

–Such natural wealth, among the ten countries in GDP/cap in 1980, 1993, 1994, 1995, 2006, 2009.

As ex-colonial countries, English, French, German, Portuguese, Belgian . . . , among the last ten percentage increase of academic independence in 1994.

Let's start with the top ten.

1. TOP TEN COUNTRIES GDP/Cap IN 1980

NO	FORMER COLONY	FREQUENCE BY 10	PRINCIPAL RELIGIOUS AFFILIATION	FREQUENCE BY 10	NATURAL RESOURCES	FERQUENCE BY 10	EXECUTIVE BRANCH	FREQUENCES BY 10
1	FRENCH	5	MUSLIM	5	OIL	6	PRESIDENT-PRIME MINISTER	5
2	BRITISH	4	CHRISTIANS	3	DIAMONDS	4	PRESIDENT	4
3	GERMAN	1	LUTHERIANS	1	URANIUM	4	KING	1
4			TRADITIONAL BELIEFS	1	IRON ORE	2		
5					COPPER	2		
6					MANGANESE	2		
7					NATURAL GAS	1		

2. THE TOP TEN COUNTRIES IN GDP/Cap IN1993

NO	FORMER COLONY	FREQUENCE ON 10	RELIGIOUS AFFILIATION	FREQUENCE ON 10	NATURAL RESOURCES	FREQUENCE ON 10	EXECUTIVE BRANCH	FREQUENCE SUR 10
1	FRENCH	5	MUSLIM	4	OIL	6	PRESIDENT-PRIME MINISTER	5
2	BRITISH	3	CHRISTIANS	2	DIAMONDS	4	PRESIDENT	4
3	GERMAN	1	ROMAN CATHOLIC CHRETIANS	2	IRON ORE	4	KING	1

4	PORTUGUESE	1	LUTHERIANS	1	URANIUM	3	
5			TRADITONAL BELIEVES	1	COPPER	3	
6					MANGANESE	2	
7					NATURAL GAS	1	

3. TOP TEN COUNTRIES GDP/Cap IN 1994

NO	FORMER COLONY	FREQUENCE ON 10	MAIN RELIGIOUS AFFILIATION	FREQUENCE ON 10	NATURAL RESOURCES	FREQUENCE	EXECUTIVE BRANCH	FREQUENCE SUR 10
1	FRENCH	5	MUSLIM	3	OIL	6	PRESIDENT–PRIME MINISTRE	6
2	BRITISH	+ 2	ROMAN CATHOLIC	3	DIAMONDS	3	PRESIDENT	3
3	GERMAN	2	CHRISTIANS	2	COPPER	3	KING	1
4	PORTUGUESE	1	LUTHERIANS	1	URANIUM	2		
5	ITALIAN	+ 1	TRADITIONAL BELIEVES	1	MANGANESE	2		
6					AGRICULTURAL PRODUCTS	2		

4. TOP TEN COUNTRIES GDP/Cap IN 1995

No	FORMER COLONY	FREQUENCE BY 10	MAIN RELIGIOUS AFFILIATION	FREQUENCE BY 10	NATURAL RESOURCE	FREQUENCE BY 10	EXECUTIVE BRANCH	FREQUENCE SUR 10
1	FRENCH	5	MUSLIMS	4	OIL	5	PRESIDENT–PRIME MINISTER	6
2	BRITISH	+3	CHRISTIANS	2	DIAMONDS	4	PRESIDENT	3
3	GERMAN	1	LUTHERIANS	1	URANIUM	3	KING	1
4	PORTUGUESE	1	ROMAN CATHOLIC	1	COPPER	3		
5	ITALIAN	+1	TRADITIONAL BELIEVES	1	MANGANESE	2		
6					NATURAL GAS	1		

5. TOP TEN COUNTRIES GDP/Cap IN 2006

No	FORMER COLONY	FREQUENCE BY 10	MAIN RELIGIOUS AFFILIATION	FREQUENCE BY 10	NATURAL RESOURCES	FREQUENCE BY 10	EXECUTIVE BRANCH	FREQUENCE SUR 10
1	BRITISH	4	MUSLIMS	3	OIL	4	PRESIDENT–PRIME MINISTER	6
2	FRENCH	4	CHRISTIANS	2	DIAMONDS	3	PRESIDENT	4

#					
3	SPANISH	1	ROMAN CATHOLIC	2	URANIUM	3
4	GERMAN	1	TRADITIONAL BELIEVES	1	LEAD	3
5			LUTHERIANS	1	ZINC	3
6					COPPER	2
7					GOLD	2
8					TEXTILES	2
9					IRON ORE	2
10					PHOSPHATES	2
11					COCO	1
12					WOOD	1
13					COFFE	1
14					FISH AND PREPARATION OF FISH	1
15					BEVERAGES AND TOBACCO	1
16					GRAIN OIL	1
17					SPICES	1

18	MANGANESE	1	
19	NICKEL	1	
20	COAL	1	
21	WINE AND FRUTS	1	
22	SUGAR	1	
23	ELECTRONIC PARTS	1	
24	KNITWEAR	1	
25	MERCURY	1	
26	TIN	1	
27	VANADIUM	1	
28	SILVER	1	
29	CALCIUM	1	
30	NATURAL GAS	1	

6. TOP TEN COUNTRIES GDP/Cap IN 2009

No	FORMER COLONY	FREQUENCE BY 10	MAIN RELIGIOUS AFFILIATION	FREQUENCE BY 10	NATURAL RESOURCES	FREQUENCE	EXECUTIVE BRANCH	FREQUENCE SUR 10
1	BRITISH	4	MUSLIMS	3	OIL	4	PRESIDENT-PRIME MINISTER	6
2	FRENCH	4	ROMAN CATHOLIC	2	DIAMONDS	3	PRESIDENT	4
3	SPANISH	1	CHRISTIANS	2	GOLD	3		
4	GERMAN	1	TRADITIONAL BELIEVES	1	URANIUM	3		
5			HINDU	1	ZINC	3		
6			LUTHERIANS	1	LEAD	3		
7					IRON ORE	2		
8					COPPER	2		
9					TEXTILES AND CLOTHINGS	2		
10					PHOSPHATES	2		
11					FISH AND PREPARATION OF FISH	1		
12					BEVERAGES AND TABACCO	1		

13	GRAIN OF OIL	1
14	SPICES	1
15	COCO	1
16	WOOD	1
17	COFFE	1
18	MANGANESE	1
19	NATURAL GAS	1
20	NICKEL	1
21	COAL	1
22	SUGAR	1
23	ELECTRONIC PARTS	1
24	KNIT WEAR	1
25	WINE AND FRUTS	1
26	IRON	1
27	CALCIUM	1
28	MERCURY	1
29	TIN	1
30	VANADIUM	1
31	SILVER	1

After the first ten, going to last ten:

1. LAST TEN COUNTRIES GDP/Cap IN 1980

No	FORMER COLONY	FREQUENCE BY 10	MAIN RELIGIOUS AFFILIATION	FREQUENCE BY 10	NATURAL RESOURCES	FREQUENCE	EXECUTIVE BRANCH	FREQUENCE SUR 10
1	FRENCH	4	MUSLIMS	5	GOLD	5	PRESIDENT–PRIME MINISTER	8
2	BELGIUM	3	TRADITIONAL BELIEVES	3	URANIUM	4	PRESIDENT	2
3	BRITISH	2	ROMAN CATHOLIC	3	DIAMONDS	2		
4	PORTUGUESE	1	CHRISTIANS	1	IRON ORE	1		
5	GERMAN	1	ETHIOPIAN ORTHODOXES	1	COPPER	1		
6					MANGANESE	1		
7					OIL	1		

2. THE LAST TEN COUNTRIES IN GDP/Cap IN 1993

No	FORMER COLONY	FREQUENCE BY 10	MAIN RELIGIOUS AFFILIATION	FREQUENCE BY 10	NATURAL RESOURCES	FREQUENCE	EXECUTIVE BRANCH	FREQUENCE BY 10
1	BRITISH	4	MUSLIM	4	URANIUM	5	PRESIDENT–PRIME MINISTER	6

No	FORMER COLONY	FREQUENCE BY 10	RELIGIOUS AFFILIATION	FREQUENCE	NATURAL RESOURCES	FREQUENCE	EXECUTIVE BRANCH	FREQUENCE SUR 10
							PRESIDENT	5
2	BELGIUM	3	ROMAN CATHOLIC	4	DIAMONDS	3		
3	FRENCH	2	TRADITIONAL BELIEFS	2	GOLD	3		
4	GERMAN	1	ETSHIOPIAN ORTHODOXES	1	OIL	2		
5	PORTUGUESE	1	CHRISTIANS	1	COPPER	2		
6					COBALT	1		

3. LAST TEN COUNTRIES IN GDP/cap IN 1994

No	FORMER COLONY	FREQUENCE BY 10	MAIN RELIGIOUS AFFILIATION	FREQUENCE BY 10	NATURAL RESOURCES	FREQUENCE	EXECUTIVE BRANCH	FREQUENCE SUR 10
1	BRITISH	5	MUSLIMS	5	DIAMONDS	3	PRESIDENT–PRIME MINISTER	6
2	FRENCH	3	ROMAN CATHOLIC	3	OIL	2	PRESIDENT	5
3	BELGIUM	2	TRADITIONAL BELIEFS	1	URANIUM	2		
4	GERMAN	1	ETSHIOPIAN ORTHODOXES	1	IRON ORE	2		
5			CHRISTIANS	1	COPPER	1		

4. LAST TEN COUNTRIES GDP/Cap IN 1995

No	FORMER COLONY	FREQUENCE BY 10	MAIN RELIGIOUS AFFILIATION	FREQUENCE BY 10	NATURAL RESOURCES	FREQUENCE	EXECUTIVE BRANCH	FREQUENCE SUR 10
1	BRITISH	4	MUSLIMS	4	URANIUM	5	PRESIDENT-PRIME MINISTER	7
2	FRENCH	3	ROMAN CATHOLIC	4	DIAMONDS	3	PRESIDENT	4
3	BELGIUM	3	TRADITIONAL BELIEFS	1	OIL	2		
4	GERMAN	1	ETSHIOPIAN ORTHODOXES	1	IRON ORE	2		
5			CHRISTIANS	1	COPPER	2		

5. LAST TEN COUNTRIES GDP/ Cap In2006

No	FORMER COLONY	FREQUENCE BY 10	MAIN RELIGIOUS AFFILIATION	FREQUENCE BY 10	NATURAL RESOURCES	FREQUENCE	EXECUTIVE BRANCH	FREQUENCE SUR 10
1	BELGIUM	3	ROMAN CATHOLIC	3	GOLD	5	PRESIDENT-PRIME MINISTER	7
2	BRITISH	2	MUSLIMS	3	URANIUM	4	PRESIDENT	3

3	FRENCH	2	CHRISTIANS	2	IRON ORE	4
4	FREE	2	CROYANCES TRADITIONAL BELIEFS	1	DIAMONDS	3
5	ITALIAN	1	ETSHIOPIAN ORTHODOXES	1	TUNGSTEN	2
6					BAUXITE	2
7					COAL	2
8					ZINC	2
9					TIN	1
10					COLOMBO-TENTALITE	1
11					RUTILE	
12					CASSITERITE	
13					CALCIUM	
14					NATURAL GAS	
15					COPPER	
16					PEANUTS	
17					PALM ALMOND	

No								
18								LEAD
19								LIGNITE
20								GRAPHITE
21								SILVER
22								COBALT
23								OIL
24								CADMINIUM
25								BASTNASITE
26								NICKEL

6. LAST TEN COUNTRIES GDP/ Cap IN 2009

NO	FORMER COLONY	FREQUENCE BY 10	MAIN RELIGIOUS AFFILIATION	FREQUENCE BY 10	NATURAL RESOURCES	FREQUENCE BY 10	EXECUTIVE BRANCH	FREQUENCE SUR 10
1	GERMAN	2	MUSLIMS	3	DIAMONDS	4	PRESIDENT– PRIME MINISTER	6
2	BRITISH	2	TRADITIONAL BELIEFS	2	URANIUM	4	PRESIDENT	4
3	FRENCH	2	ROMAN CATHOLIC	2	IRON ORE	4		
4	BELGIUM	2	CHRISTIANS	2	GOLD	4		

#	FREE / ITALIAN	PROTESTANTS	Resource	Count
5	FREE 1	1	COPPER	3
6	ITALIAN 1		COAL	3
7			PHOSPHATES	2
8			NICKEL	2
9			BAUXITE	1
10			RUTILE	1
11			NATURAL GAS	1
12			CASSITERITE	1
13			CALCIUM	1
14			PEANUTS	1
15			PALM ALMOND	1
16			BASTNASITE	1
17			SILVER	1
18			ZINC	1
19			COBALT	1
20			OIL	1
21			CADMINIUM	1
22			CHROME	1
23			ASBESTOS	1
24			EMERALD	1

Based on the above data, one can find how the mode among the top ten countries GDP/Cap.

That's how in 1980 as a way, there are the former French colonies (6/10) Muslims (5/10) for main religious affiliation, oil to natural resources, the political system where there is the President as Head of State and the Prime Minister as head of government.

In 1993 as a way, there are the former French colonies (5/10), Islam (4/10) for the main religious affiliation, oil for natural resources and the political system where there is the President as head of State and the Prime Minister as head of government to the executive branch.

In 1994 as a way, there are the former French colonies, the Muslim religion (3/10) Roman Catholic (3/10) for main religious affiliation oil to natural resources and the political system where there is the President as chief of State and the Prime Minister as head of government to the executive branch.

In 1995 as the mode, there are the former French colonies, Islam's main religious affiliation, oil to natural resources and the political system where the president is head of state and the Prime Minister is the head of government to the executive branch .

In 2006 as the mode, ex French colonies (4/10), English (4/10), the main Muslim religious affiliation oil to natural resources, and the political system where the president is the head of state Prime Minister and head of government.

In 2009 as the mode, the ex British colonies (4/10), French (4/10), the main Muslim religious affiliation, oil to natural resources and the political system where there is the president as head of state and Prime Minister as head of government to the executive branch.

On the other hand, for the last ten countries GDP/Cap:

In 1980, as the mode we have the former French colonies, the main Muslim religious affiliation, gold for natural resources and the political system where is the presiding head of state and prime minister head of government for executive branch.

In 1993 as the mode, there are the former British colonies, Catholics of the Roman Catholic religious affiliation for the primary, uranium for natural resources and the political system where the President is the Head of State and the Prime Minister head of government.

In 1994 as the mode, there are the former British colonies, the main Muslim religious affiliation, diamonds for natural resources, and the political system where the president is the head of state and prime minister, head of government to the executive branch.

In 1995 as the mode, there are the former British colonies for former colonies, Muslim (4/10) and the Catholics of the Roman Catholic religious affiliation for principal, uranium for natural resources and the system where the presiding is the head of state and prime minister head of government to the executive branch.

In 2006 as a way, there are the former Belgian colonies, Muslims (3/10) and the Catholics of the Roman Catholic religious affiliation for the primary, gold for natural resources and the political system where the president is the head of State and the Prime Minister is the head of government to the executive branch.

In 2009 as the mode, there are the former German colonies (2/10), former British colonies (2/10), former French colonies (2/10) and former Belgian colonies (2/10), the main Muslim religious affiliation , diamond (4/24), uranium (4/24), iron ore (4/24) and gold (4/24) for natural resources and the political system where the president is the head of State and the Prime Minister head of government to the executive branch.

We will now consider the proportion by group of countries colonized by the same country. For example, if 20 countries and former British colonies that six of them are among the top ten, and eight are among the last ten in some year, we can say that 30% of the ex English colonies were among the top ten and 40% were among the last ten in that year.

From this, there were:

-In 1980, a total of 41 countries which we have data. Of these 41 countries there were 14 countries such as English colonies, 16 former French colonies, three former German colonies, three former Portuguese colonies, three former Belgian colonies, a former colony that was a time in the colonization or French influence, and another time in colonization or English influence, a former colony that was a time under German influence and colonization or another time under colonial or English influence. And for these mixed cases, we give the value 0.5 instead of 1.

—In 1993, there were a total of 43 countries which we have data. Of these 43 countries, there were 15 former British colonies countries, 16 former French colonies, three former German colonies, three former Portuguese colonies, three former Belgian colonies, a former Spanish colony, a former colony which was under French influence and colonization or English, a former colony which was under colonial or English and German influence.

-In 1994, there were a total of 41 countries which we have data. Among them were 15 former British colonies, 15 former French colonies, three former German colonies, three former Belgian colonies, two former Portuguese colonies, a former Spanish colony, a former colony which was under French, and later English influence or colonization, a former colony that was under colonial or English and German influence.

—In 1995, there were a total of 43 countries which we have data. Among them were former British colonies in 14 countries, 14 former French colonies, three former German colonies, three former Belgian colonies, two former Portuguese colonies, a former Spanish colony, a country that was under colonial or English and French influence.

–In 2006, a total of 50 countries which we have data. Among them, there were 18 former British colonies, 18 former French colonies, four former German colonies, three former Portuguese colonies, three former Belgian colonies, two free countries (with no history of colonization), a former Italian colony, a former Spanish colony.

–In 2009, a total of 49 countries which we have data. Among them were former French colonies in 18 countries, 17 former British colonies, four former German colonies, three former Portuguese colonies, three former Belgian colonies, a former Spanish colony, a former Italian colony, two free (no history of colonization).

Given the above and knowing the number of ex British colonies, French, German, Belgian, Portuguese, Spanish, Italian . . . , which are among the top ten in GDP/Cap and those from the last ten years in various we can find the proportion. Then in 1980:
1. for former British colonies in the top ten countries GDP/Cap, the ratio is (3.5 x 100): 15 = 23.3%. But among the 13.3% in the last ten GDP/Cap.
2. For the former French colonies, the top ten in GDP/Cap, the ratio is (5.5 x 100) :16.5 = 33.3%. But 24.2% from the last ten.
3. For the former German colonies in the top ten in GDP/Cap, the proportion (1x100) 3.5 = 28.5%. And 28.5% from the last ten.
4. For the former Portuguese colonies in the top ten in GDP/Cap, the proportion is (0 x 100): 3 = 0%. But 33.3% among the last in GDP/Cap.
5. For the former Belgian colonies in the top ten in GDP/Cap, the proportion is (0 x 100): 3 = 0%. But 100% from the last ten.

In 1993:
1. For former British colonies in the top ten in GDP/Cap, the ratio is (3 x 100): 16.5% = 18.7. But (4 x 100): 16 = 25% from the last ten in GDP/Cap.
2. For the former French colonies in the top ten in GDP/Cap, the ratio is (5.5 x 100): 15.5% = 35.4. But (3 x100): 15.5 = 19.3% from the last ten in GDP/Cap.

3. For former German colonies are among the top ten in GDP/Cap, the ratio is (2 x100): 3.5% = 57.1. But (1 x 100) = 28.5 3.5 from the last ten.

4. For the former Portuguese colonies in the top ten in GDP/Cap, the proportion is (1 x100): 2 = 50%. And (1 x100): 2 = 50% from the last ten.

5. For the former Belgian colonies in the top ten in GDP/Cap, the proportion is (0 x 100): 3 = 0%. But (2 x 100): 3 = 66.6% from the last ten.

6. For the former Spanish colony in the top ten in GDP/Cap, the proportion (0 x100): 1 = 0%. But (0 x 100): 1 = 0% from the last ten.

In 1994:
1. For the former English colonies in the top ten in GDP/Cap, the ratio is (1.5 x 100): 15.5% = 9.6. But (5 x 100): 16 = 31.2% from the last ten.

2. For the former French colonies in the top ten in GDP/Cap, the ratio is (5.5 x 100): 15.5% = 35.4. But (3 x 100) 15.5 = 19.3% from the last ten.

3. For the former German colonies in the top ten in GDP/Cap, the ratio is (2 x 100): 3.5% = 57.1. But (1 x 100): 3.5% = 28.5 in the top ten.

4. For the former Portuguese colonies in the top ten in GDP/Cap, the proportion is (1 x 100): 2 = 50%. And (1 x 100): 2 = 50% for the last ten.

5. For the former Belgian colonies in the top ten in GDP/Cap, the proportion is (0 x 100): 3 = 0%. But (2 x 100): 3 = 66.6% from the last ten.

6. For the former Spanish colony in the top ten in GDP/Cap, the proportion is (0 x 100): 1 = 0%. And (0 x 100): 1 = 0%.

In 1995:
1. For the former English colonies in the top ten in GDP/Cap, the ratio is (2.5 x 100): 14.5% = 17.2. But (4 x 100): 14.5 = 27.5 from the last ten.

2. For the former French colonies in the top ten in GDP/Cap, the ratio is (5.5 x 100): 14.5% = 37.9. But (3 x 100): 14.5 = 20.6% from the last ten.

3. For the former German colonies in the top ten in GDP/Cap, the proportion is (1 x 100): 3 = 33.3%. And (1 x100): 3 = 33.3% from the last ten.
4. For the former Portuguese colonies in the top ten in GDP/Cap, the proportion is (1 x 100): 2 = 50%. But (0 x 100): 2 = 0% from the last ten.
5. For the former Belgian colonies, the top ten in GDP/Cap, the proportion is (0 x 100): 3 = 0%. But (3 x 100): 3 = 100% from the last ten.
6. For the former Spanish colonies in the top ten in GDP/Cap, the proportion is (0 x 100): 1 = 0% and 0% from the last ten.

In 2006:
1. For the former English colonies in the top ten, the proportion is (4 x 100): 18 = 22.22% among the top ten. But (2 x 100): 18 = 11.11% from the last ten.
2. For the former French colonies in the top ten, the proportion is (4 x 100): 18 = 22.22% among the top ten. But (2 x 100): 18 = 11.11% from the last ten.
3. For the former German colonies in the top ten, the proportion is (1 x 100): 4 = 25% for the first ten. But (0 x 100): 4 = 0% for the last ten.
4. For the former Portuguese colonies in the top ten in GDP/Cap, the proportion is (0 x 100): 3 = 0%. And (0 X 100): 3 = 0% for the top ten.
5. For the former Belgian colonies in the top ten in GDP/Cap, the proportion is (0 x 10) 3 = 0% (0 x 100): 3 = 0% for the last ten.
6. For free countries (with no history of colonization) among the top ten in GDP/Cap is the proportion (0 x 100): 2 = 0% for the top ten. But (2 x 100): 2 = 100% for the last ten.
7. For the former Spanish colony in the top ten in GDP/Cap, the proportion is (1 x 100): 1 = 100% for the top ten. But (0 x 100): 1 = 0% for the last ten.
8. For the former Italian colony in the top ten, the proportion is (0 x 100): 1 = 0%. But (1 x 100): 1 = 100% for the last ten.

In 2009:

1. For the former English colonies in the top ten GDP/Cap is the ratio (4 x 100): 17 = 23.5% among the top ten. But (2 x 100): 17 = 11.76% from the last ten.

2. For the former French colonies in the top ten in GDP/Cap, the ratio is (4 x 100): 18 = 22.22% among the top ten. But (3 x 100): 18 = 16.66% from the last ten.

3. For the former German colonies in the top ten in GDP/Cap, the proportion is (1 x 100): 4 = 25% among the top ten. And (1 x 100): 4 = 25% from the last ten.

4. For the former Spanish colony in the top ten in GDP/Cap, the proportion is (1 x 100): 1 = 100%. But (0 x 100): 1 = 0% for the last ten.

5. For the former Portuguese colonies in the top ten in GDP/Cap, the proportion is (0 x 100): 3 = 0% top ten. And (0 x 100): 3 = 0% for the last ten.

6. For the former Belgian colonies in the top ten in GDP/Cap, the proportion is (0 x 100): 3 = 0% top ten. But (2 x 100): 3 = 66.66% from the last ten.

7. For the former Italian colony in the top ten in GDP/Cap, the proportion is (0 x 100): 1 = 0%. But (1 x 100): 1 = 100% from the last ten.

8. For free countries in the top ten in GDP/Cap, the proportion is (0 x 100): 2 = 0% from the last ten. But (1 x 100): 2 = 50% from the last ten.

GDP/Cap which is the key to our ranking is the result of joint efforts of various factors in inter–influence. And proportions above may lead to the discovery that there are some former colonial powers that have been relatively favorable to the progress of their former colonies.

You can realize that Belgium had at least 66% or 100% of its former colonies among the last ten in GDP/Cap, and sometimes among the two or three last in the GDP/Cap in 2006 and 2009. This shows that somewhere the former colonial power is responsible to some extent in the bad start of Congo DRC in its march towards progress.

The DRC that was, among the six in GDP/Cap in 1980 for example, has many similarities with Gabon, which is second in GDP/cap in 1980. The DRC has almost everything and even more than what Gabon has in terms of natural resources, access to many waters, Christians as the primary religious affiliation, the same type of government and executive branch, except . . . unlike the former colonizing countries and other minor differences.

The DRC, among the last 6 in GDP/Cap in 1980, has almost everything and more than what Libya has in terms of natural resources, but Libya is first in GDP/Cap in 1980. The DRC has acces to large water, almost the same kind of executive branch, but with a difference of type of government, the main religious affiliation, former colonizing country and some minor differences.

The DRC, among the six in GDP/Cap in 1980, has almost everything and more than what Algeria has in terms of natural resources, but Algeria was the fourth in GDP/cap in 1980. The DRC has the same type of government and executive branch with Algeria. But one main difference in religious affiliation, and the former colonial power.

The DRC one of six in GDP/Cap in 1980, has almost everything and more than Tunisia in terms of natural resources. But Tunisia was sixth in GDP/cap in 1980, the same type of government and industry Executive, but differences on the main religious affiliation, the former colonial power, and other minor differences.

After all this exercise on African countries, also see what happened in other continents.
Let's start with the Asian continent.

The Asian continent

I. COLONIES OR FORMER U.S.A MANDATED

NO	COUNTRIES	DATA IN 1980				DATA IN 1993
		GDP/Cap IN U.S $	POPULATION	GRADUATED STUDENTS	% OF GRADUATED STUDENTS	GDP/CAP IN U.S $
1	PHILLIPPINES	720	48.317.000	1.276.000	2,640	830
II.	**UNDER AUSTRALIAN ADMINISTRATION**					
1	PAPWA NEW GUINEA	–	–	–	–	1.120
III.	**INDEPENDENTS**					
1	SAUDIA ARABIA	11.260	9.373.000	62	0,0006	7.510
2	IRAN	–	39.297.000	174*1979	0,0004	2.200
3	MONGOLIA	–	1.663.000	–	–	400
4	TURQUIA	1.460	44.472.000	237.000	0,5329	2.120
5	AFGHANISTAN	170	15.951.000	14.000	0,0877	280
6	JAPON	9.890	116.807.000	1.835.000	1,5709	31.450
7	NEPAL	140	14.010.000	–	–	160
8	NORTH CORREA	–	18.026.000	63.000*1960		970

#	Country					
9	SOUTH CORREA	1.520	38.124.000	648.000	1,6997	7.670
10	BHUTAN	80	1.246.000	-	-	170
IV.	UNDER TURC INFLUENCE					
1	IRAK	3.020	13.238.000	107	0,0008	1.500
2	LIBAN	-	2.670.000	9.760*1970		2.150
3	KOWEIT	22.840	1.370.000	-		23.350
V.	UNDER JAPONESE INFLUENCE					
1	TAIWAN (FORMOSE)					
VI.	FORMER BRITISH COLONIES					
1	INDE	240	675.000.000	6.016.000	0,8912	290
2	PAKISTAN	300	82.581.000	43	0,00005	440
3	BURMA (MYANMAR)	180	17.518.000*1983	162	0,0009	220
4	MALAISIA	1.670	13.697.000	61.000	0,4453	3.160
5	BENGLADESH	120	88.678.000	37.000	0,0417	220
6	SRILANKA	270	14.747.000	18.000	0,1220	600
7	QATAR	26.080	230.000	-	-	15.140
8	PORTUGUESE TIMOR	-	-	-	-	-

9	CIPRUS	3.560	627.000	418	0,0666	10.480
10	SINGAPOR	4.480	2.414.000	23.000	0,9527	19.310
11	MALDIVES	260	143.000*1977	–		820
VII.	UNDER BRITISH MANDATE OR PROTECTORATE					
1	OMAN	4.380	984.000	–		5.600
2	JORDANIA	1.420	2.923.000	37.000	1,2658	1.190
3	ISRAEL	4.500	3.878.000	59	0,0015	13.760
VIII.	FORMER FRENCH COLONIES					
1	VIETNAM	–	53.701.000	146	0,0002	170
2	LAOS	–	3.206.000	1.408	0,0439	290
IX.	UNDER FRENCH MANDATE OR PROTECTORATE					
1	THAILAND	670	46.718.000	599.000	1,2821	2.040
2	SYRIA	1.340	8.704.000	140.000	1,6084	15.892
3	CAMBODGE	70	6.401.000	9.988*1972		170
X.	FORMER NETHERLAND COLONY					
1	INDONESIA	420	147.490.000	196.000*1979	0,1328	730

DATA ON AREA km2, NATURAL

1. EX COLONIES OR COUNTRY IN TERMS/Protectorate USA

No	COUNTRIES	AREA IN Km2	NATURAL RESOURCES
1	PHILLIPPINES	300.000	Cobalt, copper, gold, nickel, oil, forests 40% of the area.
II.	UNDER AUSTRALIAN ADMINISTRATION		
1	PAPWA NEW GUINEA	461.691	Gold, copper, silver.
III.	INDEPENDENTS		
1	SAUDI ARABIA	2.149.690	Oil, gas, gold, copper, iron, crude oil reserves in 1994, bin 261 barrels.
2	IRAN	1.648.000	Chrome, oil, gas, crude oil reserves in 1994, bin 93 barrels, rubber, silk and caviar.
3	MONGOLIA	1.565.000	Coal, oil, tungsten, copper, molybdenum, gold, tin.
4	TURQUIA	780.576	Antimony, chromium, mercury, copper, coal, wool, silk, forests, reserves of crude oil in 1994 488 bin barrels.
5	AFGHANISTANT	647.497	Gas, oil, copper, coal, zinc, iron, wool, hides.

6	JAPON	370.073	
7	NEPAL	140.797	Quartz, forests.
8	NORTH CORREA	120.538	Coal, lead, tungsten, zinc, graphite.
9	SOUTH CORREA	98.477	Tungsten, coal, graphite.
10	BHUTAN	47.000	Tree, cement, wood.
IV.	UNDER TURC INFLUENCE		
1	IRAK	434.924	Oil, gas, crude oil reserves in 1994, bin 100 barrels, wool, hides.
2	LIBAN	10.400	Lime stone, iron.
3	KUWEIT	17.818	Oil, gas, crude oil reserves in 1994, bin 96.5 barrels.
V.	UNDER JAPONESE INFLUENCE		
1	TAIWAN (FORMOSE)	35.962	Coal, lime stone, marble, fishing for fish 1.2 min metric tones in 1993.
VI.	FORMER BRITISH COLONIES		
1	INDE	3.280.483	Coal, iron, manganese, mica, bauxite, titanium, chromium, petroleum, rubber, crude oil reserves in 1994 5.9 bin barrels.

#	Country	Value	Resources
2	PAKISTAN	803.943	Natural gas, iron ore, crude oil reserves 1994 203 min bin barrels, wool.
3	BURMA (MYANMAR)	678.033	Oil, lead, copper, tin, precious stones, rubber, teak reserves of crude oil barrels in 1994, 50 min.
4	MALAISIA	329.749	Tin, oil, bauxite, iron, rubber 35% of world production, reserves of crude oil barrels in 1994 4.3 bin.
5	BENGLADESH	142.776	Natural gas.
6	SRILANKA	65.610	Graphite, lime stone, pierres, phosphates, forêts, caoutchouc.
7	QATAR	22.014	Réserves du pétrole brut en 1994 3,7 bin barrels.
8	PORTUGUESE TIMOR	14.925	Graphite, lime stone, rocks, phosphates, forests, rubber.
9	CIPRUS	9.251	Copper, pyrites, asbestos.
10	SINGAPOR	581	Fishing for fish in 1992 9000 tonnes/m
11	MALDIVES 298 Fishing for fish in 1991 81.000 t/m.		
1	OMAN	212.457	85% oil exports, crude oil reserves in 1994 4.7 bin barrels.
2	JORDANIA	97.740	Phosphates, potash.
3	ISRAEL	20.700	Potassium, copper, phosphates, manganese sulphide.

VIII.	FORMER FRENCH COLONIES		
1	VIETNAM	332.559	Phosphates, coal, manganese, coal, bauxite, chrome, oil reserves of crude oil in barrels 1994 500 min, forest.
2	LAOS	236.800	Tin, Forest.
IX.	UNDER FRENCH MANDATE OR PROTECTORATE		
1	THAILAND	514.000	Largest producer of tin and tungsten, forest, teak, rubber.
2	SYRIA	185.180	Petroleum, phosphates, gypsum, crude oil reserves in 1994 1.7 bin barrels, wool.
3	CAMBODGE	181.035	Gemstones, phosphates, manganese, forests, rubber.
x.	FORMER NETHERLAND COLONIES		
1	INDONESIA	1.491.564	Nickel, tin, oil, bauxite, copper, natural gas, rubber, crude oil reserves in 1994, 50 min barrels, teak

DATA ON ACCESS TO BIG WATER, TYPE OF GOVERNMENT EXECUTIVE BRANCH OFFICIAL AND RELIGION

1. FORMER USA COLONY OR MANDATED/PROTECTORATE.

No	COUNTRIES	ACCES TO GREAT WATERS	TYPE GOVERNMENT	EXECUTIVE BRANCH		OFFICIAL RELIGIOUS AFFILIATION
				HEAD OF STATE	HEAD OF GOVERNMENT	
1	PHILLIPPINES	YES	REPUBLIC	PRESIDENT		NONE

II. INDEPENDENTS

No	COUNTRIES	ACCES TO GREAT WATERS	TYPE GOVERNMENT	HEAD OF STATE	HEAD OF GOVERNMENT	OFFICIAL RELIGIOUS AFFILIATION
1	ARABIE SAUDITE	YES	MONARCHY	KING		ISLAM
2	IRAN	YES	ISLAMIC REPUBLIQUE	PRESIDENT		ISLAM
3	MONGOLIE	NO	REPUBLIC	PRESIDENT	PRIME MINISTER	NONE
4	TURQUIE	ALMOST YES	REPUBLIC	PRESIDENT	PRIME MINISTER	NONE
5	AFGHANISTAN	NO	REPUBLIC	PRESIDENT	PRIME MINISTER	ISLAM
6	JAPON	YES	CONSTITUTIONAL MONARCHY	EMPEROR	PRIME MINISTER	NONE

#	Country		Regime	Head of State	Head of Government	Religion
7	NEPAL	NO	CONSTITUTIONAL MONARCHY	KING	PRIME MINISTER	HINDUISME
8	CORREE DU NORD	YES	SOCIALISTE REPUBLIC	PRESIDENT	PRIME MINISTER	NONE
9	CORREE DU SUD	YES	REPUBLIC	PRESIDENT	PRIME MINISTER	NONE
10	BHUTAN	No	—	KING		BUDIS MAJAHARIYAM

IV. UNDER TURC INFLUENCE

#	Country		Regime	Head of State	Head of Government	Religion
1	IRAK	ALMOST YES	REPUBLIC	PRESIDENT		ISLAM
2	LIBAN	ALMOST YES	REPUBLIC	PRESIDENT	PRIME MINISTER	NONE
3	KOWEIT	YES	CONSTITUTIONAL MONARCHY (EMIRATE)	EMIR		ISLAM

V. UNDER JAPONESE INFLUENCE

#	Country		Regime	Head of State	Head of Government	Religion
1	TAIWAN (FORMOSE)	YES	REPUBLIC	PRESIDENT	PRIME MINISTER	NONE

VI. UNDER BRITISH MANDATE OR PROTECTORATE

#	Country		Regime	Head of State	Head of Government	Religion
1	OMAN	YES	MONARCHY (SULTANATE)	SULTAN		ISLAM

#	Country		Government Type	Head of State	Head of Government	Religion
2	JORDANIE	ALMOST YES	CONSTITUTIONAL MONARCHY	KING		ISLAM
3	ISRAEL	ALMOST YES	REPUBLIC	PRESIDENT	PRIME MINISTER	NONE

VII. UNDER FRENCH MANDATE OR PROTECTORATE

#	Country		Government Type	Head of State	Head of Government	Religion
1	THAILANDE	YES	CONSTITUTIONAL MONARCHY	KING	PRIME MINISTER	BUDHISM
2	SYRIE	ALMOST YES	REPUBLIC	PRESIDENT		NONE
3	CAMBODGE		CONSTITUTIONAL MONARCHY	KING		BUDHISM

VIII. FORMER BRITISH COLONIES

#	Country		Government Type	Head of State	Head of Government	Religion
1	INDE	YES	FEDERAL REPUBLIC	PRESIDENT	PRIME MINISTER	NONE
2	PAKISTAN	YES	ISLAMIC FEDERAL REPUBLIC	PRESIDENT	PRIME MINISTER	ISLAM
3	BURMA (MYANMAR)	YES				NONE
4	MALAISIE	YES	CONSTITUTIONAL MONARCHY	PARAMOUNT RULER	PRIME MINISTER	ISLAM
5	BENGLADESH	YES	REPUBLIC	PRESIDENT	PRIME MINISTER	ISLAM
6	SRILANKA	YES	REPUBLIC	PRESIDENT		NONE

7	QATAR	YES	MONARCHY	EMIR	—	ISLAM
8	PORTUGUESE TIMOR	YES	—	—	—	—
9	CIPRUS	No	REPUBLIC	PRESIDENT		—
10	SINGAPORE	YES	REPUBLIC	PRESIDENT	PRIME MINISTER	NONE
11	MALDIVES	YES	REPUBLIC	PRESIDENT		ISLAM

IX. FORMER FRENCH COLONIES

1	VIETNAM	YES	SOCIALISTE REPUBLIC	PRESIDANT	PRIME MINISTER	NONE
2	LAOS	No	REPUBLIC	PRESIDANT	PRIME MINISTER	NONE

X. FORMER NETHERLAND COLONIES

1	INDONESIE	YES	REPUBLIC	PRESIDENT		MONOTHEISM

UNDER AUSTRALIAN ADMINISTRATION

1	PAPWA NEW GUINEA	YES	CONSTITUTIONAL MONARCHY	BRITANIC MONARC	PRIME MINISTER	NONE

RELIGIOUS AFFILIATION DATA

I. EX COLONIES AND MANDATED/Protectorate U.S.A

No	COUNTRIES	RELIGIOUS AFFILIATION
1	PHILLIPPINES	(1990) Roman Catholic 82.9%, Protestant 8.3%, Muslim 4.6%, aghipayan (Philippine church indent) 2.6%, other 1.6%.
II.	UNDER AUSTRALIAN ADMINISTRATION	
1	PAPWA NEW GUINEA	(1980) 58.4% Protestant, Roman Catholic 32.8%, Anglican 5.4%, indigenous beliefs 2.5%, Baha'i 0.6%, other 0.3%.
III.	INDEPENDENTS	
1	SAUDI ARABIA	(1980) Muslims, mainly Sunnah 98.8%, Christians 0.8%, other 0.4%.
2	IRAN	(1994) Muslim 99.1% (93.4% shits, Sunna 5.7%), Baha'i 0.6%, Christians 0.1%, zoroastriam 0.1%, Jewish 0.1%.
3	MONGOLIA	Although formal freedom of worship are all forms of traditional religions practiced Lamaist Buddhism, shamanism, Islam and others were greatly reduced during the 20th century. Data safe around the year 1994 do not exist.
4	TURQUIA	(1992) 80% Sunni Muslim, Alevi (non-Orthodox sect shite) 19.8%, Christians 0.2%.
5	AFGHANISTAN	(1990) Sunni Muslim 84%, Muslim 15% shite, other 1%.
6	JAPON	(1992) and Shinto religions for 51.3%, Buddhism 38.3%, Christian 1.2%, other 8.9%
7	NEPAL	(1991) 86.2% Hindu, Buddhist 7.8%, Muslim 3.8%, Christian 0.2%, Jain 0.1%, other 1.9%.

8	NORTH CORREA	(1980) Atheists non-religious 67.9%, traditional beliefs 15.6%, c. ondogyo 13.9% Buddhist 1.7%, Christians 0.9%.
9	SOUTH CORREA	(1991) Religious Buddhist 54.0% of which 27.6%, Protestant 18.6%, Roman Catholic 5.7%, Confucianism 1.0%, 0.3% wonberlgyo, c. ondogyo 0.2%, other 0, 6%, 46.0% non-religious.
10	BHUTAN	(1980) 69.6% Buddhist, Hindu 24.6%, Muslim 5.0%, other 0.8%.

IV. UNDER TUKISH INFLUENCE

1	IRAK	(1994) shite Muslim 62.5%, 34.5% Sunni Muslims, mainly Christians chaldéiens rite rite and Syrian Nestorian and Roman Catholic 2.7%, other 0.3% yazich synchétistes first.
2	LIBAN	*
3	KUWEIT	(1995) which Sunni Muslims 85% 45% 30% Shiah, another 10% Muslims, Christians and others mainly Hindu 15%.

V. UNDER BRITISH MANDATE OR PROTECTORATE

1	OMAN	(1984) 86% Muslim. Hindu 13%, other 1%.
2	JORDANIA	(1980) 93.0% Sunni Muslims, Christians 4.9%, other 2.1%.
3	ISRAEL	(1994) 81.4% Jews, Muslims mostly Sunni 13.9%, Christian 2.7%, 2.0% Druze and others.

VI. FORMER BRITISH COLONIES

1	INDE	(1991) Hindu 80.3%, Muslim 11% Sunni which 8.2% 2.8% shite, Christians 2.4% of which Roman Catholic 1.4%, other 1% mostly Protestant, Sikh 2.0%, 0.7% Buddhist, Jain 0.5%, zoroastria 0.01%, other 3.1%.
2	PAKISTAN	(1981) Musulamns 96.7%, Christian 1.6%, Hindu 1.5%, other 0.2%.

3	BURMA (MYANMAR)	(1990) Buddhist 89.1%, Christian 4.9%, Muslim 3.8%, other 2.2%.
4	MALAISIA	(1980) Musulamns 52.9%, Buddhist 17.3%, China folk religionists 11.6%, Hindu 7.0%, Christian 6.4%, other 4.8%.
5	BENGLADESH	(1991) 88.3% Muslim, Hindu 10.5%, Buddhist 0.6%, Christian 0.3%, other 0.3%.
6	SRILANKA	(1981) Buddhist 69.3%, Hindu, Muslim &, 6%, Christian 7.5%, other 0.1%.
7	QATAR	(1980) mainly Sunni Muslims 92.4% Christians 5.9%, Hindu 1.1%, bahaï0, 2%, other 0.4%.
8	PORTUGUESE TIMOR	
9	CIPRUS	(1990) Cypriot Orthodox 82.0%, Maronite 1.5%, other 16.5%.
10	SINGAPOR	(1991) Buddhist Taoist and other traditional beliefs 53.9%, Muslim 15.4%, Christian 12.6%, Hindu 3.6%, 14.5% non-religious.
11	MALDIVES	Virtually 100% Sunni Muslim.
VII.	SOUS INFLUENCE JAPONAISE	
1	TAIWAN (FORMOSE)	(1980) Chinese folk religionist 48.5%, Buddhist 43.0%, Christian 7.4%, Muslim 0.5%, other 0.6%.
VIII.	FORMER FRENCH COLONIES	
1	VIETNAM	(1992) Buddhist 67.0%, Roman Catholic 8.0%.
2	LAOS	(1994) Buddhist 57.8%, 33.6% tribal religion, which Christians 1.8% 0.8% Roman Catholic, Protestant 0.2%, Muslim 1.0%, atheist 1%, Chinese folk religionists 0, 9%.

IX.	UNDER FRENCH MANDATE OR PROTECTORATE
1	THAILAND	(1992) Buddhist 94.8%, Muslim 4.0%, Christian 0.6%, other 0.6%.
2	SYRIA	(1992) which Sunni Muslims 86.0% 74% Alawites (shite) 12.0%, Christian 8.9%, Druze 3.0%, other 1.0%.
3	CAMBODGE	(1994) Buddhist 95.0%, Muslim 2.0%, other 3.0%.
X.	FORMER NETHERLAND COLONIES
1	INDONESIA	(1990) Muslims 87.2% Christians 9.6% of which Roman Catholic 3.6%, Hindu 1.8%, Buddhist 1.0%, other 0.4%.

* Lebanon: official data do not exist, subsequant the 1932 census. Unofficial estimates and the CIA (1984-1986) indicate that Muslims shite 32/41% as the main group reli.

PROPORTION OF ACADEMICS IN ASIAN COUNTRIES IN 1980 IN ORDER

NO	COUNTRIES	FORMER COLONY	% OF GRADUATED STUDENTS	MAIN RELIGIOUS AFFILIATION
1	PHILLIPPINES	U.S.A	2,640	(1990) Roman Catholic 82.9%
2	SOUTH CORREA	_	1,6997	(1991) Traditional beliefs 54%
3	SYRIA	FRENCH MANDATE	1,6084	Muslim 86%
4	JAPON	_	1,5709	(1992) and Shinto religions for 51.3%
5	THAILAND	FRENCH AND CHINESE INFLUENCE	1,2821	(1992) Buddhist 94.8%
6	JORDANIA	BRITISH MANDATE	1,2658	(1980) 93% Sunni Muslims
7	SINGAPOR	BRITISH	0,9527	(1991) Buddhist Taoist and other traditional beliefs
8	INDE	BRITISH	0,8912	(1991) Hindu 80.3%
9	TURQUIA	_	0,53,29	(1992) 80% Sunni Muslims
10	MALAISIA	BRITISH	0,4453	(1980) Muslims 52.9%
11	TAIWAN	JAPONESE INFLUENCE	0,1918	(1980) Chinese folk religion 48.5%
12	AFGHANISTAN	_	0,0877	(1990) 84% Sunni Muslims

13	CIPRUS	BRITISH	0,0666	(19,900 Orthodox Ciprus 82%
14	LAOS	FRENCH	0,0439	(1980) Buddhist 57.8%
15	BENGLADESH	BRITISH	0,0417	(1991) Muslim 88.3%
16	ISRAEL	BRITISH MANDATE	0,0015	(1994) 81.3% Jews
17	BURMA	BRITISH	0,0009	(1990) Buddhist 89.1%
18	IRAK	TURKISH INFLUENCE	0,0008	(1994) 62.5% Muslims shite
19	SAUDI ARABIA	_	0,0006	(1980) mainly Sunni Muslim 98.8%
20	IRAN	_	0,0004	(1994) Muslim 99.1%
21	VIETNAM	FRENCH	0,0002	(1992) Buddhist 67%
22	PAKISTAN	BRITISH	0,00005	(1981) Muslim 96.7%

GDP/Cap ASIAN COUNTRIES IN 1980 IN ORDER (THE LARGEST TO SMALLEST

NO	COUNTRIES	GDP/Cap IN U.S $
1	QATAR	26.080
2	KUWEIT	22.840
3	SAUDI ARABIA	11.260
4	JAPON	9.890
5	ISRAEL	4.500
6	SINGAPOR	4.480
7	OMAN	4.380
8	CIPRUS	3.560

9	IRAK	3.020
10	MALAISIA	1.670
11	SOUTH CORREA	1.520
12	TURQUIA	1.460
13	JORDANIA	1.420
14	SYRIA	1.340
15	PHILLIPPINES	720
16	THAILAND	670
17	INDONESIA	420
18	PAKISTAN	300
19	SRILANKA	270
20	MALDIVES	260
21	INDE	240
22	BURMA (MYANMAR)	180
23	AFGHANISTAN	170
24	NEPAL	140
25	BENGLADESH	120
26	BHUTAN	80
27	CAMBODGE	70

GDP/Cap ASIAN COUNTRIES IN 1993 IN ORDER OF MAGNITUDE (High to Low)

NO	COUNTRIES	GDP/Cap IN U.S.$
1	JAPON	31.450
2	KUWEIT	23.350
3	SINGAPOR	19.310
4	SYRIA	15.892
5	QATAR	15.140
6	ISRAEL	13.760
7	CIPRUS	10.480
8	SOUTH CORREA	7.670
9	SAUDI ARABIA	7.510

10	OMAN	5.600
11	MALAISIA	3.160
12	IRAN	2.200
13	LIBAN	2.150
14	TURQUIA	2.120
15	TAIWAN	2.040
15	THAILAND	2.040
16	IRAK	1.500
17	JORDANIA	1.190
18	NORTH CORREA	970
19	PHILLIPPINES	830
20	MALDIVES	820
21	INDONESIA	730
22	SRILANKA	600
23	PAKISTAN	440
24	MONGOLIA	400
25	INDE	290
25	LAOS	290
26	AFGHANISTAN	280
27	BENGLADESH	220
27	BURMA (MYANMAR)	220
28	VIETNAM	170
28	CAMBODGE	170
28	BHUTAN	170
29	NEPAL	160

Using data on Asian countries in the pages above, let us see if there is a correlation between the percentage of academics and better GDP/Cap:

1. The Philippines have been colonized or were under the influence of the USA, were first in percentage of academics in 1980, but 15th in GDP/Cap the same year.

2. South Correa, the second in percentage of academics in 1980, but was 11th in GDP/Cap the same year.

3. Syria, which was under French mandate, 3rd in percentage of academics in 1980, was 14th in GDP/Cap the same year.

4. Japan, fourth in percentage of academics in 1980, was 4th in GDP/Cap of the same year.

5. Thailand has been under French influence, was 5th in percentage of academics in 1980, but 16th in GDP/Cap of the same year.

———————

Page 178 to 196 data that is in the tables have different sources:

1. The GDP/Cap in 1980. Source: protein deficiency and malnutrition. Published in 1990 by the United Nations Educational, Scientific and Cultural Organization.
    7 Place de Fontenoy, 75700 Paris, Typeset by Coupé, Sautron. Printed by Imprimerie des Presses universitaiers de France, Vendôme.
    ISBN 92-3-102083-8 c Unesco 1990 Printed in France.

2. Population in 1980. Source: Encyclopeadia Britannica. Book of the Year 1982. Events of 1981.

3. The P.N.B/Cap in 1993. Source: Encyclopeadia Britannica. Book of the Year 1996. Events of 1995. c 1996 Encyclopeadia Britannica, Inc.

4. The classification of countries according to the colonizing countries. Source: THE WORLD BOOK ATLAS. Copyright c 1965, 1964 by Field Enterprises Educational-corporate.
    Merchandise Mart Plaza, Chicago, Illinois 60654.

5. Richesses natural state religion, religious affiliation, type of government, executive branch. Source: Encyclopeadia Britannica, Inc.

6. University. Source: International Historical Statistics. Africa, Asia and Oceania 1750-2000. BR Mitchell, 5 th ed, Basingstoke: palagrave, 2003. ISNN 0-333-99412-4.

7. Area, access to many waters. Source: Follet Student Atlas. Compiled Under the leadership of Herbert H. Gross, Ph.D. Follet Publishing Company, Chicago. C 1975.

6. Jordan was under British mandate, was 6th in the percentage of academics in 1980, but 13th in GDP/Cap the same year.
7. The Singapore, a former British colony, was 7th in the percentage of academics in 1980, but 6th in GDP/Cap of the same year.
8. India, the former British colony, was 8th in the percentage of academics in 1980, but 21st in GDP/Cap the same year.
9. Turkey, was 9th in percentage of academics, but 12th in GDP/Cap of the same year.
10. Malaysia, former British colony, was 10th in percentage of the academics in 1980 and 10th in GDP/Cap of the same year.
11. The Taiwan was under Japanese influence, was 11th in percentage of the academics in 1980, but data on GDP/Cap in 1980 are not available.
12. Afghanistan, was 12th in percentage of the academics in 1980, but was 23rd in GDP /Cap the same year.
13. The Ciprus, 13th in percentage of academics in 1980, but 8th in GDP/Cap the same year.
14. Laos, former French colony, was 14th in percentage of the academics in 1980, but data on GDP/Cap in 1980 are not available.
15. Bangladesh, the former British colony, was 15th in percentage of the academics in 1980, but 25th in GDP/Cap the same year.
16. The Israel that was under British mandate, was 16th in percentage of academics in 1980, but 5th in GDP/Cap the same year.
17. Burma, former British colony, was 17th in percentage of academics in 1980, but 22nd in GDP/Cap the same year.
18. Iraq has been under Turkish influence, was 18th in percentage of academics in 1980, but 9th in GDP/Cap the same year.
19. Saudi Arabia, was 19th in percentage of the academics in 1980, but 3rd in GDP/Cap the same year.
20. Iran, was 20th in percentage of academics in 1980, but the data in GDP/Cap in 1980 are not available.
21. The former French colony in Vietnam, was 21st in percentage of the academics in 1980, but data on GDP/Cap in 1980 are not available.

22. Pakistan, former French colony, was 22nd in percentage of the academics in 1980, but 18th in GDP/Cap of the same year.

Based on the above data on the percentage of academics and GDP/Cap Asian countries in 1980, one can observe a weak correlation between the percentage of academics and a relatively good GDP/Cap. Because there are countries such as:
1. Japan, 4th in percentage of academics, was also 4th in GDP/Cap.
2. Malaysia, 10th in percentage of academics, was also 10th in GDP/Cap.
3. The Singapore, 7th in percentage of academics, was 6th in GDP/Cap.

Apart from these three countries one hand, there, poor countries occupying seats as a percentage of academics, but hold relatively good seats GDP/Cap. This applies to countries such as:
1. Saudi Arabia, 19th in percentage of academics, but was 3rd in GDP/Cap.
2. The Israel, 16th in percentage of academics, but was 5th in GDP/Cap.
3. The Ciprus, 13th in percentage of academics, but was 8th in GDP/Cap.
4. Iraq, 18th in percentage of the academics, but was 9th in GDP/Cap.
5. Pakistan, 22nd in percentage of academics, but was 18th in GDP/Cap.

On the other hand, countries occupying the best seats in the percentage of academics, but take the bad places in GDP/Cap. This applies to countries such as:
1. The Philippines, 1st in percentage of academics, but in 15th in GDP/Cap.
2. Corrée the South, 2nd in percentage of academics, but was 11th in GDP/Cap
3. Syria, 3rd in percentage of academics, but was 14th in GDP/Cap.
4. Thailand, 5th in percentage of academics, but was 16th in GDP/Cap.
5. Jordan, 6th in percentage of academics, but was 13th in GDP/Cap.

6. India, 8th percentage of academics, but was 21st in GDP/Cap.
7. Afghanistan, 12th in percentage of the academics, but was 23rd in GDP/Cap.
8. Bangladesh, 15th in percentage of the academics, but was 25th in GDP/Cap.
9. Burma, 17th in percentage of academics, but was 22nd in GDP/Cap.
10. Turkey, 9th in percentage of academics, but was 12th in GDP/Cap.

Given the above, it appears that the number of academics in a country, does not affect a large proportion of the GDP/Cap. This does not mean that the number of academics is to a large proportion for a better affect GDP/Cap. But it means that the number of academics in a country is a significant factor if used efficiently and effectively. That is to say that if the aware academics are used rationally, they will make the difference with other countries that have the same resources as natural resources, the main religious affiliation, the area . . . But a country with a significant number of scholars, can have a very low GDP/Cap if other factors, such as elements of the political, economic factors (such as natural resources, production facilities, the investment code . . .), cultural factors . . . are malfunctioning.

Now let us see on the one hand, the top ten Asian countries in GNP/Cap, and also in the other hand the last ten GDP/Cap in 1980, 1993.

THE TOP TEN IN ASIAN COUNTRIES GDP/Cap IN 1980

NO	COUNTRIES	GDP/Cap IN U.S $
1	QATAR	26.080
2	KUWEIT	22.840
3	SAUDI ARABIA	11.260
4	JAPON	9.890
5	ISRAEL	4.500
6	SINGAPOR	4.480
7	OMAN	4.380

8	CIPRUS	3.560
9	IRAK	3.020
10	MALAISIA	1.670

After the first ten in GDP/Cap in 1980, now see the last ten.

LAST1 TEN ASIAN COUNTRIES IN GDP/Cap IN 1980

NO	COUNTRIES	GDP/Cap IN U.S $
1	PAKISTAN	300
2	SRILANKA	270
3	MALDIVES	260
4	INDE	240
5	BURMA (MYANMAR)	180
6	AFGHANISTAN	170
7	NEPAL	140
8	BENGLADESH	120
9	BHUTAN	80
10	CAMBODGE	70

THE TOP 10 ASIAN COUNTRIES IN GDP/cap IN 1993

	COUNTRIES	GDP/Cap IN U.S $
1	JAPON	31.450
2	KUWEIT	23.350
3	SINGAPOR	19.310
4	SYRIA	15.892
5	QATAR	15.140
6	ISRAEL	13.760
7	CIPRUS	10.480
8	SOUTH CORREA	7.670
9	SAUDI ARABIA	7.510
10	OMAN	5.600

THE TEN LAST ASIAN COUNTRIES IN GDP/CA IN 1993

NO	COUNTRIES	GDP/Cap IN U.S $
1	MALDIVES	820
2	INDONESIA	730
3	SRILANKA	600
4	PAKISTAN	440
5	MONGOLIA	400
6	INDE	290
6	LAOS	290
7	AFGHANISTAN	280
8	BENGLADESH	220
8	BURMA (MYANMAR)	220
9	VIETNAM	170
9	CAMBODGE	170
9	BHUTAN	170
10	NEPAL	160

As was done for African countries, we do also for the Asian continent and we'll do it for the other remaining continents.

This allows us to discover: first, what former colonizing country has the largest number of countries that were among the top ten in GDP/Cap in 1980, 1993. On the other hand what former colonizing country has the largest number of countries that were among the last ten in GDP/Cap in 1980, 1993.

Let's start with the top ten.

THE TOP TEN IN ASIAN COUNTRIES GDP/Cap IN 1980

No	FORMER COLONY	FREQUENCE BY 8	MAIN RELIGIOUS AFFILIATION	FREQUENCE BY 10	NATURAL RESOURCES	FREQUENCE	EXECUTIVE BRANCH	FREQUENCE BY 10
1	BRITISH	6	MUSLIMS	6	Oil	6	King, Emir, Sultan, President	6
2	TURKISH INFLUENCE	2	SHINTO RELATED RELIGIONS	1	Gas	3	President-Prime minister	4
3			BOUDDHISTES	1	Copper	3		
4			JEWS	1	Iron	2		
5			ORTHODOXES OF CIPRUS	1	Gold	1		
6					Phosphates	1		
7					Sulphur	1		
8					Pyrite	1		
9					Manganese	1		
10					Fishing fish	1		
11					Asbestos	1		

THE TOP TEN IN ASIAN COUNTRIES GDP/Cap IN 1993

No	FORMER COLONY	FREQUENCE BY 7	MAIN RELIGIOUS AFFILIATION	FREQUENCE BY 10	NATURAL RESOURCES	FREQUENCE	EXECUTIVE BRANCH	FREQUENCE SUR 13
1	BRITISH	5	MUSLIMS	5	OIL	7	PRESIDENT-PRIME MINISTER	8
2	FRENCH	1	SHINTO AND RELATED RELIGIONS	1	RUBBER	5	KING OR PRESIDENT	5
3	TURKISH INFLUENCE	1	BOUDDHISTES TAOISTES AND OTHER TRADITIONAL BELIEVES	1	FORESTS	5		
4			ORTHODOXES OF CIPRUS	1	COPPER	4		
5			JEWS	1	NATURAL GAS	3		
6			TRADITIONAL BELIEFS	1	PHOSPHATES	3		
7					BAUXITE	3		
8					TIN, FISH FISH, NICKEL.	(3),(1),(1)		

LAST TEN COUNTRIES GDP/Cap IN 1980

No	FORMER COLONY	FREQUENCE BY 7	MAIN RELIGIOUS AFFILIATION	FREQUENCE BY 10	NATURAL RESOURCES	FREQUENCE BY 10	EXECUTIVE BRANCH	FREQUENCE BY 8
1	BRITISH	6	MUSLIMS	4	PETROLE	4	PRESIDENT– PRIME MINISTER	5
2	FRENCH	1	BOUDDHISTES	4	RUBBER	4	PRESIDENT	3
3			HINDU	2	NATURAL GAS	3		
4					COPPER	2		
5					IRON ORE	1		

LAST TEN COUNTRIES GDP/Cap IN 1993

NO	FORMER COLONY	FREQUENCE BY 10	MAIN RELIGIOUS AFFILIATION	FREQUENCE BY 14	NATURAL RESOURCES	FREQUENCE BY 14	EXECUTIVE BRANCH	FREQUENCE SUR 9
1	BRITISH	6	BOUDDHISTES	6	OIL	7	PRESIDENT–PRIME MINISTER	8
2	FRENCH	3	MUSLIMS	5	RUBBER	5	PRESIDENT	1
3	NETHRLAND	1	HINDU	2	TIN	4		
4					COPPER	4		
5					FORESTS	4		
6					NATURAL GAS	4		
7					BAUXITE	3		
8					FISH FISHING	1		
9					NICKEL	1		

From the above, find patterns among the top ten Asian countries in GDP/ cap in 1980 and 1993: the former British colony is the mode with 6/8, the Muslim religion with 6/10 is the mode for the primary affiliation Religious oil with 6/9 is the mode for natural resources, the political system where there is the king/Emir/Sultan/President as head of state and prime minister as head of government, is the fashion with 6/10 for the executive branch in 1980.

In 1993, the former colony with 5/7 is the mode, the Muslim religion with 5/10 is the mode, oil with 7/10 is how the political system where the president is the head of state and Prime Minister head of government is the way to the executive branch.

On the other hand, among the last ten in GDP/Cap: the former British colony with 6/10 is the mode, Muslim 4/10 and Buddhism 4/10 are the mode, oil 4/10 and Rubber 4/10 are the mode, the political system where the president is the head of state and prime minister head of government 5/8 is the mode in 1980.

In 1993, the former British colony 6/10 is the mode, Buddhism 6/10 is the mode, oil 7/14 is how the political system where the president is the head of state and Prime Minister the head of government 5/8 is the mode.

After that now study the proportion by group of countries colonized by the same country.

In 1980 there were a total of 20 Asian countries which we have data. Among them, there were 13 former English colonies, two former French colonies and 0.5, two who were under Turkish influence, 0.5 under Chinese influence, a former Dutch colony.

In 1993, there were a total of 24 Asian countries which we have data, including 13 former British colonies, four former French colonies and 0.5, 0.5 eg Chinese colony, three who were under Turkish influence, a under

Dutch influence, an influence on Japanese 1, under the influence of the USA

Knowing the number of ex British colonies, French, under Turkish influence, Japanese . . . which are among the top ten in GNP/Cap and those t's from the last ten in GNP/Cap, we can find the proportion.

Let's start with the proportion of the top ten:
In 1980
1. The former British colonies = (6 x 100): 13 = 46.1%
2. The former French colonies = (0 x 100): 2.5% = 0
3. Under Turkish influence = (2 x 100): 2 = 100%
4. Under Chinese influence = (0 x 100): 0.5% = 0
5. Influenced by Dutch = (0 x 100): 1 = 0%
6. Under the influence of U.S.A = (0 x 100): 1 = 0%

In 1993:
1. The former British colonies = (5 x 100): 13 = 38.4%
2. The former French colonies = (1 x 100): 2.5 = 40%
3. Under Turkish influence = (1 x 100): 2 = 50%
4. Under Chinese influence = (0 x 100): 0.5% = 0
5. Influenced Dutch = (0 x 100): 1 = 0%
Then the proportion of the last ten:

In 1980:
1. The former British colonies = (6 x 100): 13 = 46.1%
2. The former French colonies = (1 x 100): 2.5 = 40%
3. Influenced Turkish = (0 x 100): 0.5% = 0
4. Under Chinese influence = (0 x 100): 0.5% = 0
5. Influenced Dutch = (0 x 100): 1 = 0%
6. Under the influence of U.S.A = (0 x 100): 1 = 0%
In 1993:
1. The former British colonies = (6 x 100): 13 = 46.1%
2. The former French colonies = (3 x 100): 4.5% = 66.6
3. Under Chinese influence = (0 x 100): 0.5% = 0
4. Influenced Dutch = (1 x 100): 1 = 100%

5. Influenced Turkish = (0 x 100): 3 = 0%
6. Under the influence of U.S.A = (0 x 100): 1 = 0%

After the Asian continent, let us move to the North American continent.

THE NORTH AMERICAN CONTINENT'S GDP/CAP, POPULATION, GRADUATED STUDENTS

1. FORMER ENGLISH COLONIES OR UNDER ENGLISH CROWN

NO	COUNTRIES	DATA IN 1980				DATA IN 1993
		GDP/Cap IN U.S $	POPULATION	GRADUATED STUDENTS	% OF GRADUATED STUDENTS	GDP/Cap IN U.S.$
1	CANADA	10.130	23.936.000	628.000	2.6236	20.670
2	HONDURAS	560	3.691.000	24.000	0.6502	580
3	DOMINICAN REPUBLIC	1.140	5.400.000	42.000 1978	0.7777	1.080
4	BELIZE	1.080	141.000	_	_	2.440
5	BAHAMAS	3.300	234.000	_	_	11.500
6	JAMAIQUE	1.030	2.192.000	4.548	0.2074	1.190
7	TRINIDADE AND TOBAGO	4.370	1.080.000	2.923	0.2706	3.730
8	BARBADOS	3.040	312.000	1.587	0.5086	6.240
II.	FORMER FRENCH COLONIES					
1	GUADELOUP	1.060	1.060.000	_	_	8.400
2	MARTINIC	320	320.000	_	_	9.500
III.	FORMER SPANISH COLONY					
1	EL SALVADOR	1.730	4.801.000	13.000	0.2707	1.320

IV.	FORMER OR UNDER COLOMBIAN INFLUENCE				
1	PANAMA	1.730	1.825.000	40.000	2.1917	2.610

V.	INDEPENDENTS					
1	U.S.A	11.360	226.505.000	12.097.000	5.3407	24.750
2	MEXICO	2.130	67.382.600	840.000	1.2466	3.750
3	NICARAGUA	720	2.732.000	33.000	1.2079	360
4	CUBA	–	9.740.000	152.000	1.5605	1.170
5	GUATEMALA	1.110	7.262.000	51.000	0.7022	1.110
6	COSTARICA	1.730	2.232.000	47.000	2.1057	2.160
7	VIRGIN ISLANDS (U.S)	–	–	–	–	–

AREA AND NATURAL RESOURCES

1. FORMER ENGLISH COLONIES OR ENGLISH CROWN

NO	COUNTRIES	AREA IN Km2	NATURAL RESOURCES
1	CANADA	9.976.139	Nickel, zinc, copper, gold, lead, molybdenum, potash, silver, crude oil reserves (1994) 5.1 bin barrels.
2	HONDURAS	112.088	Gold, silver, copper, lead, zinc, iron, antimony, coal, wood.
3	DOMINICAN REPUBLIC	48.734	Nickel, gold, silver.
4	BELIZE	22.965	Sugar is the main export.
5	BAHAMAS	13.935	Salt, lobsters
6	JAMAIQUE	10.962	Bauxite, limestone, gypsum.
7	TRINIDADE AND TOBACO	5.128	Asphalt, oil, gas, crude oil reserves (1994) 466 min barrels.

8	BARBADOS	431	Oil, gas, fish.

II. FORMER FRENCH COLONIES

1	GUADELOUP	1.779	
2	MARTINIC	1.102	

III. FORMER SPANISH COLONY

1	EL SALVADOR	21.393	hydrolic power

IV. FORMER COLONY OR UNDER COLOMBIAN INFLUENCE

1	PANAMA	75.650	Copper, forests (mahogany), (shrimp).

V. THE INDEPENDENTS

1	U.S.A	9.363.123	Coal, copper, lead, molybdenum, phosphates, uranium, bauxite, gold, iron, mercury, nickel, potash, silver, tungsten, zinc, crude oil reserves (1994) 24 bin barrels.
2	MEXICO	1.972.547	Silver, lead, zinc, gold, oil, natural gas, crude oil reserves (1994) 51 bin barrels.
3	NICARAGUA	130.000	Gold, silver, copper, tungsten, forests, (shrimp).
4	CUBA	114.524	Cobalt, nickel, iron, copper, manganese, salt, forests.
5	GUATEMALA	108.889	Oil, nickel, rare woods, crude oil reserves (1994) 207 min barrels, fish (chicle).
6	COSTARICA	50.700	Gold, salt, fish, forests.
7	VIRGIN ISLANDS (U.S)	344	

ACCESS TO WATER MAIN TYPE OF GOVERNMENT, INDUSTRY EXECUTIVE, OFFICIAL RELIGION

1. FORMER COLONIES OR ENGLISH CROWN

No	COUNTRIES	ACCES TO GREAT WATERS	TYPE OF GOVERNMENT	EXECUTIVE BRANCH		OFFICIAL RELIGION
				HEAD OF STATE	HEAD OF GOVERNMENT	
1	CANADA	YES	PARLEMENTARY AND FEDERAL STATE	CANADIAN G.G	PRIME MINISTER	NONE
2	HONDURAS	YES	REPUBLIC	PRESIDENT		NONE
3	REPUBLIQUE DOMINICAINE	YES	REPUBLIC	PRESIDENT		NONE
4	BELIZE	YES	CONSTITUTIONAL MONARCHY	BRITISH MONARC	PRIME MINISTER	NONE
5	BAHAMAS	YES	CONSTITUTIONAL MONARCHY	BRITISH MONARC	PRIME MINISTER	NONE
6	JAMAIQUE	YES	CONSTITUTIONAL MONARCHY	BRITISH MONARC	PRIME MINISTER	NONE
7	TRINIDADE AND TOBAGO	YES	REPUBLIC	PRESIDENT	PRIME MINISTER	NONE
8	BARBADOS		CONSTITUTIONAL MONARCHY	BRITISH MONARC	PRIME MINISTER	

II.	FORMER FRENCH COLONIES					
1	GUADELOUPE		OVER SEA DEPARTMENT	FRENCH PRESIDENT	36	
2	MARTINIC		OVER SEA DEPARTMENT	FRENCH PRESIDENT	36	
III.	FORMER SPANISH COLONY					
1	EL SALVADOR	YES	REPUBLIC	PRESIDENT		NONE
IV.	FORMER COLONY OR UNDER COLOMBIAN INFLUENCE					
1	PANAMA	YES	REPUBLIC	PRESIDENT		NONE
V.	LES INDEPENDANTS					
1	U.S.A	YES	FEDERAL REPUBLIC	PRESIDENT		NONE
2	MEXICO	YES	FEDERAL REPUBLIC	PRESIDENT		NONE
3	NICARAGUA	YES	REPUBLIC	PRESIDENT		NONE
4	CUBA	YES	SOCIALISTE REPUBLIC	PRESIDENT		NONE
5	GUATEMALA	YES	REPUBLIC	PRESIDENT		NONE
6	COSTARICA	YES	REPUBLIC	PRESIDENT		ROMAN CATHOLICISM
7	VIRGIN ISLANDS (U.S0	-	U.S TERRITOIRE	PRESIDENT OF U.S.A	GOVERNOR	-

RELIGIOUS AFFILIATION

1. FORMER COLONIES OR UNDER ENGLISH CROWN

No	COUNTRIES	RELIGIOUS AFFILIATION
1	CANADA	(1991) Roman Catholic 45.7%, 36.3% Protestant, Eastern Orthodox 1.5%, Jewish 1.2%, Muslim 1%, Buddhist 0.7%, Hindu 0.6%, non-religious 12.4%, other 0.6%.
2	HONDURAS	(1986) Roman Catholic 85% Protestant (mainly fundamentalists, Moravian and Methodist) 10%, other 5%.
3	DOMINICAN REPUBLIC	(1992) Roman Catholic 91.2%, other 8.8%.
4	BELIZE	(1991) 57.7% Roman Catholic, Protestant, Anglican 34.3% of which 7%, Pentecostal 6.3%, Methodist 4.2%, 7th day Adventist 4.1%, Mennonite 4%, other Christian 1.7% other unregistered 6%.
5	BAHAMAS	(1980) Non-Anglican Protestants 55.2% 32.1% which Baptist, Methodist 6.1%, Church of God (Anderson Ind) 5.7%, Anglican 20.1%, Roman Catholic 18.8%, other 5 , 9%.
6	JAMAIQUE	(1982) 55.9% Protestant Church of God of which 18.4%, Baptist 10%, Anglican 7.1%, 7th day Adventist 6.9%, pentecôtistes5, 2%, 5% Roman Catholic, non-religious or atheists 17 , 7%, not reported 11.2%, other 10.2% of whom Rastafarians 5%.

7	TRINIDADE AND TOBAGO	(1990) 6 larger Protestant bodies which 29.7% Anglican 10.9%, Pentecostal 7.5%, Roman Catholic 29.4%, Hindu 23.7%, Muslim 5.9%, other 11.3%.
8	BARBADOS	(1980) Anglican 39.7%, other Protestant 25.6% which pentecôtistes7, 6%, Methodist 7.1%, non-religious 17.5%, Roman Catholic 4.4% undeclared 2.7%, other 10, 1%.

II. FORMER FRENCH COLONIES

1	GUADELOUPE	(1992) romaine85 Catholic, 9%, other 14.1%.
2	MARTINIC	(1993) Roman Catholic 84.6%, other (mainly 7th day Adventists, Jehovah's Witnesses, Hindu, syncretistic and non-religious) 15.4%

III. FORMER SPANISH COLONY

1	EL SALVADOR	(1993) Roman Catholic 75%, other (mostly fundamentalist Protestants, Mormons or Jehovah's Witnesses) 25%

IV. FORMER COLONIES OR UNDER COLOMBIAN INFLUENCE

1	PANAMA	(1992) Roman Catholic 80%, Protestant (mainly evangelical s) 10%, Muslim 5%, Baha'i 1%, Jewish 0.3%, other 3.7%.

V. INDEPENDENTS

1	U.S.A	(1995) 85.3% Christian 57.9 5 which Protestants, Roman Catholic 21%, other Christian 6.4%, Jewish 2.1%, Muslim 1.9%, non-religious 8.7%, other 2%.
2	MEXICO	(1990) 89.7% Roman Catholic, Protestant (Evangelical included) 4.9%, Jewish 0.1%, other 2.1%, no religion 3.2%.
3	NICARAGUA	(1992) Roman Catholic 89.3%, other (mostly Baptists, Pentecostals and Moravian) 10.7%.
4	CUBA	(1980) Non religious 48.7%, Roman Catholic 39.6%, atheist 6.4%, Protestant 3.3%, Afro-Cuban syncretic 1.6%, other 0.4%.
5	GUATEMALA	(1986) Roman Catholic 75% which syncretistic Traditional Catholic 25%, Protestant (mostly fundamentalist) 25%.
6	COSTARICA	(1992) 80% Roman Catholic, Evangelical Protestant 15%, other 5%.
7	VIRGIN ISLANDS (U.S)	—

PROPORTION OR PERCENTAGE OF ACADEMICS, COUNTRIES OF NORTH AMERICA IN 1980 IN ORDER (GREATEST TO SMALLEST)

NO	COUNTRIES	% OF ACADEMICS	MAIN RELIGIOUS AFFILIATION
1	U.S.A	5.3405	(1995) Christian 85.3%
2	CANADA	2.6236	(1991) Roman Catholic 45.7%
3	PANAMA	2.1917	(1992) Roman Catholic 80%
4	COSTARICA	2.1057	(1992) Roman Catholic 80%
5	CUBA	1.5605	(1980) Non religious 48.7%
6	MEXICO	1.2466	(1980) Non-Religious 48.7%
7	NICARAGUA	1.2079	(1992) Roman Catholic 89.3%
8	DOMINICAN REPUBLIC	0.7777	(1992) Roman Catholic 91.2%
9	GUATEMALA	0.7022	(1992) Roman Catholic 91.2%
10	HONDURAS	0.6502	(1986) Roman Catholic 85%
11	BARBADOS	0.5086	(1980) 39.7% Anglican
12	EL SALVADOR	0.2707	(1993) Roman Catholic 75%
13	TRINIDADE AND TOBACO	0.2706	(1990) Protestant 29.7%
14	JAMAIQUE	0.2074	(1982) Protestant 55.9%

GNP/Cap COUNTRIES NORTH AMERICA IN 1980 IN ORDER

NO	COUNTRIES	GDP/Cap IN U.S $
1	U.S.A	11.360
2	CANADA	10.130
3	TRINIDADE ET TOBACO	4.370
4	BAHAMAS	3.300
5	BARBADOS	3.040
6	MEXICO	2.130
7	COSTARICA	1.730
7	EL SALVADOR	1.730
7	PANAMA	1.730
8	GUATEMALA	1.110
9	BELIZE	1.080
10	JAMAIC	1.030
11	NICARAGUA	720

GNP/Cap COUNTRIES NORTH AMERICA IN 1993 IN ORDER

NO	COUN TRIES	GDP/Cap IN U.S $
1	U.S.A	24.750
2	CANADA	20.670
3	BAHAMAS	11.500
4	MARTINIQUE	9.500
5	GUADELOUPE	8.400
6	BARBADOS	6.240
7	MEXICO	3.750
8	TRINIDADE AND TOBACO	3.730
9	PANAMA	2.610
10	BELIZE	2.440
11	COSTARICA	2.160

12	EL SALVADOR	1.320
13	JAMAIQUE	1.190
14	CUBA	1.170
15	GUATEMALA	1.110
16	DOMINICAN REPUBLIC	1.080
17	NICARAGUA	360

At this point let us see the relationship between the percentage of academics and its impact on GDP/Cap. Based on data in the tables above:

1. The U.S., as a percentage of first academics in 1980, was 1st in GDP/Cap in 1980 and 1993.
2. Canada, second in percentage of academics in 1980, was 2nd in GDP/Cap in 1980 and 1993.
3. Panama, third in percentage of the academics in 1980, was 7th in GDP/Cap in 1980, 9th in 1993.
4. The Costarica, fourth in percentage of the academics in 1980, was 7th in GDP/Cap in 1980, 11th in 1993.
5. Cuba, fifth in percentage of academics in 1980, no data on GDP/Cap in 1980, 14th in 1993.
6. The Mexico, sixth in percentage of academics in 1980, was 6th in GDP/cap in 1980, 7th in 1993.
7. Nicaragua, seventh in percentage of academics in 1980, was 11th in GDP/cap in 1980, 17th in 1993.
8. The Dominican Republic, 8th in percentage of academics in 1980, has no data on GNP/Cap in 1980, 16th in 1993.
9. Guatemala, ninth in percentage of the academics in 1980, was 8th in GDP/cap in 1980, 15th in 1993.
10. Honduras, tenth in percentage of the academics in 1980, has no data on GDP/Cap in 1980 and 1993.
11. The Barbados, eleventh in percentage of the academics in 1980, was 5th in GDP/Cap in 1980, 6th in 1993.
12. The Elsalvador, twelfth in percentage of academics in 1980, was 7th in 1980, 12th in 1993.

13. Trinidad and Tobaco, thirteenth in percentage of academics in 1980, was 3rd in GDP/cap in 1980, 8th in 1993.
14. Jamaica, the fourteenth in percentage of the academics in 1980, was 10th in 1980, 13th in 1993.

From the data above, one can observe that there are countries that have occupied almost the same place, or around, in percentage of the academics in 1980 and in GDP/Cap in 1980 and 1993. This applies to USA, Canada, Mexico, El Salvador and Jamaica. However one hand, there are countries that have occupied the best seats in percentage of the academics in1980, but find themselves beyond in the seats occupied for GDP/cap. This applies to: Panama, Costarica, Cuba, Nicaragua, Dominican Republic, Guatemala, Honduras. On the other hand, there are countries that have occupied the best seats in GDP/Cap in 1980, 1993 than the seats occupied in percentage of academics in 1980. It is the case of Barbados, Trinidad and Tobaco.

At this point let us see the top five countries in GDP/cap in 1980, the first eight countries in GDP/cap in 1993 on the one hand, and the other hand the last five countries in GDP/Cap in 1980 and in the last eight GDP/Cap in 1993.

THE TOP FIVE COUNTRIES IN NORTH AMERICAN GDP/Cap IN 1980

NO	COUNTRIES	GDP/Cap IN U.S $
1	U.S.A	11.360
2	CANADA	10.130
3	TRINIDADE AND TOBACO	4.370
4	BAHAMAS	3.300
5	BARBADOS	3.040

THE LAST FIVE COUNTRIES IN NORTH AMERICAN GNP/Cap IN 1980

NO	COUNTRIES	GDP/Cap IN U.S $
1	COSTARICA	1.730
1	EL SALVADOR	1.730
1	PANAMA	1.730
2	GUATEMALA	1.110
3	BELIZE	1.080
4	JAMAIQUE	1.030
5	NICARAGUA	720

THE FIRST EIGHT NORTH AMERICAN COUNTRIES IN 1993

NO	COUNTRIES	GDP/Cap IN U.S $
1	U.S.A	24.750
2	CANADA	20.670
3	BAHAMAS	11.500
4	MARTINIC	9.500
5	GUADELOUPE	8.400
6	BARBADOS	6.240
7	MEXICO	3.750
8	TRINIDADE AND TOBACO	3.730

THE LAST EIGHT COUNTRIES IN NORTH AMERICAN GDP/Cap IN 1993

NO	COUNTRIES	GDP/Cap IN U.S $
1	BELIZE	2.440
2	COSTARICA	2.160
3	EL SALVADOR	1.320
4	JAMAIQUE	1.190
5	CUBA	1.170
6	GUATEMALA	1.110
7	DOMINICAN REPUBLIC	1.080
8	NICARAGUA	360

At this level, as was done with the other continents in the preceding pages, let find the mode on one hand for the five, eight first countries in GDP/Cap and the other hand for five, eight last in GDP/Cap in 1980 and 1993.

I. FIVE OR EIGHT FIRST IN GDP/Cap

1. in 1980

No	EFORMER COLONY	FREQUENCE BY 4	MAIN RELIGIOUS AFFILIATION	FREQUENCE BY 5	NATURAL RESOURCES	FREQUENCE	EXECUTIVE BRANCH	FREQUENCE BY 5
1	BRITISH	4	CHRITIANS	1	OIL	4	PRESIDENT/ BRITAIN MONARC / CANADIAN G.G–PRIME MINISTER	4
2			ROMAN CATHOLIC	1	POTASSE	2	PRESIDENT	1
3			PROTESTANTS	1	ZINC	2		
4			PROTESTANTS NON ANGLICANS	1	COAL	1		
5			ANGLICANS	1	MOLYBDENE	1		
6					PHOSPHATES	1		
7					URANIUM	1		
8					BAUXITE	1		
9					IRON	1		

No	Resource	Frequency
10	MERCURY	1
11	SILVER	1
12	TUNGSTENE	1
13	ASPHALTE	1
14	SALT	1
15	LOBSTERS	1
16	GAS	1
17	FISH	1
18	COPPER	2
19	LEAD	2
20	GOLD	2
21	NICKEL	2

2. In 199

No	FORMER COLONY	FREQUENCE BY 6	MAIN RELIGIOUS AFFILIATION	FREQUENCE BY 8	NATURAL RESOURCES	FREQUENCE	EXECUTIVE BRANCH	FREQUENCE SUR 8
1	BRITISH	4	ROMAN CATHOLIC	4	OIL	5	PRESIDENT/ BRITAIN MONARC/G.G CANADIAN–PRIME MINISTER	6

#	FRENCH	CHRETIENS	LEAD	PRESIDENT
2	FRENCH — 2	CHRETIENS — 1	LEAD — 3	PRESIDENT — 2
3		PROTESTANTS NON ANGLICANS — 1	GOLD — 3	
4		ANGLICANS — 1	ZINC — 3	
5		PROTESTANTS — 1	GAS — 3	
6			COPPER — 2	
7			MOLYBDENE — 2	
8			NICKEL — 2	
9			POTASSE — 2	
10			SILVER — 2	
11			COAL — 1	
12			PHOSPHATES — 1	
13			URANIUM — 1	
14			BAUXITE — 1	
15			IRON — 1	
16			MERCURY — 1	
17			TUNGSTENE — 1	
18			SALT — 1	
19			LOBSTERS — 1	
20			FISH — 1	

THE LAST FIVE OR EIGHT COUNTRIES GDP/Cap

1. in 1980

No	FORMER COLONY	FREQUENCE BY 4	MAIN RELIGIOUS AFFILIATION	FREQUENCE BY 7	NATURAL RESOURCES	FREQUENCE	BRANCHE EXECUTIVE BRANCH	FREQUENCE SUR 6
1	BRITISH	2	ROMAN CATHOLIC	6	FORESTS	3	PRESIDENT	4
2	SPANISH	1	PROTESTANTS	1	SHRIMP	2	PRESIDENT-PRIME MINISTER	2
3	COLOMBIAN	1			SALT	1		
4					HYDROELECTRIC POWER	1		
5					MAHOGANY	1		
6					OIL	1		
7					NICKEL	1		
8					WOOD RARE	1		
9					SUGAR	1		
10					BAUXITE	1		

11		ROUGH STONES	1
12		GYPSUM	1
13		SILVER	1
14		TUNGSTENE	1
15		GOLD	2
16		FISH	2
17		COPPER	2

In 1993

NO	FORMER COLONY	FREQUENCE BY 4	MAIN RELIGIOUS AFFILIATION	FREQUENCE BY 8	NATURAL RESOURCES	FREQUENCE	EXECUTIVE BRANCH	FREQUENCE SUR 5
1	BRITISH	3	ROMAN CATHOLIC	6	OIL	4	PRESIDENT/G.G CANADIAN/ PRESIDENT FRENCH/ MONARC BRITAIN-PRIME MINISTER	4
2	SPANISH	1	PROTESTANTS	1	COPPER	2	PRESIDENT	1

#	Item	Value
1	NO RELIGIOUS	1
2	LEAD	2
3	MOLYBDENE	2
4	GOLD	2
5	NICKEL	2
6	POTASSE	2
7	ZINC	2
8	COAL	1
9	PHOSPHATES	1
10	URANIUM	1
11	BAUXITE	1
12	IRON	1
13	MERCURY	1
14	SILVER	1
15	TUNGSTENE	1
16	LOBSTER	1
17	ASPHALTE	1
18	GAS	1
19	FISH	1
20		

Now, from the above data, we can find on the one hand modes of five or top eight countries in GDP/Cap and the other hand for the last five or eight. Let's start with the top five or eight.

In 1980–the former British colony 4/4 was the mode for former colonies.

-Christians, Catholics, Protestants, non-Anglican Protestants find itselves with 1/5 each.

−Oil with 4/5 is the mode for natural resources.

−The political system where there is the president as head of state and prime minister as head of government with 4/5 is the way to the executive branch.

In 1993, the former British colony 4/6 is the mode, with Roman Catholic 4/8 is the mode, oil with 5/6 is the mode, where the political system is the presiding head of state and the first Minister head of government 6/8 is the mode.

Now we can find the proportions as we know that in 1980 there were eight countries whose we have data among which: six were former British colonies, a former Spanish colony and a former Colombian colony.

In 1993 there were 11 countries whose we have data, among them: seven former British colonies, two former French colonies, a former colony and a Colombian former Spanish colony.

From this, it was for the top five or eight:
In 1980:
−The former British colonies = (4 x 100): 6 = 66.6%
−The former Spanish colony = (0 x 100): 1 = 0%
−The former Colombian colony = (0 x 100): 1 = 0%

In 1993:
Ex-British colonies = (4 x 100): 7 = 57.1%

Ex-French colonies = (2 x 100): 2 = 100%
−Former Colombian colony = (0 x 100): 1 = 0%
−The former Spanish colony = (0 x 100): 1 = 0%

For the last five or eight were
In 1980:
−The former British colonies = (2 x 100): 6 = 33.3%
−The former Spanish colony = (1 x 100): 1 = 100%
−The former Colombian colony = (1 x 100): 1 = 100%

In 1993:
Ex-British colonies = (3 x 100): 7 = 42.8%
Ex-French colonies = (0 x 100): 2 = 0%
−The former Colombian colony = (0 x 100): 1 = 0%
−The former Spanish colony = (1 x 100): 1 = 100%

This brings us to the countries of South America.

THE SOUTH AMERICAN CONTINENT.

THE P GDP/Cap, PEOPLE, ACADEMICS

I. FORMER SPANISH COLONIES AND INFLUENCE

No	COUNTRIES	DATA IN 1980				DATA IN 1993
		GDP/Cap IN U.S $	POPULATION	GRADUATED	% OF GRADUATED	GDP/Cap IN U.S $
1	ARGENTINE	2.390	28.237.000	398.000	1.4094	7.290
2	PEROU	930	17.295.000	258.000	1.4917	1.490
3	COLOMBIA	1.180	25.892.000	235.000	0.9076	1.350
4	BOLIVIA	570	5.600.000	61	0.0010	770
5	VENEZUELA	3.630	15.024.000	243.000	1.6174	2.840
6	CHILE	2.160	11.145.000	119.000	1.0677	3.070
7	PARAGUAY	1.340	3.147.000	25	0.0007	1.500
8	ECUADOR	1.220	8.123.000	264	0.0032	1.170
9	URUGUAY	2.820	2.914.000	36.000	1.2354	3.910

II.	FORMER COLONY PORTUGUESE					
1	BRESIL	2.050	121.286.000	1.378.000	1.1361	3.020

III.	FORMER BRITISH COLONY					
1	GUYANNE	690	865.000	1.681	0.1943	350

IV.	FORMER NETHERLAND COLONY					
1	SURINAME	2.840	352.000	—	—	1.210

V.	FORMER FRENCH COLONY					
1	GUYANNE	—	—	—	—	—

AREA AND NATURAL RE1SOURCES

I. FORMER COLONIES OR UNDER SPANISH INFLUENCE

C	COUNTRIES	AREA IN Km2	NATURAL RESOURCES
1	ARGENTINA	2.776.889	Oil, lead, zinc, iron, copper, tin, uranium, crude oil reserves (1994) 1.6 barrels bin
2	PEROU	1.285.215	Copper, silver, gold, oil, wool, sardines, crude oil reserves (1994) 381 min barrels.

3	COLOMBIA	1.138.914	Oil, Gas, Emerald 50% of world exports, gold, copper, lead, coal, iron, nickel, salt, crude oil reserves (1994) 1.9 bin barrels, rubber (Balsan), (copaiba, dye-wood , hydropower).
4	BOLIVIA	1.098.581	Antimony, tin, tungsten, silver, zinc, oil, gas, iron, crude oil reserves (1994) 108 min barrels, rubber (cinchona bark)
5	VENEZUELA	912.050	Oil, gas, iron (extensive reserves and production), gold, crude oil reserves (1994) 63 bin barrels, fishing Fish (1991) 353.000tone per meter.
6	CHILE	756.945	Copper (world producer), molybdenum, nitrate, Iodine (half of world production), iron, coal, oil, gas, gold, manganese, salt, sulphide, forests.
7	PARAGUAY	406.752	Iron, manganese, limestone, forests.
8	ECUADOR	283.561	Oil, gas, copper, iron, lead, silver, gold, crude oil reserves (1994) 2 bin barrels, rubber bark.
9	URUGUAY	186.926	Fishing Fish (1992) 126.000 tone/meter.
II.	FORMER PORTUGUESE COLONY		
1	BRESIL	8.511.965	Iron, manganese, phosphate, uranium, gold, nickel, tin, bauxite, petroleum, crude oil reserves (1994) 3.6 bin barrels.
III.	FORMER BRITISH COLONY		
1	GUYANNE	214.969	Bauxite, gold, diamonds, timber, (shrimp).
IV.	FORMER NETHERLAND COLONY		
1	SURINAME	163.265	Bauxite, forests, (shrimp).
V.	FORMER FRENCH COLONY		
1	GUYANNE	91.000	Bauxite, gold, diamonds, timber, (shrimp).

ACCESS TO WATER, MAIN TYPE OF GOVERNMENT, EXECUTIVE BRANCH, OFFICIAL RELIGION

I   FORMER COLONIES OR UNDER SPANISH INFLUENC

No	COUNTRIES	ACCES TO GREAT WATERS	TYPE OF GOVERNMENT	EXECUTIVE BRANCH		OFFICIAL RELIGION
				HEAD OF STATE	HEAD OF GOVERNMENT	
1	ARGENTINA	YES	FEDERAL REPUBLIC	PRESIDENT		ROMAN CATHOLIC
2	PEROU	YES	REPUBLIC	PRESIDENT		ROMAN CATHOLIC
3	COLOMBIA	YES	REPUBLIC	PRESIDENT		NONE
4	BOLIVIA	No	REPUBLIC	PRESIDENT		ROMAN CATHOLIC
5	VENEZUELA	YES	FEDERAL REPUBLIC	PRESIDENT		NONE
6	CHILE	YES	REPUBLIC	PRESIDENT		NONE
7	PARAGUAY	No	REPUBLIC	PRESIDENT		NONE
8	ECUADOR	YES	REPUBLIC	PRESIDENT		NONE

9	URUGUAY	YES	REPUBLIC	PRESIDENT	NONE
II.	FORMER PORTUGUESE COLONY				
1	BRESIL	YES	FEDERAL REPUBLIC	PRESIDENT	NONE
III.	FORMER BRITISH COLONY				
1	GUYANNE	YES	COOPERATIVE REPUBLIC	PRESIDENT	NONE
IV.	FORMER NETHERLAND COLONY				
1	SURINAME	YES	REPUBLIC	PRESIDENT	NONE
V.	FORMER FRENCH COLONY				
1	GUYANNE	YES	OVER SEA DEPARTMENT (France)	FRENCH PRESIDENT	NONE

RELIGIOUS AFFILIATION

I   FORMER COLONIES OR UNDER SPANISH INFLUENCE

NO	COUNTRIES	RELIGIOUS AFFILIATION
1	ARGENTINA	(1992) Roman Catholic 91.6%, other 8.4%.
2	PEROU	(1989) Roman Catholic 92.5%, Protestant 5.5%.
3	COLOMBIA	(1993) Roman Catholic 93.1%, other 6.9%.
4	BOLIVIA	(1992) Roman Catholic 85%, Protestant 11%, other 4%.
5	VENEZUELA	(1991) Roman Catholic 92.1%, other 7.1%.
6	CHILE	(1992) Roman Catholic 76.7%, 13.2% Protestants, atheists and non-religious 5.8%, other 4.3%.
7	PARAGUAY	(1991) Roman Catholic 93.1%, other 6.9%.
8	ECUADOR	(1992) Roman Catholic 93%, other 7%
9	URUGUAY	(1988) Roman Catholic 66%, Protestant 2%, Jewish 0.8%, non-religious and atheist 31.2%.
II.	FORMER PORTUGUES COLONY	
1	BRESIL	(1995) 70% Roman Catholic, Evangelical Protestant 19%, other 11%.
III.	FORMER BRITISH COLONY	
1	GUYANNE	(1990) which Protestant Christians 52% 34% (Anglican 17% included), Roman Catholic 18%, Hindu 34%, musulamns 9%, other 5%.

IV.	FORMER NETHERLAND COLONY	
1	SURINAME	(1983) 26% Hindu, Roman Catholic 21.6%, Muslim 18.6%, mainly Protestant Moravian 18%, other 15.8%.
V.	FORMER FRENCH COLONY	
1	GUYANNE	(1990) which Protestant Christians 52% 34% (Anglican 17% included), Roman Catholic 18%, Hindu 34%, Muslim 9%, other 5%.

PROPORTION (PERCENTAGE) OF THE ACADEMICS, COUNTRIES SOUTH AMERICA IN 1980 IN ORDER OF MAGNITUDE

NO	COUNTRIES	% OF ACADEMICS
1	VENEZUELA	1.6174
2	PEROU	1.4917
3	ARGENTINA	1.4094
4	URUGUAY	1.2354
5	BRESIL	1.1361
6	CHILE	1.0677
7	COLOMBIA	0.9076
8	GUYANNE (BRITISH)	0.1943
9	ECUADOR	0.0032
10	BOLIVIA	0.0010
11	PARAGUAY	0.0007

GDP/Cap COUNTRIES OF SOUTH AMERICA IN 1980 IN ORDER SIZE

NO	COUNTRIES	GDP/Cap IN U.S $
1	VENEZUELA	3.630
2	SURINAME	2.840
3	URUGUAY	2.820
4	ARGENTINA	2.390
5	CHILE	2.160
6	BRESIL	2050
7	PARAGUAY	1.340
8	ECUADOR	1.220
9	COLOMBIA	1.180
10	PEROU	930
11	GUYANNE	690
12	BOLIVIA	570

GDP/Cap COUNTRIES OF SOUTH AMERICA IN 1993 IN ORDER

NO	COUNTRIES	GDP/Cap IN U.S $
1	ARGENTINA	7.290
2	URUGUAY	3.910
3	CHILE	3.070
4	BRESIL	3.020
5	VENEZUELA	2.840
6	PARAGUAY	1.500
7	PEROU	1.490
8	COLOMBIA	1.350
9	SURINAME	1.210
10	ECUADOR	1.170
11	BOLIVIA	770
12	GUYANNE (BRITAIN)	350

From the data in tables that are in the pages above, let us see the relationship that exists between the percentage of academics and GDP/Cap.

1. Venezuela, first in percentage of the academics in 1980, was the first in GDP/Cap in 1980, 5th in 1993.
2. Peru, 2nd in percentage of academics in 1980, was 10th in GDP/cap in 1980, 7th in GNP/Cap in 1993.
3. The Argentine, 3rd in percentage of academics in 1980, was 4th in GDP/cap in 1980, first in 1993.
4. Uruguay, fourth in percentage of academics in 1980, was 3rd in GDP/cap in 1980, 2nd in 1993.
5. Brazil, 5th in percentage of the academics in 1980, was 6th in GDP/cap in 1980, 4th in 1993.
6. Chile, 6th in percentage of the academics in 1980, was 5th in GDP/Cap in 1980, 3rd in 1993.
7. British, 7th in percentage of the academics in 1980, was 9th in GDP/Cap in 1980, 8th in 1993.
8. Guyana English, 8th in percentage of the academics in 1980, was 11th in GDP/Cap en1980, 12th in 1993.
9. The Ecuador, 9th in percentage of the academics in 1980, was 8th in GDP/Cap en1980, 10th in 1993.
10. Bolivia, 10th in percentage of the academics in 1980, was 12th in GDP/cap in 1980, 11th in 1993.
11. Paraguay, 11th in percentage of the academics in 1980, was 7th in GDP/Cap in 1980, 6th in 1993.

Based on the foregoing, there is a strong correlation between the proportion of academic performance and GDP/Cap. One can observe that apart from Peru, 2nd in the percentage of academics in 1980, was 10th in GDP/cap in 1980, 7th in 1993. And the two countries: Chile and Paraguay who have occupied the best places in GDP/Cap in 1980, 1993 than they had occupied in percentage of the academics in 1980. Almost every country we have the data, have regarding the GDP/Cap, kept their places or around the places they occupied in percentage of the academics in 1980.

After that, let us see in one hand, the first four South American countries in GDP/Cap and also the last four in GDP/Cap in the other.

THE TOP FOUR SOUTH AMERICAN COUNTRIES IN GDP/Cap IN 1980

NO	COUNTRIES	GDP/Cap IN U.S $
1	VENEZUELA	3.630
2	SURINAME	2.840
3	URUGUAY	2.820
4	ARGENTINA	2.390

THE SOUTH AMERICAN COUNTRY LAST FOUR IN GDP/Cap IN 1980

NO	COUNTRIES	GDP/Cap IN U.S $
1	COLOMBIA	1.180
2	PEROU	930
3	GUYANNE	690
4	BOLIVIA	570

THE TOP FOUR SOUTH AMERICAN COUNTRIES IN GDP/Cap IN 1993

NO	COUNTRIES	GDP/Cap IN U.S $
1	ARGENTINA	7.290
2	URUGUAY	3.910
3	CHILE	3.070
4	BRESIL	3.020

THE SOUTH AMERICAN COUNTRY LAST FOUR IN GDP/Cap IN 1993

NO	COUNTRIES	GDP/Cap IN U.S $
1	SURINAME	1.210
2	ECUADOR	1.170
3	BOLIVIA	770
4	GUYANNE (BRITAIN)	350

As it was done for the other continents, let us seek the mode for the first four on the one hand and the last four on the other.

I. THE FIRST FOUR

in 1980

NO	FORMER COLONY	FREQUENCE BY 4	MAIN RELIGIOUS AFFILIATION	FREQUENCE BY 4	NATURAL RESOURCES	FREQUENCE	EXECUTIVE BRANCH	FREQUUR 4
1	SPANISH	3	ROMAN CATHOLIC	3	OIL	3	PRESIDENT	4
2	NETHERLAND	1	HINDU	1	GOLD	3	PRESIDENT-PRIME MINISTER	0
3					COPPER	2		
4					IRON	2		
5					CAOUTCHOUC	2		
6					GAS	1		
7					EMERAUDES	1		
8					LEAD	1		
9					COAL	1		
10					NICKEL	1		
11					SALT	1		
12					BALSAN	1		
13					CAPAIBA	1		

No		Frequence
14	DYE-WOOD	1
15	PUISSANCE HYDRO ELECTRIQUE	1
16	LAINE	1
17	SARDINES	1
18	BAUXITE	1
19	DIAMOND	1
20	WOOD	1
21	SHRIMP	1
22	CINCHONA	1

IN 1993

No	FORMER COLONY	FREQUENCE BY 4	MAIN RELIGIOUS AFFILIATION	FREQUENCE BY 4	NATURAL RESOURCES	FREQUENCE BY 4	EXECUTIVE BRANCH	FREQUENCE BY 4
1	SPANISH	3	ROMAN CATHOLIC	2	BAUXITE	2	PRESIDENT	4
2	PORTUGUESE	1	HINDU	1	SHRIMP	2	PRESIDENT-PRIME MINISTER	0
3			CHRITIANS	1	OIL	2		

#	Resource	Value
4	GAS	2
5	IRON	2
6	SILVER	2
7	GOLD	2
8	RUBBER	2
9	FORESTS	1
10	COPPER	1
11	LEAD	1
12	BARK	1
13	ANTIMONY	1
14	TIN	1
15	TUNGSTEN	1
16	ZINC	1
17	Cinchona	1
18	DIAMOND	1
19	WOOD	1

II. THE LAST FOUR

IN 1980

NO	FORMER COLONY	FREQUENCE BY 4	MAIN RELIGIOUS AFFILIATION	FREQUENCE BY 4	NATURAL RESOURCES	FREQUENCE	EXECUTIVE BRANCH	FREQUENCE BY 4
1	SPANISH	3	ROMAN CATHOLIC	3	OIL	3	PRESIDENT	4
2	BRITISH	1	CHRISTIANS	1	GAS	2		
3					GOLD	2		
4					COPPER	2		
5					IRON	2		
6					RUBBER	2		
7					SILVER	2		
8					EMERALD	1		
9					LEAD	1		
10					COAL	1		
11					NICKEL	1		
12					SALT	1		
13					BALSAN	1		
14					CAPAIBA	1		

15		DYE-WOOD	1
16		HYDRO POWER ELELCTRIQUE	1
17		WOOL	1
18		SARDINES	1
19		BAUXITE	1
20		DIAMONDS	1
21		WOODS	1
22		SHRIMP	1
23		ANTIMONY	1
24		TIN	1
25		TUNGSTEN	1
26		ZINC	1
27		CINCHONA	1

IN 1993

NO	FORMER COLONY	FREQUENCE SUR 4	PRINCIPALE AFFILIATION RELIGIEUSE	FREQUENCE BY 4	NATURAL RESOURCES	FREQUENCE	EXECUTIVE BRANCH	FREQUENCE SUR 4
1	SPANISH	2	ROMAN CATHOLIC	2	BAUXITE	2	PRESIDENT	4

#						
2	NETHERLAND	1	CHRISTIANS	1	SHRIMP	2
3	BRITISH	1	HINDU	1	OIL	2
4					IRON	2
5					SILVER	2
6					GOLD	2
7					RUBBER	2
8					GAS	2
9					FORESTS	1
10					COPPER	1
11					LEAD	1
12					BARK	1
13					ANTIMONY	1
14					TIN	1
15					TUNGSTEN	1
16					ZINC	1
17					BARK Cinchona	1
18					DIAMOND	1
19					WOOD	1

From the above, one can find the mode for the first four on one side and the other last.

1. THE FIRST FOUR

In 1980, the former Spanish colony 3/4 is the mode, Roman Catholic ¾ is the mode, the political system where only the President 4/4 in the executive branch is the mode, oil 3/4 is mode for natural resources.

In 1993, the former Spanish colony 1/4 is the mode, the Catholic Church 2/4 is the mode, oil, gas, iron, bauxite, silver, rubber and shrimp share 2/4 for natural resources, the political system where the president is the only player in the executive branch with 4/4 is the mode.

At this level one can find the proportions as we know that in 1980 there were 12 countries which we have data, among which: former Spanish colonies in nine countries, a former Dutch colony, a former Portuguese colony and a former British colony.

In 1993, there were 12 countries among which: nine former Spanish colonies, a former Portuguese colony, a former Dutch colony and a former British colony.

Based on the foregoing, we have for the first four:
−In 1980:
1. The former Spanish colonies = (3x100): 9 = 33.3%
2. The former English colony = (0x100): 1 = 0%
3. The former Dutch colony = (1x100): 1 = 100%
4. The former Portuguese colony = (0x100): 1 = 0%

−In 1993:
1. The former Spanish colonies = (3x100): 9 = 33.3%
2. The former Portuguese colony = (1x100): 1 = 100%
3. The former Dutch colony = (0x100): 1 = 0%
4. The former English colony = (0x100): 1 = 0%

This brings us to the European continent.

I. EUROPEAN COUNTRIES

No	COUNTRIES	DATA IN 1980				DATA IN 1993
		GDP/Cap IN U.S $	POPULATION	GRADUATED STUDENTS	% OF GRADUATED STUDENTS	GDP/Cap IN U.S $
1	U.S.S.R	4.550	262.436.000 1979			2.350
2	FRANCE	11.730	54.273.000 1982	864	0.0015	22.760
3	SPAIN	5.350	37.617.000 1981	424	0.0011	14.230
4	SWEDEN	13.520	8.318.000	158	0.0018	24.830
5	GERMANY	13.590	–	948		23.630
6	FINLAND	9.720	4.788.000	84,2	0.0017	16.840
7	POLAND	3.900	35.061.000 1979	131	0.0003	2.270
8	ITALY	6.480	56.557.000 1981	764	0.0013	19.620
9	YOUGOSLAVIA	2.620	22.425.000 1981	411	0.0018	1.000
10	UNITED KINGDOM	7.920	49.155.000 1981	340	0.0006	17.920
11	ROUMANIA	2.340	21.560.000 1977	193	0.0008	1.090
12	GREECE	4.520	9.740.000 1981	64,2	0.0006	7.390
13	TSCHECOSLOVAQUIA	5.820	15.283.000	152	0.0009	2.730
14	BULGARIA	4.150	8.948.000 1985	85,8	0.0009	1.160
15	NETHERLAND	11.470	14.091.000	153	0.0010	20.710
16	HONGRIA	4.180	–	45,4	–	3.330
17	Portugal	2.350	9.883.000 1981	84,1	0.0008	7.890

18	AUSTRIA	10.230	7.555.000 1981	121	0.0016	23.120
19	IRELAND	4.880	3.443.000 1981	–	–	12.580
20	DANEMARK	12.950	5.073.000 1976	49,1	0.0009	26.510
21	SWITZERLAND	16.440	6.366.000	49,7	0.0007	36.410
22	BELGIUM	12.180	–	95,2	–	21.210
23	ALBANIA	–	3.238.000 1989			340
24	LUXEMBURG	14.510	365.000 1981			35.850
25	ANDORA	–				14.000
26	MALTA	3.470				7.280
27	LIECHTENSTEIN					33.510
28	SAN MARINO					16.000
29	MONACO					16.000
II.	DANISH INFLUENCE					
1	NORWAY	12.650	4.091.000	40,6	0.0009	26.340
2	ICELAND	11.330	229.000	–	–	23.620

AREA, NATURAL

I. EUROPEAN COUNTRIES

No	COUNTRIES	AREA IN Km2	NATURAL RESOURCES
1	U.R.S.S	22.402.200	Manganese, mercury, potash, bauxite, cobalt, chromium, copper, coal, gold, lead, molybdenum, nickel, phosphate, silver, tin, tungsten, zinc, oil, gas, potassium, crude oil reserves (1994) 157 barrels bin , forestry, fishing for fish (1992) 5.3 min tone/meter.
2	FRANCE	547.026	Bauxite, iron, coal, crude oil reserves (1994) 177 min barrels, forest.
3	SPAIN	504.782	Lignite, uranium, lead, iron, copper, zinc, coal, forests.
4	SWEDEN	449.750	Zinc, iron, lead, copper, silver, Forests (half the country) produces a quarter of exports, fishing, fish (1993) 334 000 t/m.
5	GERMANY	355.744	Coal, potash, lignite, iron, uranium, crude oil reserves (1994) 449 min barrels, fishing, fish (1992) 258.000 t/m.
6	FINLAND	337.009	Copper, iron, zinc, forest 40% of exports, fishing, fish (1991) 82.813 t/m.
7	POLAND	312.677	Coal, copper, silver, sulphide, natural gas, fishing for fish (1991) 457.000 t/m.

#	Country	Value	Resources
8	ITALIA	301.225	Mercury, potash, sulphide, crude oil reserves (1994) 621 min barrels.
9	YOUGOSLAVIA	255.804	Oil, gas, coal, antimony, lead, nickel, gold, copper, chrome, fishing for fish (1991) 37,000 tonnes/m.
10	UNITED KIGDOM	244.044	Coal, tin, oil, gas, limestone, iron, salt, clay, crude oil reserves (1994) 4.6 barrels bin, fishing for fish (1991) 823 000 t/m.
11	ROUMANIA	237.500	Oil, gas, coal, crude oil reserves (1994) 1.6 bin barrels, wood.
12	GREECE	131.944	Bauxite, lignite, petroleum, manganese, crude oil reserves (1991) 149.000 tons/m.
13	TCHECOSLOVAQUIA	127.869	Coal, lignite.
14	BULGARIA	110.912	Bauxite, copper, zinc, lead, coal, fishing, fish (1993) 27 000 t/m.
15	HONGRIA	93.030	Bauxite, coal, natural gas.
16	PORTUGAL	92.082	Yungstène, uranium, iron, forests (the world leader in cork production, fishing, fish (1991) 325 000 t/m.
17	AUSTRIA	83.849	Iron ore, petroleum, manganese, forests, hydro-electric power.
18	IRLAND	70.283	Zinc, lead, gas fish fishing (1991) 241.000 tons/m.

19	DANEMARK	43.069	Oil, salt, fish poisons (1992) 1.8 min tones/m.
20	SWITZERLAND	41.288	Salt, potential hydro-electric power.
21	NETHERLAND	40.844	Natural gas, petroleum, crude oil reserves (1994) 132 min barrels.
22	BELGIUM	30.513	Coal, gas, forestry, fishing and fish (1991) 40 226 t/m.
23	ALBANIA	28.748	Chrome, coal, oil, gas, forests.
24	LUXEMBOURG	2.586	D.N.D
25	ANDORA	453	D.N.D
26	MALTA	316	D.N.D
27	LIECHTENSTEIN	157	D.N.D
28	SAN MARINO	61	D.N.D
29	MONACO	1.5	D.N.D
30	CITY OF VATICAN	0.44	D.N.D
II.	UNDER DANISH INFLUENCE		
1	NORWAY	324.219	Oil, copper, pyrites, nickel, iron, zinc, lead, wood, crude oil reserves (1994) 9.3 min barrels.
2	ICELAND	103.000	Fish fishing (1991) 1.1 min t/m.

DND: in the above table means data not available.

ACCESS TO WATER, MAIN TYPE OF GOVERNMENT, EXECUTIVE BRANCH, OFFICIAL RELIGION.

I. EUROPEAN COUNTRIES

No	COUNTRIES	ACCES TO GREAT WATERS ?	TYPE OF GOVERNMENT	EXECUTIVE BRANCH		OFFICIAL RELIGION
				HEAD OF STATE	HEAD OF GOVERNMENT	
1	U.R.S.S	YES	FEDERAL REPUBLIC	PRESIDENT	PRIME MINISTER	NONE
2	France	YES	REPUBLIC	PRESIDENT	PRIME MINISTER	NONE
3	SPAIN	YES	CONSTITUTIONAL MONARCHY	KING	PRIME MINISTER	NONE
4	SWEDEN	YES	CONSTITUTIONAL MONARCHY	KING	PRIME MINISTER	SWEDISH CHURCH
5	GERMANY	YES	FEDERAL REPUBLIC	PRESIDENT	PRIME MINISTER	NONE
6	FINLAND	YES	REPUBLIC	PRESIDENT	PRIME MINISTER	NONE
7	POLAND	YES	REPUBLIC	PRESIDENT	PRIME MINISTER	NONE
8	ITALIA	ALMOST YES	REPUBLIC	PRESIDENT	PRIME MINISTER	NONE

#	Country					
9	YOUGOSLAVIA	ALMOST YES	FEDERAL REPUBLIC	FEDERAL PRESIDENT	PRIME MINISTER	NONE
10	UNITED KINGDOM	YES	CONSTITUTIONAL MONARCHY	MONARC	PRIME MINISTER	(1)
11	ROUMANIA	No	REPUBLIC	PRESIDENT	PRIME MINISTER	NONE
12	GREECE	ALMOST YES	REPUBLIC	PRESIDENT	PRIME MINISTER	EASTERN ORTHODOXES
13	TCHECOSLOVAQUIA	No	REPUBLIC	PRESIDENT	PRIME MINISTER	NONE
14	BULGARIA	No	REPUBLIC	PRESIDENT	PRIME MINISTER	NONE
15	HONGRIA	No	REPUBLIC	PRESIDENT	PRIME MINISTER	NONE
16	Portugal	YES	PARLEMENTARY STATE	PRESIDENT	PRIME MINISTER	NONE
17	AUSTRIA	No	FEDERAL REPUBLIC	PRESIDENT	CHANCELOR	NONE
18	IRLAND	YES	REPUBLIC	PRESIDENT	PRIME MINISTER	NONE
19	DANEMARK	YES	CONSTITUITONAL MONARCHY	MONARC	PRIME MINISTER	EVANGELIC LUTHERIANS
20	SWITZERLAND	No	FEDERAL STATE	PRESIDENT F.C		NONE
21	NETHERLAND	YES	CONSTITUTIONAL MONARCHY	MONARC	PRIME MINISTER	NONE
22	BELGIUM	No	FEDERAL CONSTITUTIONAL MONARCHY	MONARC	PRIME MINISTER	NONE

23	ALBANIA	ALMOST YES	REPUBLIC	PRESIDENT	PRIME MINISTER	NONE
24	Luxembourg	No	CONSTITUTIONAL MONARCHY	GREAT DUC	PRIME MINISTER	NONE
25	ANDORA	–	PARLEMENTARY CO-PRINCIPALITY	HEAD OF GOVERNMENT		NONE
26	MALTA	–	REPUBLIC	PRESIDENT	PRIME MINISTER	ROMAN CATHOLICISM
27	LIECHTENSTEIN	–	CONSTITUTIONAL MONARCHY	PRINCE	HEAD OF GOVERNMENT	NONE
28	SAN MARINO	–	REPUBLIC	CAPTAINS-REGENT		NONE
29	MONACO	–	CONSTITUTIONAL MONARCHY	PRINCE	STATE MINISTER	–
30	CITY OF VATICAN	–		–	–	–
II.	UNDER DANISH INFLUENCE					
1	NORWAY	YES	CONSTITUTIONAL MONARCHY	KING	PRIME MINISTER	EVANGELIC LUTHERIANS
2	ICELAND	YES	–	PRESIDENT	PRIME MINISTER	EVANGELIC LUTHERIA
		YES				

(1) Official religion in the United Kingdom official: Churches of England and Scotland "established" (protected by the state, but not "officialy" in their respective countries, no established churches in Northern Ireland or Wales.

RELIGIOUS AFFILIATION

I. EUROPEAN COUNTRIES

No	COUNTRIES	RELIGIOUS AFFILIATION
1	U.R.S.S	D.N.D
2	France	(1980) Roman Catholic 76.4%, other Christian 3.7%, atheist 3.4%, Muslim 3%, other 13.5%.
3	SPAIN	(1993) Roman Catholic 94.9%, Muslim 1.2%, Protestant 1.5%, other 3.4%.
4	SWEDEN	(1993) Swedish Church 87.3% (nominally 30% non-practicing), Roman Catholic 1.7%, Pentecostal 1.1%, other 9.9%.
5	GERMANY	(1987) Old (Western Germany) Roman Catholic 42.9%, Lutherans, Reformed and Lutheran 41.6%, Muslim 2.7%, 0.6% reformed traditionalists, Jewish 0.1%, other 12.1 %. Former East Germany (1990) 47% Protestant, Roman Catholic 7%, 46% more unified.
6	FINLAND	(1995) Evangelical Lutheran 85.9%, finish (Greek) Orthodox 1.1%, non-religious 12%, other 1%.
7	POLAND	(1993) Roman Catholic 90.5%, Orthodox 1.5%.
8	ITALIA	(1980) Roman Catholic 83.2%, 13.6% non-religious, atheist 2.6%, other 0.6%.
9	YOUGOSLAVIA	(1991) Most believers are affiliated with the Orthodox Church Serbien. There are also Muslim, Roman Catholic and Protestant minorities.

No	Country	Religious Data
10	UNITED KINGDOM	(1980) The religious participation of about 8,400 active members only. Christians 80% of which 21% Roman Catholic, Anglican 20%, 14% Presbyterian, Methodist 5%, Baptist 3%, Muslim 11%, 4% Sikh, Hindu 2%, Jewish 1%, other 2%.
11	ROUMANIA	(1992) Romanian Orthodox 86.8%, 5% Roman Catholic, Greek Orthodox 3.5%, Pentecostal 1%, Muslim 0.2%, other 3.5%.
12	GREECE	(1980) which Orthodox Christians 98.1% East 97.6%, Roman Catholic 0.4%, Protestant 0.1%, Muslim 1.5%, other 0.4%.
13	TCHECOSLOVAQUIA	(1991) 39% Catholic, Protestant 4.3%, which the brothers reformed Czechoslovak Czechoslovak Hussite% 2 1.7%, Silesian Evangelical 0.3%, Orthodox Eastern 0.2%, Greek Catholic 0.1% , other Christian 0.3%, sub-denominational 39.9%, other 16.2%.
14	BULGARIA	(1992) Eastern Orthodox 87%, Muslim 12.7%, other 0.3%.
15	HONGRIA	(1992) Christian 92% of which Roman Catholic 67.8%, 25.1% Protestants, atheists and non-religious 4.8%, other 2.3%.
16	Portugal	(1981) Christian 96% of which Roman Catholic 94.5%, Protestant 0.6%, other Christian Catholic Apostolic mainly Jehovah's Witnesses 0.9%, non-religious 3.8%, Jewish 0.1%, Muslim 0, 1%.
17	AUSTRIA	(1991) Roman Catholic 78%, non-religious and atheist 8.6%, Lutheran 4.8%, Muslim 2%, Jewish 0.2%, other mainly Christian 2.7%, unknown 3.7%.
18	IRLAND	(1991) 91.6% Roman Catholic, Church of Ireland (Anglican) 2.3%, Presbyterian 0.4%, other 5.7%.
19	DANEMARK	(1993) Evangelical Lutheran 87.7%, other Christian 1.6%, Muslim 1.4%, other 9.3% non-religious.
20	SWITZERLAND	(1990) Roman Catholic 46.2%, Protestant 40%, Muslim 2.2%, 1% Orthodox Christians, Jews 0.3%, other 10.3%.

21	NETHERLAND	(1993) Roman Catholic 32%, Dutch Reformed Church 15%, Calvinist 7%, Muslim 3.7%, other 2.3%, no religion 40%.
22	BELGIUM	(1980) Roman Catholic 90%, Muslim 1.1%, Protestant 0.4%, non-religious and atheist 7.5%, other 1%.
23	ALBANIA	(1992) A significant portion of the population is non-religious believers identify themselves as Muslims 65%, 20% Orthodox, Roman Catholic 13%, other 2%.
24	LUXEMBURG	(1990) Roman Catholic 94.9%, Protestant 1.1%, other 4%.
25	ANDORA	(1992) Roman Catholic 92%, Protestant 0.5%, Jewish 0.4%, other 7.1%.
26	MALTA	(1992) Roman Catholic 98.6%, other 1.4%
27	LIECHTENSTEIN	(1994) Roman Catholic 80.3%, Protestant 7.1%, 7.9% unreported.
28	SAN MARINO	(1980) Roman Catholic 95.2%, non-religious 3%, other 1.8%.
29	MONACO	—
30	CITY OF VATICAN	—
	UNDER DANISH INFLUENCE	
1	NORWAY	(1980) Lutheran 87.9%, non-religious 3.2%, other 8.9%.
2	ICELAND	(1994) Protestant Evangelical Lutheran 95.7% of which 91.8%, other 3.2% Lutheran, Roman Catholic 1%, non-religious 1.4%, other 1.9%.

PROPORTION (PERCENTAGE) OF ACADEMICS OF EUROPEAN COUNTRIES

IN ORDER IN 1980

NO	COUNTRIES	% OF GRADUATED STUDENTS
1	TCHECOSLOVAQUIA	9.9456
2	NORWAY	9.9242
3	Portugal	9.883*
4	DANEMARK	9.6786*
5	BELGIUM	9.6659*
6	BULGARIA	9.5887*
7	ROUMANIA	8.9517*
8	SWITZERLAND	7.8071
9	UNITED KINGDOM	6.9168*
10	GREECE	6.5913*
11	POLAND	3.7363*
12	SWEDEN	1.8994
13	YOUGOSLAVIA	1.8327*
14	FINLAND	1.7585
15	AUSTRIA	1.6015
16	ITALIA	1.3508*
17	NETHERLAND	1.0857

The asterixis * in the column percentage of academics mean that these proportions do not reflect reality because the population in 1980 was not available, we had to take it around 1980, 1977, 79, 81, 82 apart from the 1976 for Denmark, Bulgaria and Albania 1985 1989.

GDP/Cap EUROPEAN COUNTRIES IN 1980 IN ORDER OF MAGNITUDE

NO	COUNTRIES	GDP/Cap IN U.S $
1	SWITZERLAND	16.440
2	LUXEMBOURG	14.510
3	GERMANY	13.590
4	SWEDEN	13.520
5	DANEMARK	12.950
6	NORWAY	12.650
7	BELGIUM	12.180
8	FRANCE	11.730
9	NETHERLAND	11.470
10	ICELAND	11.330
11	AUSTRIA	10.230
12	FINLAND	9.720
13	UNITED KINGDOM	7.920
14	ITALIA	6.480
15	TCHECOSLOVAQUIA	5.820
16	SPAIN	5.350
17	IRLAND	4.880
18	U.R.S.S	4.550
19	GREECE	4.520
20	HONGRIA	4.180
21	BULGARIA	4.150
22	POLAND	3.900
23	MALTA	3.470
24	YOUGOSLAVIA	2.620
25	PORTUGAL	2.350
26	ROUMANIA	2.340

GDP/Cap EUROPEAN COUNTRIES IN 1993 IN ORDER OF MAGNITUD

NO	COUNTRIES	GDP/Cap IN U.S.$
1	SWITZERLAND	36.410
2	LUXEMBOURG	35.850
3	LIECHTENSTEIN	33.510
4	DANEMARK	26.510
5	NORWAY	26.340
6	SWEDEN	24.830
7	GERMANY	23.630
8	ICELAND	23.620
9	AUSTRIA	23.120
10	FRANCE	22.760
11	BELGIUM	21.210
12	NETHERLAND	20.710
13	ITALIA	19.620
14	UNITED KINGDOM	17.920
15	FINLAND	16.840
16	SAN MARINO	16.000
16	MONACO	16.000
17	SPAIN	14.230
18	ANDORA	14.000
19	IRLAND	12.580
20	PORTUGAL	7.890
21	GREECE	7.390
22	MALTA	7.280
23	HONGRIA	3.330
24	TCHECOSLOVAQUIA	2.730
25	U.R.S.S	2.350
26	POLAND	2.270
27	BULGARIA	1.160
28	ROUMANIA	1.090
29	YOUGOSLAVIA	1.000
30	ALBANIA	340

Referring to the data that is in the preceding pages, we may examine the relationship between the percentage of the academics and performance GDP/Cap.

1. Czechoslovakia, first in percentage of the academics in 1980, was 15th in GDP/cap in 1980, 24th in 1993.
2. The Norway, the second in percentage of the academics in 1980, was 6th in GDP/cap in 1980, 5th in 1993.
3. Portugal, the third in percentage of the academics in 1980, was 25th in GDP/Cap in 1980, 20th in 1993.
4. Denmark, fourth in percentage of the academics in 1980, was 5th in GDP/Cap in 1980, 4th in 1993.
5. Belgium fifth, in percentage of the academics in 1980, was 7th in GDP/Cap in 1980, 11th in 1993.
6. Bulgaria, sixth in percentage of the academics in 1980, was 21st in GDP/cap in 1980, 27th in 1993.
7. Romania, seventh in percentage of the academics in 1980, was 26th in GDP/cap in 1980, 28th in 1993.
8. Switzerland, the eighth in percentage of the academics in 1980, was the first in GDP/Cap in 1980 and 1993.
9. The United Kingdom, ninth in percentage of the academics in 1980, was 13th in GDP/cap in 1980, 14th in 1993.
10. Greece, tenth in percentage of the academics in 1980, was 19th in GDP/Cap in 1980, 21st in 1993.
11. Poland, eleventh in percentage of the academics in 1980, was 22nd in GDP/cap in 1980, 26th in 1993.
12. Sweden, twelfth in percentage of the academics in 1980, was in 4th in GDP/cap in 1980, 6th in 1993.
13. Yugoslavia, the thirteenth in percentage of the academics in 1980, was 24th in GDP/cap in 1980, 29th in 1993.
14. Finland, the fourteenth in the percentage of academics in 1980, 12th in GDP/cap in 1980, 15th in 1993.
15. Austria, thefifteenth in percentage of the academics in 1980, was 11th in GDP/cap in 1980, 9th in 1993.
16. Italy, Sixteenth in percentage of the academics in 1980, was 14th in GDP/cap in 1980, 13th in 1993.

17. The Netherlands, Seventeenth in percentage of academics in 1980, was 9th in GDP/Cap in 1980, 12th in 1993.

From the above, one can observe a low correlation. Because apart from a few countries that have the same place or around a percentage of the academics in 1980 and GDP/Cap in the case of 1980, 1993: Norway, Denmark, United Kingdom, Finland, Italy; there are in one hand, countries that occupied the best seats in percentage of the academics in 1980, but with places in GDP/Cap in 1980, 1993 far different from those obtained in percentage of academics in 1980. This is the case of: Czechoslovakia, Portugal, Belgium, Bulgaria, Romania, Greece, Poland, Yugoslavia. On the other hand there are countries that seats occupied in GDP/Cap in 1980, 1993 are better than those occupied in percentage of academics in 1980. This is the case of: Switzerland, Sweden, Austria, the Netherlands.

This chapter has been dominated by two assumptions:
–The number of years between colonization and independence would be very crucial in the future life of the former colonized countries.
–The number, the percentage of academics, infrastructure (roads, health, production . . .) bequeathed to independence would be a factor in the future life of the country former colony.
In this chapter, you have realized that:
1. the number of years of colonization is not an absolute condition for good performance in the future life of the country that was colonized, because as we have seen, although there are countries such as Gabon (121 years), Algeria (132 years), South Africa (105 years), Namibia (106 years), with average of many years of colonization, had a strong performance in GDP/cap in 1980.

Countries such as Tunisia (75 years), Ivory Coast (78 years), Botswana (81 years), Nigeria (99 years), Congo Brazzaville (50 years), Cameroon (76 years), Egypt (40 years), Zambia (40 years), which had relatively fewer years of colonization, had however relatively a good performance in GNP/Cap in 1980, than countries with many years of colonization, such as Angola, Cape Verde, Mozambique, Senegal, Ghana . . .

2. The number of the academics at independence or around the years after independence in different countries or different continents did not have all positively correlated. This is to say that this factor and others as the number of years of settlement, infrastructure, legacy of independence, need to interact with other factors to be truly rational, effective and efficient. Because even the best infrastructure, if not a qualified staff to manage them efficiently and effectively will not be profitable and will be short-lived.

Similarly a country with a large number of intellectuals, academics, skilled . . . can miss to receive this benefit if the political structures of the stifle, if the political, economic, ideological, do not allow university intellectuals to express themselves, to give what they can do. Some times, some political regimes may even misuse some unconscious academics, intelectuals in the political system to be more intellectual collaboration to marginalize and impoverish the population. And then these intellectuals are contradictory in what they do, as there is discrepancy between words and action. And it devalues the intellectual in general. And that associated with other ailments, causes the crisis, the problems.

That is why in Chapter 3 we will discuss about the current situation in Congo.

From page 228 to 242, the data that is in the tables have different sources:
1. The GDP/Cap in 1980. Source: Protein deficiency and malnutrition. Published in 1990 by the United Nations Educational, Scientific and Cultural Organization. 7 Place Fontenoy, 75700 Paris, Typeset by Coupé, Sautron. Printed by the Printing Presses Universitaires de France, Vendôme. ISBN 92-3-102083-8 c Unesco 1990 Printed in France.
2. Area and access to many waters. Source: Follet student Atlas: Ibid

3. Natural Resources, official religion, religious affiliation, type of government, executive branch. Source: Encyclopaedia Britannica. Book of the Year 1996. Ibid

4. The classification of countries according to the colonizing countries. Source: The New Universal Family Encyclopaedia. Ibid.

5. The G.D.P/Cap in 1993. Source: Encyclopaedia Britannica. Book of the Year 1996. Ibid.

6. Academics in 1980. Source: International Historical Statistics: Africa, Asia and Oceania 1750-2000 BR Mitchell-5th Ed-Basingstoke: palagrave, 2003. ISBN 0-333-99412-4.

7. Population in 1980. Source: Encyclopaedia Britannica. Book of the Year 1982. Events of 1981.

CHAPTER 3

THE CURRENT SITUATION IN THE CONGO

In Chapter 1 you were able to realize that the Congo is potentially rich in men, basement, flora, fauna, hydrography . . . Obviously the Congo is cited as potentially rich country, but now among the countries that are poorest. The Congo is in crisis, as you will see in this chapter when we talk about the political, economic and even social situation in Congo. But you will find the political, economic and even social events dating back since 2001 and before. This is to allow you to enter the current political system since its inception.

POLITICAL SITUATION

After the assassination of the late president Laurent Kabila in January 2001, January 26 of that year, his "son" Major-General Joseph Kabila found himself at the head of the country as the presiding republic.

It can be asked questions why Joseph Kabila had to succeed his "father" as if the Congo was a monarchy or a kingdom? The real reasons that had pushed for this choice were unknown to the Congolese population that is nevertheless the first concerned. This is very easy to understand especially when it is known that the fate of Congo is decided largely out of Congo.

In fact the succession of the late President Laurent Désiré Kabila by his "son" Joseph Kabila was confirmed by unanimous vote of the Congolese parliament. This could not surprise people observing rationally what is happening in the politics of Congo. It is not a secret that "most parliamentarians had been had picked by the late President Laurent Désiré Kabila." [69] What can the country expected from such parliamentarians, who as appointed by Laurent Désiré Kabila, could do nothing if is only pleasing their boss, than listerning to the cries of martyred people. That is how they confused Congo to a kingdom or a monarchy where the son/daughter can succeed his/her fatherd after his death.

To justify this hostage, some have argued that the advent of Joseph Kabila was necessary to avoid a bloodbath in the Congo. He had a point solution to avoid a bloodbath in the country. The reason of the strongest is always the best told. It is here that there is still reason to ask: was it because Joseph Kabila was probably the person to whom the army and loyal to Laurent Kabila could listen and obey, or because it was probably the person in whom the West could trust for latent political and economic reasons?

We will get an idea of the reasons that have campaigned for this choice later in what follows when we speak about causes.

The period of Joseph Kabila was also characterized by attacks here, and there, insecurity here, and there, as a legacy of previous regimes. Weapons in the country had not ceased to be heard, consuming the poor population, always found, martyred sacrificed. Meanwhile, systematic lootings are organized in the country. This was confirmed among others by the report [70] of the UN released in April 2001, late October 2002, and July 2003 on the illegal exploitation of Congo's resources by the nations involved in the Congo war.

Although peace negotiations were held here and there, however insecurities, fightings were going on as we can read:"despite peace agreements

---

69. Conrad Bo Painting in Superstroke/ Congo, Democratic Republic of the (DROC)-History.

70. Democratic Republic of Congo.
    Vol. 15 No. 11(A)-July 2003.

purportedly ending the five year-old Congolese war, fighting in northeastern DRC intensified in late 2002 and early 2003. [71]

In November 2002, the inter-congolese dialogue resumed in Pretoria, South Africa and in December the same year they signed an agreement that will lead to the adoption of a two years new constitution of transition on the 4 April 2003. Negotiations with the various rebel groups resulted in the formation of a government of national union in 2003.

By the way it can also be remembered that the inaugural speech of the transition in Congo was given by the late Mobutu, chairing of the Republic at the time, on the 24th April 1990. Coincidentally the adoption of the so-called new constitution (that of the Inter Congolese Dialogue), was made in April 4, 2003. Although years are different, however a similarity is drawn between the two dates: April 24 1990 and 24 April 2003, when one questions the value of the texts in these dates, especially with regard to respect for these texts by their authors. Can we say that the date of April 1st, the day known as the fool day influence the political life in the Congo? It's still ridiculous somewhere if this is the case. We must understand that it is rather an issue of honesty of men. Men are able to turn a mountain into a valley or a plain in a mountain.

We can recall here that it is from that agreement signed at Sun City in South Africa, that the country went through a political monster where by, there was one president and four vice presidents, a formula unic at my knowledge in politics of countries. Fortunatly, that, there were brave and heroic leaders who have understood and refused to take the people in hostage, by signing the so called agreement.
Starting from the Inter-Congolese agreement of December 2002, April 7, 2003, Major-General Joseph Kabila had seen its days long at the head of the country to lead the transition. The agreement provided for the transition:

---

71. DR Congo:chronology.
   August 21 2009.

1. President of the Republic who has the supreme command of the armed forces, the power to appoint and dismiss ministers and judges, governors and deputy governors . . . in accordance with the transitional constitution published in the Official Gazette of the Democratic Republic of Congo (DRC) 44th year, Special Issue April 5, 2003.
2. Said a government of national unity, composed of members from the outgoing government, armed groups, unarmed political parties and civil society.
3. A bicameral parliament composed of 500 members of the lower house (National Assembly) and 120 members upper house (senate). Like any transitional body, the parliament also consists of members from different components: the outgoing government, armed groups, unarmed political parties and civil society.

Regarding the duration of the transitional institutions, it is stated in the transitional constitution, Title VI: Transitional and Final Provisions. Article 196: the duration of the transition is 24 months. It runs from the formation of the transitional government and ends with the inauguration of President elected after the elections marking the end of the transitional period in the Democratic Republic of Congo. However due to problems specifically related to the organization of elections, the transition may be extended for a period of six months, renewable once, if circumstances so require, on a proposal from the independent electoral commission and a joint decision and duly grounds of the National Assembly and Senate. Was this constitution scrupulously respected ? Most of all Congolese and sincere man know that it was not.

That's how, in principle, the transition was expected to end June 30, 2005. But it has been extended to June 30, 2006. It should be noted that until that time (in April 2003 which saw Joseph Kabila adding his days as head of the country) Congo was thirteen years in the political transition process characterized by untold suffering of all kinds. The population has long been martyred, has seen all the colors. But lack of a better she had to rely on the patience though many were already pessimistic about the political scheme proposed by the members who participated in the Inter-Congolese agreement.

It may need to be recalled here that over 70% of those who gathered at the inter-Congolese dialogue did not go to defend the interests of the people but rather to consolidate their interests or those of their masters. That's how they took out the formula $4 + 1 = 5$, which means 1 President + 4 Vice-Presidents, a formula almost unique in the world.

And much of the population considered that $1 + 4 = 0$ to express their pessimism, their distrust on this scheme thinking it will fail. But some said that this formula has had the merit to exist for us to avoid the worst. What worse that the people has not yet seen live? While the inter-Congolese dialogue had the merit to exist because in addition to seeking a consensus on the transitional institutions, it would have avoided endless quarrels among others, potential fighting between various armed groups, but for a short time.

Even the $1 + 4$ formula in my opinion, was a anthropogenic Negu mechanism, the social expansion, made to hold the population hostage and extend the transitional period, which greatly benefits the enemies of democracy, of the welfare of the Congolese.

But as the group opposed to the interests of the people is very tricky, it is very risky to make an analysis contrary to their scheme without being treated pessimistic, as some one who wants to disturb the transition, an enemy of democracy . . . This group of interest has the means to support his scheme. Knowing that their scheme will not result in a successful outcome for Congo, they pretend to be concerned about the situation, but prefer this time of political confusion that benefits them in terms of country's resources at lower cost.

However, there are those who think it is better to enter big business in peace with credible institutions in peacefull times than in times of political uncertainty. For those of course they want to see one day the Congo acquiring credible political institutions and begin a normal life.

But for those who want to enjoy in times of political confusion or a regime loyal to them, they invest their time to either extend the political confusion or seek to legalize those who can work in their pay. And for that they have systematic mechanisms. They put barriers to any person or group of people with the desire to see the country get back on track. They seek to cover every way abuses by the group of people working in their pay. But as the social fact is stubborn, abuses always end up being discovered. It's like a faucet that has a hole where the water gushes with pressure. If you want to prevent the escape of the water trying to stifle the hole, as the pressure continues, there will be signs that the water escape until the technique are tired, then you have to remove your hand.

Given the above, in less than a month people began to live the opposite of the agreements signed in Pretoria in December 2002, and later over abuses of power were registered. For example, the 20/12/2002 we could hear the RFI say, "four days after the Pretoria Agreement, the weapons speak in South Kivu. According to Adolf Onusumba, the Mayi-Mayi attack the DRC from Ruzizi Makobola. In Ituri, Jean Pierre Bemba said they were also attacked by pro-government MNCL.

"In 2003 Uganda People's Defence Forces, supported by ethnic Lendu and Ngiti militias, ousted the Union des patriots Congolais (UPC) from city of Bunia, following several hours of intense fighting. HRV said that the UPC, generally identified with the Hema ethnic group, while opposing political and military groups associated with the Lendu and Ngiti. It added that during years of fighting for control of this resource–rich region, various local forces and their more powerful supporters had frequently targeted civilians, often on an ethnic basis, regarding them as supporters of other contenders. "Many military operations in this area have turned into slaughter of civilians or other kinds of abuses, like rape, torture and pillage", said Alison Des Forges, the senior adviser to the Africa Division of HRW." [72]

It is only after pressure "from the South African government, that the Ugandan armed forces left the country and the UPC attacked Bunia after

---

[72] Reports on Ethnic Relations.

fierce fighting during which many civilians were massacred by the armies of both opposite sides. [73]

In May/June 2004:" General Laurent Nkunda, with the support from Rwanda, takes control of Bukavu in South Kivu, claiming to protect Tutsi civilians under attack. MONUC peacekeepers fail to halt Nkunda's advance. After intense diplomatic pressure, Nkunda withdraws from Bukavu four days later, but across the country, MONUC staff are attacked by angry crowds protesting the UN's failure to act." [74]

The attitude of MONUC in these events, reminds us of the questions asked by NGIJOL GILBERT [75] about what happened in Rwanda in the first half of 90: "Why: 1. the same Security Council, after the outbreak of a predictable war, rather drastically reduced military strength of UNAMIR I? 2. after the RPF (Rwandan Patriotic Front) military vicyory, the Security Council finally flooded Rwanda with large contingents to deal only with humanitarian missions?
3. these peacekeepers remained as indifferent and passive in the face of organized and planned slaughtering of more than 2,000 Hutu refugees from camps in Kibeho, 22 April 1995 by the Rwandan Patriotic Army?"

It is without coment, we give you the latitude to judge. In September 2004 there was the HRW report [76], alleging "violation of human rights against the civilians by armed groups. In December 2004, Rwandan President Paul Kagame threatened twice to redeploy its forces in Congo, if neither MONUC nor the Congolese army, does nothing against the FDLR". That's how there

73. Europa Regional Surveys of the World, Africa South of Sahara 2006, 35thEdition.
74. DR Congo: chronology.
    August 21, 2009.
75. GILBERT Ngijol: op cit
76. Europa Regional Surveys of the World, Africa South of Sahara 2006. 35th Edition.

were reports of military movements along the Rwandan/congolese border and inside the Congo. And this could show disharmony between the two countries. Meanwhile, "fighting broke out in Kanyabayonga (North Kivu) between the RCD-Goma and government armed forces resulting in the killing, and about 60,000 people to be displaced" [77].

The same year, the Transitional Government promulgated a new law on nationality stating that "every person belonging to, an ethnic group whose members or territory, was in Congo at independence, has Congolese nationality, realizing the main application of the RCD-Goma and the Rwandan government." [78] For members of RCD/G knew, "it was likely for them as they could receive many votes from the Banyamulenge being citizen during an election." [79]

But "many Congolese are skeptical that the Banyamulenge deserve citizenship, believing that they are still loyal to Rwanda." [80]

And here some Congoleses, awakened by the events began to understand that the war against Congo is already inside the government institutions. For, you must know that there are matters that can not be handled rationaly than only by the government to be office after the fair and transparent elections.

While the government's mandate was driving to an end, Mr Anzuluni Bembe pointed out: "from the analysis of the budget's debate in parliament for 2004, it emerged that many topics related to elections, have not attracted the attention of the government institutions, or parliament. The same for the constitutional referendum organization, the census and national identification . . . Priority sectors to fight against poverty such as

---

77. Idem

78. Ibidem.

79. Cable Reference ID #04 Kinshasa 1141.
Reference ID 04 Kinshasa aka wikileaks ID # 18005 ?

80. Idem.

education, health, access to drinking water, road infrastructure and other basic infrastructure have not experienced substantial credit." [81]

"You may also notice that the formation of a restructured and integrated national army is not effective. National reconciliation is far from being achieved.

And the fight is opened against any person seeking to know and inform the public. The independent press was muzzled, independent journalists threatened, beaten, tortured . . .". [82]

The domestication of information, violence, terror, . . . , planted by the government, disputes between members of different components on the shared responsibility for public enterprises and parastatals, the territorial, diplomatic, . . . , corruption is common.

We have said that nothing is said about the people who hire agreements the country with other countries. In this regard, the following is a sample: Monday, August 15, 2005, at the television in Namibia "Talk of the Nation" program transmitted on Monday at 9:00 p.m., the Ambassador of Namibia in the Democratic Republic of Congo, responding to a question from a listener, acknowledged that the government of Laurent Kabila had given a grant to Namibia for diamonds in Kasai-Oriental and that the Namibian experts after prospecting qualified the concession very rich. It is amazing that in the 21st century, there are presidents who access to the head of the country to distribute in the name of nationalism, national land, to foreign countries without even informing the people. And Joseph Kabila who has inherited the situation does not make any effort to inform and explain why, to people which is nevertheless the first concerned.

---

81. Anzuluni Bembe ISILONYONI: Press conference on the peace process in Democratic Republic of Congo. Dated 1st May 2004 in Kinshasa.
82. ANZULINI BEMBE ISILONYONI: op cit.

The population is sacrificed. In the words of Mr. Anzuluni Bembe "employees, although they spent nearly three months to go on strike, althougth the Mbudi agreements, have not seen their situation improve.

Yet the presidential circle has been allocated substantial funds both in terms of compensation as operating costs.

In fact it appeared that budget that will restore a new political order does not appear. The presidential circle has not only higher pay credit to what was announced by the Government in presenting the 2004 budget, but also has other loans ill-defined, such as special funds. The old methods and practices decried by the Sovereign National Conference and the new political class: secret funds, civil lists, allocations are not subject to overall control. The press, both written and audio-visual has not hesitated to treat the budget as the budget of shame, antisocial, budget of managers, not for the poor, less for people". [83]

But to believe the words of those in power, the transitional institutions are at work, serving the people. Until some six months after the end of the mandate of the transition-extension put apart-Apollinaire Malu-Malu, chairman of the electoral commission announced early in January 2005 that the electoral calendar was behind the forecast, implying that the election process will be delayed. Tired of seeing his misery prolonged by a government in which he does not trust, people replied to the speech of Malu-Malu by protests in Kinshasa and other cities, protests were suppressed by security forces.

That's how having arrived on 30 June 2005, the people once again accepted the chore even to the last extension. And the regime of Joseph Kabila was still remained in place until 30 June 2006, date at which elections should have been already organized.

One might think having arrived on June 30, 2005, President Joseph Kabila would have at least apologized to the nation for not having fulfilled his solemn promise to the people and also make amends for the future. What

---

[83]   Anzuluni Bembe ISILONYONI: op cit

has not been the case, and the government continued its momentum destroying the country even more. More money is used to purchase things that are far from democratic set, such as buying weapons and that at large discretion. For example according to the BBC Tuesday, July 5, 2005, Congo is a rich country in the world in terms of mining, but that money is used to buy weapons. According to the RFI's Morning Edition April 25, 2006 (6:30), a Radio Okapi journalist was violently hit by the presidential guard. According to Radio Okapi in the April 29, 2006, morning edition, the presidential guard had exchanged a shot with the army in Equateur province.

Given the above, you may have to briefly report on the government's behavior in few months around the date set for the elections.

As we said in the introduction to this book, the international community, countries and different institutions have in general not only supported the 2006 elections in Congo,-" the European Commission, U.S. and UN had invested heavily in the electoral process and were zealous to have a real winner that can bring legitimacy [84]–but also the elected government.

And it seems that the support or external intervention in the crisis/conflict in the DRC was "based on the assumption that the situation facing the Congo is unacceptable and should be changed." [85] It is apparently based on this philosophy that the European Commission and the United States as the "largest donors in humanitarian assistance and development" [86], and other institutions like the UN, have actively supported the Congo.

---

[84] Democratic Republic of Congo: European Commission and U.S. Approaches to Linking Relief, Rehabilitation and Development. Taken from google, Foreign funding to DRC's government from 2007 to 2011.
[85] Democratic Republic of Congo: Idem.
[86] Democratic Republic of Congo: Ibid.

That's how there was different funding for the DR Congo, and we here give just some samples: "18.5 million Euro under stabilizing the situation of fragility, have been allocated for 2006-2008. [87] For all operations in the DRC in 2008 according to the ECHO, the European Commission has committed the following funds:

ECHO

Global plan 2008: 30 million Euro
Food aid: 13.3 million Euro
Echo flights: 8 million Euro.

DELEGATION OF THE EUROPEAN UNION

–European Development Fund: 388 million+100 million Euro (2003-2007)
–Food safety: 23 million Euro (2007-2013)
I nstruments Stability: 18.5 million Euro (2006-2008) [88]
–Emergency Reserve (globally to 239 million Euro in 2008) [89]

UNITED STATES

In contrast to the UK, who walked most of its humanitarian assistance to the DRC through the bottom of the UN jointly managed (US $ 58 million in 2008 according to the system of the track financial OCHA) all the European commission and the United States had preferred to fund billateraly. On top of that the U.S. government had paid large sums of development assistance to the DRC. The U.S. State Department and USAID have jointly asked Congress for $ 105 million in 2008 and $ 95 million in 2009 for operations in the DRC, excluding humanitarian assistance as it is called short-term. [90]

---

[87] Democratic Republic of Congo: Ibid.

[88] Democratic Republic of Congo: Ibid.

[89] Democrati Republic of Congo:Ibid.

[90] U.S. (2008) Congressional Budget Justification 2009, page 212. Taken from google, DRC foreign funding to DRC's government from 2007 to 2011.

According to the DRC's report December 2007 by the Office of Government Accounting, the State and USAID had reported for 80% of all U.S. assistance to the DRC in the years 2006-2007. [91]

OTHER INSTITUTIONS

On 11 December 2009, the IMF Executive Board had approved an arrangement of three years (July 2009–June 2012 for the DRC under the program of poverty reduction and growth facility (PRGF). The amount was about 551 million U.S. and also $ 73 million USD to enhance the Heavily Indebted Poor Countries Initiative, to reduce the payment of debt service of the DRC to the IMF. [92]

IMPACT OF REACHING THE COMPLETION POINT

_____(In billions of U.S. dollars) 2010-2012

1. RESOURCES FOLLOWING APPROVAL PROGRAM 9500
    Debt Relief – 1600
    Restructuring of outstanding Paris Club 1600 –
    Financial aid mobilized – 6300
    External support (WB, ADB, EU, China and other – 5700
    IMF support to the BCC – 0.600 –
2. BENEFIT OF ACHIEVING THE COMPLETION POINT – 21,000
    Resources related to program approval – 9500
    Debt cancellation – 11,500 [93].

---

91. GAO (2007), page 13. Taken from google, foreign funding to DRC's governemnt from 2007 to 2011. Democratic Republic of Congo: European Commission and U.S. Approaches to Linking Relief, Rehabilitation and Development. Page 174, paragraph 4.
92. Google, foreign funding to DRC's government from 2007 to 2011. DRC Economic Report. Page 4 Paragraph 9 to page 5 paragraph 1.
93. Google, foreign funding to DRC's government from 2007 to 2011. DRC Mining Industry News page 2 of 12.

These are some examples of funds which some, date back many years even before the 2006 elections and beyond. All these efforts can translate good intentions of the international community, countries, different institutions to see the Congo (DRC) living democracy, which can stimulate the development of the country.

But the fear may be that all these efforts are to put in the law of the falling rate of profit, that consists of losing deliberately some of its properties money, used to let sleep, feed the exploited for them to believe that the exploiter spends his money, properties in the interests of the exploited, while the exploiter agrees to spend that as long as his company works.

This is where the international community, countries, national and international institutions that supported not only the electoral process of 2006, but also its results can blame something in their consciousness, if their efforts in supporting this process were really sincere in the interest of the Congolese people. If we objectively assess the regime of President Joseph Kabila in his governance from 2006 and even around, up to these days, the world, the international community can now see that although the efforts [financial support (and the Cancellation of debt even small be it), material, technical, moral], provided by some Western powers, financial institutions to support President Joseph Kabila, the DRC is still:

1. LIVING AWAY FROM DEMOCRACY (GOOD GOVERNANCE, THE BALANCE BETWEEN GOVERNING INSTITUTIONS)

Through the second half of 2006 and early 2007 the scores of those suspected sympathizers or supporters of the opposition were arbitrarily arrested and detained. There were attacks against the offices of opposition political parties and media stations across the country. [94]

In April 2007, the political opposition temporarily suspended its participation in parliament, citing continuing intimidation by security forces. [95]

---

[94]   Democratic Republic of Congo: idem, page 307.
[95]   Democratic Republic of Congo: idem, page 308, 326

Many journalists, cameramen are targets of intimidation, arbitrary detention and cruel, inhuman and degrading treatment by agents of state security. [96] attacks the media. [97]

Personnel or official, pastor or important personalities which they dout about their connivence with the presidential, are subject of intimidation, arrest and detention and even discret execution. This is the case among the arrested: "Pastor Kutino, Pastor Timothée Bompere, Junior Ngandu, Anne-Marie Lisasi an election official". (15[98])

Good governance can be seen through the balance that can be observed between different powers that make up the system, the independence of powers between them, but in a collaboration established by the constitution.

That's why here we try to see if the actual balance and independence enshrined in the constitution between the Presidency, the executive, the legislative and the judicial are real in business management in these powers. Because the lack to respect that balance and independence may cause the malfunction of one of these power system components, so that if something is malfunctioning, the malfunctioning of one of the elements can lead to failure in the system.

Having lost that we have said, one can observe that already in 2007, the DRC government was inactive. "To notice it and think of how the new government was headed, see: Antoine Gizenga, 90 days of inactivity, in an editorial in Kinshasa, Le Potentiel, 24 May 2007.
See http://fr.allafrica.com/stories/200705240244.html.

Indeed it is even at the beginning of term as it says, "by appointing Antoine Gizenga to the post of head of government at the beginning of

---

96.   Idem, p. 339-343
97.   If you want to know more about the media attacks, see Journalists in Danger (JED) the ratio of Journalists in Danger (JED), freedom of the press during the election period, November 2006.
98.   Democratic Republic of Congo, general election 2006: ibid, page 316-321.

the mandate, Kabila seeks a head of government unable to perform his duties. Octogenarian physically weak Gizenga can not take the amount of work corresponding to its function or impose its authority in the corridors of power. PALU his party is formally the third force in the parliament after President PPRD and ML Jean Pierre Bemba, but has only 34 deputies and two senators. Kabila soon began chairing many government meetings in the absence of the Prime Minister. Criticized even within the presidential majority in Parliament because of his inaction, Gizenga resigned September 25, 2008 and gave way to Muzito, his deputy in the management of his party. Although the appointment of a new government 26 October 2008, relations between the President and the Prime Minister does not rebalance. A letter from the Office of the President by the press reported June 5, 2009 Muzito asked not to incur expenses without prior approval of the Head of State." [99]

We could also observe the rule of advisors of the Presidency over the Government, "three major inner circles have power and influence within the government and around Kabila." [100]

Security affairs especially, escape the formal channels of decision-making. "Between December 2006/january 2007, shortly after taking office, Kabila sent General John Numbi, the head of Air force to Rwanda to secretly negociate a deal with Nkunda. The two sides meet in Rwanda and agree to integrate Nkunda's rebel troops into the national army (in what is called mixage) and permit them to stay in the Kivu provinces". [101] What about the chief of the FARDC's General Staff?

[99.] See Marie-France Cros, "a year of elected government, little progress," La Libre Belgique, March 11, 2008. "Kabila place Muzito supervised financial RFI June 5, 2009.

[100.] Transformation DR Congo.
Congo, Democratic Republic, Country Report.

[101.] DR Congo:Chronology
More coverage: More human Rights Watch reporting on the Democratic Republic of Congo.

In this imbroglio, the effectiveness of government can only be affected negatively. That's how the national and provincial "structures are unable to provide basic security, transparent management of resources and wealth for communities." [102]

———————

Can we expect good governance in such a system?
That is how DRC is mostly regarded as poor governance example. "regularly found in the bottom of the good governance, transparency, respect for human rights, development indicators table". [103]

While, when Joseph kabila became the "first" democratically elected president in 2006 "the international community celebrated this election as a milestone in the peace process,–hope of good governance, democratic political culture etc-, but today checks and balances barely exist, civil liberties are regularly threatened, the key institutional reforms, the security sector . . . have made no significant progress. [104] It was then a new government but with more conflict. [105]

———————

Alluring to be a democrat, the President Joseph kabila is far from being democrat as you can read: "rather than pushing through steps towards decentralization set out in the constitution, analysts say Kabila's rule has seen a concentration of power and rising political oppression". [106]

While on paper, the Constitution establishes the semi-presidential system, "the semi-presidential system was established by the constitution" [107]

---

102. Google, witness.Voices World is on Genocide Prevention.
103. World is Witness, voices on Genocide Prevention.
104. Congo: A Stalled Democratic Agenda.
    8 April 2010.
105. DR Congo: Chronology; op cit.
106. Katrina Manson. Journalist, December 3 2010.
107. Presidential powers, from Wikipedia.

President Kabila wants to fly beyond all powers." He is contemplating amending the constitution on the pretext of addressing difficulties in implementing decentralization. But, anyconstitutional amendment aiming at concentrating more power for the presidency or controlling dissenting voices, however, would pose a threat to already weakened mechanisms of checks and balances. [108]

A government official, Olivier Kamitatu, Minister of Planning, finaly made it clear saying that the: "situation in Congo needs to move from a semi-presidential to a presidential system hard to give more power to a president whose term of office should be extended." [109] Then it is easy to understand why "during the last three years, presidentialization power has increased".[110]

Section 220, which was according to the constitution an article lock, as said "in order to guard the democratic principles contained in the constitution against political vicissitudes and untimely amendements, the constitution entrenches some of its provisions that may not be subject to any amendement", is suffering. However this article is balanced by article 218 that gives, provision for amendement requiring either "a national referendum or a super-majority (three fifths) of both houses of parliament, voting collectively as a congress".[111]

"President Joseph Kabila has so far established a system to reduce securitocratique kleptocratic and in silence any voice of opposition in the country. Extra-judicial killings, arbitrary arrests, kidnapping politicians are some of his tactics to lead as King in the DRC." [112]

---

108. Congo: A Stalled Democratic Agendas.
    8 April 2010.
109. World is Witness, op cit.
110. See Marie-France Cros, "a year of elected government, little progress"
111. Hauser Global Law School.
112. Gustavemoke's blog. Wednesday, April 13, 2011. Africa-Power: Fathers to sound: a Dictatorship rising game.

Faced with all this, the parliament often seems nonexistent. Dominated in numbers by the presidential majority, the members of the National Assembly appear to have accountability to President Joseph Kabila than to the people they are "derive from". For example, "the Christian Democrats, Alliance of Christian Democrats have complained about the resumption of the Prime Minister's office by the President and claimed that the only obstacle to getting the executive branch any power in the country was the National Assembly." [113]

"After the events of Bundu dia Kongo, a parliamentary commission of inquiry was made. The report and the results were discussed in the National Assembly in May 2007, but further discussion was suspended and the report was never made public." [114]

While the government tried to downplay the incident of Bundu dia Kongo, the occupation of Kahemba by Angolan troops at the beginning of 2007 caused a fierce reaction from Congolese parliamentarians. They have formed a bipartisan commission of inquiry and have questioned the conciliatory attitude of the interior minister at the time, Denis Kalume, in respect of Luanda. In denouncing the incursion, the parliamentarians also antagonized Kabila. (3[115])

It was agreed that Chinese companies are making infrastructure projects worth six billion dollars and invest three billion dollars as part of a joint venture with Gecamines. [116]

---

[113] Gustavemoke's blog. Wednesday, April 13, 2011. Africa-Power: Fathers to sons: a dictatorship rising game.

[114] Democratic Republic of Congo, genral elections 2006. Page 358.

[115] Report of the Task crisis in the DRC: consolidating peace.

[116] World is Witness. Voices on Genocide Prevention.

"Six months after the episode of the Chinese contract (, Kamerhe outspoken critic of President Kabila's decision to allow a Rwandan involvement in a military operation against the FDLR January 21, 2009. He described as "serious" entry of Rwandan troops in North Kivu and warns against the risk of collateral damage. In February 2009, 260 members of the National Assembly, including members of the MPA signed a petition calling for a debate and more transparency on the contents of the agreement signed by Kabila with his Rwandan counterpart. Kamerhe reached a limit. "The Chinese contracts in the DRC: the opposition MPs slams the door." [117]

And President Kabila decided through the Majority Parliamentarian Alliance MPs to let Kamerhe go".

"According to several sources, the Presidency had paid each officer of the Assembly $ 200,000 to leave their office. Althought that other members have not resigned, it is widely believed that the pressure will be clicked on them to force them to do this. A group of Kabila's sent entered also in action talking with Kamerhe to request his resignation." (3[118])

"The determination of President Kabila to drive out Vital Kamerhe was quickly becoming a political crisis and probably constitutional that should be resolved one way or another on March 15 when the parliament was to open its session." [119]

———————————

"Observers believe that now, Kamerhe has the right to hold office if he does not resign. Many have pointed out however that efforts to buy the

[117] Agence France-Presse, May 13, 2008. See also the interview Kamerhe had granted the magazine Jeune Afrique "Chinese contracts: Miracle or mirage", May 19, 2008. See François Sudan, "Kabila-Kamerhe: a chronicle of disenchantment," Jeune Afrique February 17, 2009. Quoted From page 126.

[118] Gustavemoke's blog. Wednesday, April 13, 2011. Africa-Power: Fathers to sound: a dictatorship rising game.Page 305

[119] Gustavemoke's blog. Wednesday, April 13, 2011. Africa-Power: Fathers to sound: a dictatorship rising game. Page 304

votes are usually effective in this highly corrupt political culture and the tide in the National Assembly could quickly turn against Kamerhe." [120]

And "on 25 March 2009, following two months of pressure from his party and President Kabila, Vital kamerhe, the president of the Congo National Assembly, resigned his office". [121]

According to a diplomatic cable obtained by Wikileaks and published Monday in a Belgian newspaper. The president of the National Assembly, Vital Kamerhe, long close to Joseph Kabila, had resigned March 25, 2009 after being pressurized by the presidential majority for criticizing the entry of Rwandan troops in eastern DRC in a joint operation with the Congolese army. The U.S. ambassador at the time, William Garvelink said in a cable sent to Washington three weeks before his resignation, that the "presidency" of the Republic of Congo paid "$ 200,000 to each member of the office of the National Assembly" so that they leave their function and thus lead to the departure of Kamerhe. This was not immediately successful "our greatest fear concerning reports corroborated by several sources indicating that the president's men are now using intimidation and physical threats to push Kamerhe to quit the stage," added U.S. ambassador in cable published by the daily De Standaard

http://standaard.be/extra/wikileaks/cablekabila, cited by Gustavemoke's blog. Wednesday, April 13, 2011. Africa-Power: Fathers to sons: a dictatorship rising game. Page 303.

As for the judiciary, the song is the same: "impunity within the security system allows serious human rights violations, including sexual and genderbased violence, to go unchecked. This culture of impunity with the law enforcement and security services must change to render the security

---

[120.] Gustavemoke's blog. Wednesday, April 13 2011.Africa-power: Fathers to sound: a dictatorship rising game. Page 305

[121.] Repot of mission in DRC, a Semblance of State in ruins.
Kris Berwouts, director Eur AC.

system a protector of Congolese citizens'rights rather than the principal abusers".[122]

The UN Special Rapporteur on the independence of judges and lawyers, Leandro Despouy, after a visit April 2007 in DRC, concluded: "the interference by the executive and the military in court proceedings was very common and the judicial system of the Congo was rarely effective".[123]

"Another commentator provides some historical perspective on violence and justice together in the eastern DRC, noting that the coalition around political and social justice in the DRC are now very weak and fragile compared to five or six years ago. There was a simultaneous growth in the entrenchment of violence with economic interests, especially trade and mining". [124]

"In the DRC, to legal action against the perpetrators of rape is also challenging. There are a lot of impunity in the DRC. Ms. Kembe notes: we have filed many complaints. We have even identified the perpetrators. We report to the police a few days later you see them free. This is especially the case if they are military or ex-combatants. [125]

With more dysfunctional than good functioning in all four governing institutions, with some institutions abusing their powers for selfish interests, encroaching on the power of other institutions, most of these institutions instead of being open to positive collaboration in the national interest, instead of managing efficiently and effectively, are confined to distrust the other institutions which are nevertheless part of the system.

[122.] IFP Security cluster. Country case study: DRC Justice-sensitive security System Reform in the Democratic Republic of Congo.
Laura Davis
February 2009.

[123.] Google, World is Witness, voicess on Genocide Prevention.

[124.] Human Rights Abuses in DRC from2009 up to 2011.Google Page 210

[125.] Congolese women Confront Legacy of war rape and sexual violence leave survivors in desperated Need. By Mary Kimani Page 303.

That's how "four years after the 2006 election, the promises to reform governance, to strengthen democracy and implement the constitution are mostly not fulfilled." [126]

And with extreme poverty for the majority of Congolese "Religion has provided a significant refuge from the harsh reality of daily life. Churches are one of the most important institutions of influence. There are many sects and revivalist churches, whose financial sources are not always transparent." [127] And the politicians in power find it, a fertile ground to manipulate consciences to their advantage. It is not uncommon to hear so-called men of God, justifying the Kabila regime, while the bible asks us to be faithful to the truth.

It is true that to some extent the power could still do something even slightly. That's how you can hear "that there are spaces in the DRC that are relatively well-governed, such as Butembo and Katanga." [128] However, this relatively good governance is not without reference to political alliances beneficial to power. And often in the logic of the law of the falling rate of profit which is to accept to lose some of its profits to maintain the entity, or regions to support political power.

While impunity, injustice is often obvious in the Congo (DRC), some cases which might be seen as positive could be registered. It is the case on March 5, 2009 of the commander Mai–Mai, Gedeon Kyungu Mutanga together with his co-defendants, were convicted by a military court in Katanga for crimes against humanity and other charges. The same month, eleven soldiers in Walikale, North Kivu, were convicted for rape as a crime against humanity." [129] "On July 27, in a rare case against an officer, Colonel Ndayambaje Kipanga was doomed—failing to appear, to imprisonment for life for crimes against humanity, on charges of rape. He escaped from jail before trial. (January 26, 2009), the ICC (International Criminal Court) began its first

---

126. Google, World is Witness, voicess on Genocide Prevention.
127. Google, World is Witness, voices on Genocide Prevention.
128. Human Rights Abuses in DRC from 2009 up to 2011. Page 210
129. Google, Human Rights Abuses in DRC, from 2009 up to 2011. Section 4 Page 191–192.

trial ever seen. Former Congolese warlord Thomas Lubanga had faced the charges of war crimes for his use of child soldiers in the conflict in Ituri. The opening day of the trial was broadcast or televised across the country. The trials of two other gentlemen in Ituri Germain Katanga and Mathieu Ngudjolo, began November 24, 2009." [130]

Although there have been some cases where the decision was rendered against the perpetrators of crimes, impunity is still observed in the DRC. Even in cases where the perpetrators were charged, this was not often regardless of political affiliation.

From the above, we can realize that the dysfunction of the leadership public institutions is real. Independence of these institutions is a dead letter. Since these institutions are different elements that make up the system, the system can suffer.

2. COUNTRY STILL LIVING IN INSECURITY, VIOLENCE AND WARS

As we read:"MONUC reported that on 3 August 2006, the third day of vote counting, a fire in suspicious an important center of Kinshasa made to worry about the transparency of results.

On August 5, 2006 thousands of people in the east of the country were fleeing clashes between the national army and the forces affiliated with General Laurent Nkunda." [131]

"On August 20 after counting the votes of nearly all 169 constituencies, it was reported automatic gunfire in Kinshasa and representatives of the MLC (Movement for the Liberation of Congo) had accused the Republican

---

130. Ditto

131. Concerns over election result in Congo, Radio NewZeland, August 6, 2006 in Democratic Republic of Congo, general election in 2006. Page 271 wikipedia, the free encyclopedia.

Guard of Joseph Kabila to have of his men killed one and wounded three police." [132]

As of August 20, 2006 there were heavy weapons in Kinshasa between loyal forces to Kabila and Bemba, the two sides accusing each other of having started. On August 21, 2006, during a meeting in Kinshasa between Bemba and ambassadors representing the International Committee for Support of transition to democracy (CIAT), explodes arms fire from Kabila's forces and those of Bemba. And Bemba's residence where the meeting took place was attacked. According to a diplomat in the residence, this attack consisted of artillery and heavy weapons. Bemba and diplomats were moved to a secure place in the residence and there were no injuries. The private helicopter of Bemba had been destroyed during the attack. Several hours later, the spokesman for the UN in DRC, Jean Tobias Okala announced that foreign diplomats including the head of MONUC, William Swing, were evacuated to the headquarters of the United Nations by the Spanish and uruguayen guards peacekeeping force after a general of Kabila and the commander of UN forces had cooperated to allow their safe passage. [133]

The rescue is completed, the battle ensued in the capital of the DRC, and August 22, 2006, two tanks of the Congolese army were reported seen heading towards the residence of Bemba. [134]

The European Union began sending more troops to maintain peace in Kinshasa and Swing, the head of MONUC called for an immediate

---

132. "Congo poll heads for runoff, gunfire in Kinshasa. "Reuters, August 20, 2006. In Democratic Republic of Congo, general election 2006, page 273. Taken from wikwpedia, the free encyclopedia, google.

133. "UN frees diplomats trapped in Congo attack", CBC, August 21, 2006.In Democratic Republic of Congo. General Elections 2006 page 276.Taken from google Wikipedia, the free encyclopedia.

134. "Congo–Kinshasa: After fresh fighting in DRC SA Envoy Rescued" Cape Argus, page 276 August 22.2006. In Democratic Republic of Congo, general elections, 2006 page 276.Taken from google, wikipedia the free encyclopedia.

ceasefire. (135) At least three people had died in combat Tuesday. Sixteen were reported killed during the fight and police reported of bodies found. (136)

On August 24, 2006, the ceasefire remained in effect, with the armed forces loyal to the two candidates remaining in the barracks, but the situation remains unstable. (137)
Later that day, police fired into the air to disperse angry mobs calling for the reopening of two Bemba's television stations. (138)

In late October 2006, they expressed increasing concerns about security as they approached the second round of presidential elections. On October 26, 2006 the IEC (Independent Electoral Commission) declared that the province of North Kivu could face the threat of insecurity. While MONUC said it has no plans to see "major problems", the next day, October 27, Secretary General Kofi Annan said he was "very concerned about the rising level of violence as election day approached. (139)

135. "UN presses Congo factions to end fighting Kinshasa" SABC, August 24, 2006.In Democratic Republic of Congo, general elections 2006. Google, Wikipedia, the free encyclopedia.

136. "DRC police fire shots as delicate truce hold," Mail & Guardian, August 24, 2006.In Democratic Republic of Congo, general election 2006. Google Wikipedia, the free encyclopedia.

137. "Fragile DRC ceasefire holding" SABC, August 24, 2006.In Democratic Republic of Congo, general elections. Google Wikipedia, the free encyclopedia.

138. DRC police fire shots as delicate truce hold "Mail & Guardian, August 24, 2006.In Democratic Republic of Congo, general elections 2006. Google Wikipedia, the free encyclopedia.

139. "Congo–Kinshasa: Annan 'Very Concerned' At Rising Violence Ahead of Sunday's elections", United Nations, October 27, 2006.In Democratic Republic of Congo, general elections 2006. Google Wikipedia, the free encyclopedia, page 285.

During the first day of the vote, there was heavy fighting resulting in two victims. [140]

On October 30, 2006 as vote counting began, MONUC had reported that a soldier killed two workers in the polling station in the town of Fataki, Ituri province. This resulted in looting that led to the destruction of forty-three polling stations. The reason for the shooting was unclear, but it appeared that the soldier was drunk and he was tried and scooped the death sentence for murder. [141]

November 11, a shooting took place several hours after police had fired into the air to disperse Bemba's partisans who were demonstrating near the residence of Bemba in Kinshasa, protesting against the counting of votes during the second round. These shots ceased after the MONUC organized a mediation between representatives of both groups. At least four people were reported to have been killed in this battle. [142]

On 13 November 2007, police arrested 337 of the DRC people including 87 children, suspected to have been involved in clashes on 11 November. [143]

On November 21, 2006, part of the local Supreme Court justice was burned in a shootout during a short session where the spirit was to review complaints of electoral fraud. The direct cause of the fire was unclear. But it happened after the manifestation of Bemba's partisans seeking to enter the

---

140. "DRC election marred by violence" News 24, October 29, 2006.In Democratic Republic of Congo, general elections page 284. Google Wikipedia, the free encyclopedia.

141. "DRC hit by post election riots," News 24, October 30, 2006.In Democratic Republic of Congo, general elections 2006. Google Wikipedia, the free encyclopedia page 286.

142. "Calm returns to DRC capital after election-related violence" People's Daily, November 12.2006.In Democratic Republic of Congo, general elections 2006. Google Wikipedia, the free encyclopedia page 286.

143. "DRC: Police arrest 337 over Kinshasa clashes," Reuters, November 13, 2006.In Democratic Republic of Congo, general elections 2006. Google Wikipedia, the free encyclopedia page 287.

premises. MONUC, which had evacuated the judges, lawyers and officials of the CIS, had attributed the incident to uncontrolled elements. [144]

On November 25, 2006, forces loyal to General Laurent Nkunda engaged over 2,000 soldiers against the army of the Congo (DRC), the Eleventh Brigade around the town of Sake (near Goma) in the province of North Kivu. Three soldiers and three civilians were killed and about 20 people were injured. MONUC had sent 1,000 soldiers to secure the place. According to the UN, "15,000 and 20,000 people were displaced by the fighting. [145]

The elections, however, had not brought peace. Violence intensified in the Kivu region as Kabila's army fighting against a new insurgency, as well as land disputes with neighboring Rwanda. Millions were displaced and thousands killed on all sides. [146]

There was intense fighting in the east of the country in September 2007 between the forces of Laurent Nkunda and the FARDC (Armed Forces of the Republic of Congo). It made displaced nearly 500,000 civilians . . . [147]

In the East the war was never completely finished. A string forces continue to perpetrate violence against civilians, including forced displacement, abduction, looting, forced recruitment and use of children as soldiers and sexual violence in mass. According to the UN 27,000 sexual assaults were reported in the province of South Kivu alone. These data represent only those assaults that were reported officially. [148]

---

144. "DRC: Part of the suprem court burnt Amid gunshots," IRIN, November 21, 2006.In Democratic Republic of Congo, general elections 2006. Google Wikipedia, the free encyclopedia page 288.
145. "Congo Warlord's Fighters Attack Forces," Washington Post, November 26, 2006.In Democratic Republic of Congo, general elections 2006. Google Wikipedia, the free encyclopedia.
146. Democratic Republic of Congo, general elections 2006.Page 298. Google Wikipedia, the free encyclopedia.
147. Idem, page 311.
148. Ibid, page 439.

The dense jungle in eastern Congo (DRC) remains the home of many organizations of rebels who have histories and complex agendas. Responsible for committing atrocities against civilians in mass, including massacres, rape, abduction and suffering in recent years.FDLR (Democratic Forces for the Liberation of Rwanda), CNDP (National Congress for the Defence of the People) and LRA (the Lord's Resistance Army). Some times, each organization receives government support from different countries in the region, and many rebels have taken advantage of the generous continued exploitation of abundant natural resources. Any prey on the civilian population. Layer scattered throughout the north-eastern Congo, the largest UN force in the world for peacekeeping is largely unable to stop attacks.Congolese armed forces, themselves responsible for large atrocities in 2009, is largely an obstacle to achieving peace and security in the region. [149]

After the peace agreement had failed and there were fresh clashes in 2007 and 2008 the intensification of international pressure finally forced the DRC and Rwanda to address the deteriorated situation together. January 20, 2009, the Rwandan army entered the eastern Congo (DRC) as a joint mission with the UN and the Congo (DRC) against the FDLR. The operation itself was a humanitarian disaster. It caused the Revenge (killing and rape) and drained more than 900,000 people from their homes. Just a month after the operation took place, the FDLR had returned to its former capacity. [150]

Deterred by the attention of the Ugandan army, the Congolese army, MONUC, the SPLA and the Lord's Resistance Army continue to terrorize, kidnap, rape and murder to civilians throughout the region. [151]

A new confidential report published by a group of experts mandated by the UN, said most troubling dimension to the images of mournful eastern

---

149. Preventing genocide-Who is at risk? DR Congo: current situation Archive. Google, were the 2006 DRC elections fair? Page 44
150. Idem, page 449.
151. Idem, page 455.

Congo. The report of the sorry record of the situation described cases where groups of charity convey money to the rebel soldiers attacking and raping civilians, the army commanders receiving $ 250,000 per month fee for the movement of the exploitation of resources and support from senior rebel officers into the Congolese army and neighboring nations. [152]

Responsible for extensive atrocities in the months following the military operation, the Congolese army had clearly targeted civilians, according to the head of the peacekeeping United Nations, Alain Le Roy. [153]

The FDLR, a Rwandan Hutu militia groups and FARDC (Armed Forces of the Democratic Republic of Congo) had all committed widespread atrocities. Since January, more than 1,000 civilians were killed, 7,000 women and girls were subject of rape and external sexual violence, and around 900,000 people were forced to flee their homes. Satellite images collected by the American Association for the Advancement of Science showed extensive destruction of homes and villages as recent as September. Since launching the offensive, more than 6,000 homes were burned in the eastern provinces (North and South Kivu). [154]

The coalition of the Congo advocacity had calculated that for every rebel fighter disarmed, a civilian was killed and seven women and girls were raped, six houses burnt and destroyed, and 900 people forced to flee their homes. According to UN statistics, only 1,071 FDLR rebels, a force as large as 6,000 to 7,000 fighters, had filed since January. Many reports indicate that the FDLR has recruited continuously to maintain its numbers. [155]

[152.] "Messy and Ragged" S.A Gloomy Report on the Congo.December 1, 2009 from Chris Mc Greal page 456.

[153.] Congolese Army Uses vaccination sites as Bait. November 9, 2009. From MC Chris Greal, page 457.

[154.] A Humanitarian Disaster Backed by the UN, October 15, 2009.From MC Chris Greal, page 458.

[155.] Idem, page 459.

In October 2006, the Assistant Secretary General of the UN for the operations of peacekeeping, Jean Marie Guéhemo had reported that 12000 women and girls were raped in only six months. [156]

Slaughter of 500,000 homes in eastern DRC, July and August 2010, 242 reported rapes in and around Luvungi, a village far from camp No. of peacekeepers from the UN, more than 260 rapes were being to light at Uvira and other parts of North and South Kivu, 74 attacks in a village called Miki, in South Kivu. The victims including 21 children, all (girls aged between seven and fifteen years) and six men. [157]

After this, let still proceed with the events of violence and killing:
"In March 2010, there was killing, 100 people in the district of High-Uele in Eastern Province." [158]

"As i understand it, they do not hurt, they kill, so we do not get injured. "Mattia Novella, Doctors without Borders (MSF) field Coordinator, on the attack (LRA) in eastern DRC." [159]

"The UN statistics show that in three months, 1244 cases of sexual violence were reported throughout the DRC—or an average of 14 attacks per day (UNHCR Briefing Notes 23 April 2010). Most attacks have happened in North and South Kivu. The UNHCR spokeswoman Melissa Fleming believes that these numbers are a gross underestimate, given the scandal

---

[156.] Congolese women cofront Legacy of war and sexual violence Rape Survivors in Desperate Need leave.

[157.] (1). Source: BBC News, 8 September 2010.Cited by Human Rights Watch, Covered in blood,
http://www.hrw.org/sites/default/files/reports/DRC0703.pdf,

[158.] Source: The Guardian 2 May 2010. Quoted by Human Rights Watch, Covered in blood.

[159.] Source, the Guardian, 2 May 2010.In Human Rights Watch, Covered in blood,
http://www.hrw.org/sites/default/files/reports/DRC0703.pdf

associated with rape. A similar number of sexual assaults were recorded in the same period last year." [160]

"At the end of the month of October 2009, disturbances erupted in the province of Equateur. Since summer 2009, trying ethnic rose sharply in the area of the town of Dongo on the basis of socio-economic demands ignored by the political authorities since the 1940s. Violating a conflict between tribes and Enyele Munzaya causes another massacre of civilians on October 29 and a massive displacement of population. Nearly 130,000 Congolese crossed the border with the neighboring Republic of Congo to find refuge. November 27, 2009, the FARDC and MONUC evacuated under fire the city of Dongo. Enyele groups progress to the town of Gemena.

In response, the military decided to redeploy Congolese troops across the country with the support of MONUC to take control of the western province.

The report of an agent of an international NGO that carried out a humanitarian assessment in the town of Dongo in February 2010 report that between 200 and 500 civilians were killed in Dongo. In a report of UN Secretary General to the Security Council dated 30 March 2010, the total of Congolese always displaced since the clashes of October 2009 is estimated at around 200,000.

See "31st report of the Secretary-General on the Mission of the United Nations in the Democratic Republic of Congo ". S/2010/164, 30 March 2010, Page 4.

Taking temporary control of the airport of the city and killing three officers of MONUC personnel, rebels dramatically demonstrate the difficulties faced by the Congolese government to end local conflicts in the DRC." [161]

---

160. Idem.
161. Idem.

The organization Doctors Without Borders (MSF) has provided specialized care to 53 men, women and children who were violated in a series of incidents that came between 19 and January 21 in South Kivu in the DRC "in space only a few weeks, the MSF has provided medical treatment of about 100 men, women and children—all of which were violated in a mass attack, "said Anne Marie Loof, head of mission for MSF in South Kivu ". We are extremely concerned about the fate of civilians in this place—normal people who have nothing to do with the conflict but bringing much of the recent surge of violence and insecurity in this part of eastern DRC." [162]

"The brutal violence and abuse of human rights have increased in the DRC through 2009." [163] And "MONUC, the strength of the peacekeeping Congo, struggled to balance its mandate to protect civilians to support the operations of the Congolese army." [164]

"In October 2009 the military had succeeded in demobilizing fighters 1100 the ranks of the FDLR force estimated at 6000. But it had reached a high price: from January to September more than 1,300 civilians were killed in North and South Kivu. The majority were women, children and the elderly. Of thousands of civilians were subject and pressed into forced labor, and more than 900,000 people had fled for their lives. The FDLR and Congolese soldiers had looted their property and burned an estimated 7,000 homes to the ground. Already poor, the civilians were left with nothing." [165]

"In March 2009, the killings by the LRA and the kidnaping of civilians continued, resulting in a displacement of over 200,000 people across the worst affected areas of Upper and Lower Uele in the Eastern Province". [166]

---

162. Idem.
163. Human Rights Abuses in DRC from 2009 up to April 2011.World Report 2010–Democratic Republic of Congo.
164. Human Rights Abuses in DRC from 2009 up to April 2011.World Report 2010–Democratic Republic of Congo
165. Idem.
166. Idem.

"The eastern DRC continues to be characterized by widespread violence and violence perpetrated against civilians by all government forces and militias, and large-scale displacement. In light of continuing attacks on civilians, including the persistent high level of sexual violence against women and girls, and failure to provide security, the Council shall not introduce some changes in the mandate of MONUC could jeopardize the protection of civilians." [167]

"The sexual violations and gender-based crimes, committed in the DRC, including attacks Walikale, requires a clear and strong action to ensure that MONUSCO, the UN mission, fulfilling its mandate." [168]

"Amnesty International is dismayed because of the recent reports of rape and sexual violence committed mass Walikale in North Kivu between July 30 and August 2 According to the UN, over 150 civilians in 13 villages were raped by members of armed groups, including the FDLR." [169]

"Reports indicate that the level of brutality against women and girls is growing, with survivors describing being subject to mutilation and torture by gangs of rapists and kidnaping by armed groups." [170]

"It is estimated that 8,000 women and girls were raped in eastern DRC in 2009." [171]

"This report of 183 pages documenting in detail the deliberately killing over 1400 civilians between January and September 2009 for two successive operations of the Congolese army against the Hutu militia in Rwanda (FDLR)." (2[172])

---

[167] Idem, (Monthly Action Points on Women, Peace and Security for May 2011.

[168] Idem.

[169] Idem.

[170] Idem.

[171] Democratic Republic of Congo, general elections 2006, page 303. Google Wikipedia, the free encyclopedia.

[172] Idem, page 304.

3. THE HUMAN RIGHT ABUSES

The torture and killings* by agents of state security are endemic. During and after the election period, the population has been the subject of serious human rights violations. In particular the report highlights two government security forces which were responsible for the majority of politically motivated violations against all the real and supposed political opponents of President Joseph Kabila and his ruling party. These two forces are, the Directorate of General Intelligence and Special Services of the police and Republican Guard (GR) under the control of President Joseph Kabila.

Many people arrested by the two services were held in detention, without communication, suffered torture and other cruel, inhuman or degrading treatment. Many of these individuals remain in custody without trial. Many were detained because of their origin in the province of Equateur, Jean Pierre Bemba province, or because they are the same ethnic as Jean Pierre Bemba. Such arbitrary arrests and detentions are continually reported in Kinshasa.

In the East, where conflict has not ended, serious violations of human rights continue to be committed by government forces as well as political groups of foreign armies. [173]

Violations of human rights are legion in the Congo (DRC), if you want more information, see Democratic Republic of Congo general elections 2006. Page 316-343. In the conclusion of this report, it was said that there was some progress observed in regard to respect for human rights in 2007.

In protest against alleged corruption in the provincial election of the governor, the Bunda Dia Kongo (BDK), a political religious movement in south-west of the province of Bas-Congo, called for a wide day of protest

---

*   There is no reliable record of deaths. NGO sources in Kinshasa. Basing their estimates on surveys conducted in hospitals and mortuaries, they put the statistics to 500. MONUC officials have estimated around 400, while diplomatic sources say up to 600, page 365.

[173.]   Idem, page 346.

Feb. 1, 2007. The protests became violent and the police and the army made disproportionate use of force and unlawful killings to suppress the protests. To date, no member of the security forces has been brought to justice for violating human rights during these events. [174]

The report of the Special Rapporter (SR) of the board of Human Rights of the UN, presented at the thirteenth session (March 2010), noted several trends of concern in relation to the environment of activities for the right defenders. [175]

Human Rights in the DRC continue saying: "in all areas of Congo, the Human Rights record remained poor, and numerous serious abuses were committed. Unlawful killings, disappearances, torture, rape, and arbitrary arrest and detention by security forces increased during the year." (1) Human Rights in the Democratic Rep of the Congo.

Mvemba Dizolele, an expert politic analyst, reflected on the danger of focusing exclusively on the east of the Republic: "when we miss the story that happens in 80% of the country, so we miss the picture," said Dizolele ". Because what happens in the East is about to happen just because of what does not happen in the rest of the country ".Broadening the lens of analysis Dizolele described the failures of the Congolese government in Kinshasa to meet the needs of its total population, which suffers from insecurity and poverty, regardless of region." [176]

---

174. For the details of the Bas-Congo violence, see the UN (MONUC) special investigation report, http://www.ohchr.org/english/docs/rep bascongo.doc. See also statement by Human Rights Watch to the DRC Parliamentary Commission Investigating Events in Bas Congo, general elections 2006, page 307.

175. Human Rights in the Democratic Republic of the Congo.

176. DRC: Wikileaks exposes the corruption of "Joseph Kabila" The UN Human Rights.Council Report Card: 2009-2010 Special Report. September 15, 2010. Page 66

"There is still war, rape and violence. The Observatory of Human Rights has released its World Report 2011."[177]

"The observatory Media Reporters without Borders says that media workers face arrest, threats and violence." (4[178]) There are times when local media might seem free, however, the regular interventions of ANR remind media's workers the type of government that rules the country.

As already said, civil society activists, journalists, poor persons who make the "mistakes" by making any analyse contrary to the government point of view are victims of either the ANR,–an intelligence service used by the government as a repressive machine against government "enemies"-, judicial, or other government's repressive machines. For example "on 12th July 2009, the Human Rights association ASADHO/Katanga, issued a report on the history of illicit mining at Shinkolobwe." [179]

"Previously ASADHO reported that Areva, a French nuclear power plant firm, signed a deal with the DRC's government in March to prospect and mine for uranium in Katanga. A deal condemned by ASADHO because its terms were secret and provided no assurance regarding worker safety or environmental impacts. The deal was finalized during the visit of the French President, Nicola Sarcozy to Kinshasa in late March." [180]

As one could expect, in Joseph Kabila's regime where democratie is a myth: "the president of ASADHO/Katanga, Mr Golden Misabiko, was arrested on 24 July 2009 together with his deputy on 13 July 2009. [181] And "the court in Lubumbashi/ Kamalondo sentenced him to one year

---

[177.] Idem.

[178.] Idem

[179.] Decommissioning Projects-Africa.
Congo, Democratic Republic of the.

[180.] Congo Resources,
Wednesday, July 15, 2009.

[181.] Frontline issues alert on detention of HR defender in the DR Congo.

imprisonment, suspended for eight months, charged with endangering the security of state. [182]

That's how the Amnesty International can speak, under the title defenders of human rights under attack in the DRC ". Instead of addressing the concerns of human rights, the Congolese officials at the national and provincial organizations continue to attack that ercet them." [183]

Let's talk about the economic situation.

ECONOMIC

Economically, life in Congo as we have already said, is in contrast with the country's potential. As you can read:"DRC is often cited example of de so called "paradox of plenty." Extremely rich in natural resources (80 % of world wide resources of coltan, 10 % of world wide resources of copper), the population suffers of extreme poverty (80 % of the congolese population lives of less than US$ 0, 20 a day). [184]

Different companies are present in Congo as you can see:
–Oil and gas companies: Chevron corp, Total, Eni, Inpex (Japan), Perenco, Tullow Oil, Heritage Oil.
–Mining companies: Anglo American, AngloGold Ashanti, Debeers, Freeport McMoran Copper & Gold, Gold Fields, Katanga Mining Ltd, First Quantum Minerals, Moto Gold Mines, Mwana Africa plc, Metorex Ltd, Glencore International, Central African Mining and Exploration (Camec). [185]

The mining sector is one of the main contributor of the country's economy. And within the mining sector, "the key natural resources in the DRC include copper, cobalt, petroleum, diamonds, gold, silver, zinc, manganese, tin,

---

182. Decommissioning Projects-Africa.
    Congo, Democratic Republic of the
183. DRC: Wikileaks: op cit.
184. EITI Democratic Republic of Congo.
185. EITI Democratic Republic of Congo: op cit

uranium and coal, among others. However, copper and cobalt products are the primary revenue generators." [186]

For example, "the copper sector has long been a vital component of the Congolese economy and has the potential to make an even greater contribution to the nation's economy and overall development. In recent years, the mining sector has registered reforms: implementation of the new Mining code in 2002, the restructuring of the state mining company Gécamines, the investigation into irregularities in mining contracts that began in 2007 and resulted in the review of 61 contracts and subsequent renegotiations that in some cases remain on-going.

While many of these reforms have added transparency and efficiency to the mining sector, a degree of uncertaincy continues to overshadow the copper industry in the DRC, not only due to the problems stemming from the global financial crisis and economic downturn and accompanying copper price volatility, but also due to the challenges endemic to DRC. DRC is facing enormous obstacles to development. Chief among those challenges is the need for peace and security. Other challenges include widespread corruption, the need for infrastructure development, high poverty levels etc." [187]

Besides what is said above, "corruption and misguided have for decades, fostered a clandestine economy in the DRC individuals and businesses in the formal sector operated with high costs under arbitrary enforced laws. As a consequence, the informal sector now dominates the economy." [188]

"The diamond sector, currently account for about 10 % of the export's revenue, which both gem and industrial–grade diamond sales were around $ 875 million in 2008 and were projected to approach an estimated $ 1

[186.] METOREX LIMITED Positioned for growth Democratic Republic of the Congo ICSG Insight, ICSG secretariat briefing paper. February 2010-N0-9

[187.] METOREX LIMITED:op cit.

[188.] US Department of State.
    September 30, 2011 Bureau of African Affairs.
    Background Note: Democrati Republic of the Congo.

billion in 2009. The production by the DRC parastatal, MIBA (Minière de Bakwanga), has significantly declined from the past decades; operations stopped during 2009 due to technical and financial difficulties. MIBA is currently working to restructure its operations and administration. Nearly all diamond production in the DRC is artisanal and takes place in the Kasaï regions." [189]

Gold also is assumed to contribute significantly to national income. But because of the insecurity, the official production of gold fell to just 26.5 kg in 2002 and was suspended in 2003. However during 2003, the new development suggested that the DRC could become a significant producer.

"Congo's economic performance in 2010 owes a great deal to the increase in its oil production. The latter reached a record level, estimated at 115 million barrels compared to 99 million in 2009." [190] The Congo's oil production "is yet the number one economic asset of the country. With 90 % of the country's exports mainly on oil and petroleum products. Its growing production of oil and petroleum products makes the Republic of Congo one of the top oil producing countries in Africa." [191]

The geography and the climate favors of Congo put potentially the country in very good position for agriculture. But agriculture is "the mainstay of the Congolese economy, accounting for 42.5 % of GDP in 2007." [192]

While there may be some differences on certain points regarding the economic situation in the country, it happens almost total agreement on the remarkable poverty of road, railway, water ways as a handicap to economic development. Yet for the construction of its road, port . . . Congo has

---

[189] US Department of State
     September 30, 2011
     Bureau of African Affairs
     Background Note: Democratic Republic of the Congo.
[190] Congo Republic.
[191] The economy of Congo.
[192] US Depatment of State: op cit

no need to import everything, because there are many materials available locally, the case of the bitumen. In April 2004, "Congo-bitumen announced it would begin extracting bitumen at Movuma in Lower Congo, aiming to meet the demand." [193] for domestic paved road and export the surplus.

The potential in electrical's energy in the Congo is to be envied. The hydro-electric power should be among the sectors contributing to national income. Inga is known for its large capacity and has one of the greatest potentials of world hydro-electric power. In addition to Inga, there are hydro-electric stations in different regions which can supply power not only to the country but also to the neighboring countries.

This is the case, among others, of the hydroelectric power station of the Ruzizi 1.

"On July 11, 2004, Burundi, Congo and Rwanda in CPGL negotiated the rehabilitation of the hydroelectric power station of the Ruzizi 1. This was to allow the station Ruzizi 1 to sell electricity to the Rwandan society Electrogaz. In February 2005 ESCOM, a South African company presented plans to produce power from the Congo River." [194]

Managed efficiently and effectively, Inga will be profitable not only for the Congo but also Africa and even beyond, because with its potential, it can supply electrical power to Congo and beyond: Africa and as much a part of Europe and even Asia.

But while this giant has almost unused potential, it is not uncommon to hear that there is electricity crisis, here and there. This is the case as an example of Ghana as we can read in the New African (New African of 20 June 2007): "Ghana has started load-shedding played since August of last year and the situation goes from bad to worse. The cause is mainly attributed

---

193. Europa Regional Surveys of the World, Africa South of Sahara 2006, 35th Edition.

194. Europa Regional Surveys of the World, Africa South of Sahara 2006, 35th Edition.

to the lower volume of water supplied by the lake at the Akosombo Dam which is the main source of electricity supply in Ghana." [195]

It is also the case of Namibia where local sources of electricity are not sufficient to provide the entire country. To compensate for that deficiency, Namibia was importing power from South Africa, which unfortunately, has announced in 2007 to Namibia not to count from 2008 on the supply of electricity produced by South Africa since the South Africa wants to use the share of energy that was sent to Namibia in local need of South Africa. [196]

Perhaps the issue here might be what is, the electrical potential and the management of Inga electricity have to do with politics?

In response to this question, is that if we want to achieve a positive goal in the interest of society, there is a need to understand the merits of the approach undertaken to attract not only the complicity but also the participation of the said society, said people for success, the realization of this project. And for this there must be consensus on the merits, on the rationality, the interest of the said project. And politics as say Rod Hague and Martin Harrop, is an "activity whereby a society comes to collective decisions for the direction of this society". [197]

So as we said in the preceding pages, as the political management of public affairs largely influences the others. When politics is sick, the others are affected. Here it must be said that whatever good will of donors, regardless of the availability of experts, of some potential for a project, if the country's politics is not rational, favorable, understood by the said society, the project can only suffer and eventually fail or be doomed to outright failure.

---

195. The New African June 20, 2007. Page 40-41

196. Talk of the Nation in January 2008. Talk of the Nation is a television program where they invite specialists from different areas on the plateau of the television to speak on a topic that may fall within their field. And there is also a phone open to public participation.

197. (4). Rod Hague and Martin Harrop: Comparative Government and Politics. An introduction. 6th Edition 2004. England.

In April 2005 a Japanese company HUNDAI also expressed its interest in the Inga high voltage power project to provide electricity to the south, central, eastern, northern Africa, southern Europe and the Middle East.

Among the companies generating revenues, which should participate in national income, there are transport and communication's companies such as ONATRA, SNCC, RVM . . . , but they are not outstanding in their responsabilities. This is understandable as we know that when the political instance sicks it affects as well the other instances, economic and even cultural.

It is evident that because of exportations and importations the country need to have adequat transport and communication infrastructure and means capable of insuring both local and foreign transactions. But because of the political crisis in Congo, the country had to rely on ways like the Benguela railway, leading to the port of Lobito (Angola). But "as a result of the civil war in Angola, the Benguela railway, 1348 km, the shortest route, was closed. Until some times back, the country used the national route linking Matadi (Bas-Congo) and Katanga. Because of poor maintenance, fuel shortages and insecurity, the use of this route was very hypothetical.

In April 2003, the Namibian authorities "made efforts to attract the interest of the Congolese government to draft Walvis Bay-Ndola-Lubumbashi-. The goal was to win regional support for external funding to construct a railway line at Shesheke Zambia-Namibia. According to the Namibian government, the railway would complement the existing road to allow mining companies in Katanga and Zambia to benefit from a second passage for exports, pending the rehabilitation of the Benguela Railway. [198]

Congo exports diamonds, copper, cobalt, gold, coffee, and crude oil to countries such as China, Belgium, Finland, USA and Zambia, with China being its leading export trading partner. Although the Congo has enough number of resources, it still imports food, mining products, machinery, transport equipment, and fuel from other countries like South Africa,

---

[198.] Europa Regional Surveys of the World, op cit.

Belgium, Zambia, Zimbabwe, China, Kenya and France, with South Africa being its number one import trading partner." [199]

According to the government speeches, "the government continues to build on economic reforms initiated in 2001 aimed at stabilizing the macroeconomic situation and promoting economic growth. The DRC's economy grew by 5.6 % in 2006, 6.32 % in 2007, and 6.15 % in 2008. Inflation was reduced from over 501 % in 2001 to approximately 27.6 % in 2008. The annual inflation in 2009 stood at 53.44 %, 10 % in 2010.

But the world can witness that "the Congolese population suffers of extreme poverty, (80 %) lives of less than US $ 0.20 a day". [200]

The social poverty is high and almost general in the Congo. There are people who lack, even the basic needs in terms of food, housing, education, primary health care . . . Poverty is so severe that there are people who lack almost everything. This is understandable when we know that unemployment, low productivity, the wide disparity between rural and urban areas, the gap between on the one hand a tiny minority made up mainly by rich men in power, their families or friends, and on the other hand, the majority of extremely poor . . . are topical in the Congo. And we can say without fear of contradiction that not one day passes without having seen a scene of poverty. Here we can join what was said by a former secretary general of the UN, his excellence Boutros-Ghali. [201]

Because the economy is sick, affected by the politics, many families have their children deprived of education because they can not go to school for lack of means. For those who can send their children to school must pay special contributions for the motivation of teachers often poorly paid or

---

199. The Economy of Congo.

200. EITI

Democratic Republic of Congo, op cit.

201. Boutros-Ghali: ancient Secretary General of the UN, cited by Tousy Namised in Towards Creating a Sustainable Culture of Human Rights. Lumumba–kasongo, Tukumbi. © Individual contributors 1998 Windhoek: Gamsberg Macmillan, 1998.

unpaid for several months. And to send a child to school they must be paid classical objects including uniforms and it is not easy for many parents who miraculously manage to get food for their families.

On the other hand there is a relatively significant increase of private schools, and this can be encouraged. However there must be discipline in this sector because we can not establish private schools for business reasons, as business has a different logic to some extent from what should be in the education sector.

On paper, the primary school is officially compulsory. But those who live in Congo know that this is a mystery, especially when we now know that teachers whose monthly salary is less than $ 11, have already lost hope of being paid regularly. "According to estimates made in 2007 21 % of the population had no schooling, 46 % had primary schooling, 30 % had secondary schooling, and 3 % had university schooling." [202]

The health sector is not at rest. The State hospitals no longer inspire confidence. There is lack of a better, knowing they will face unpaid medical personnel, pharmacies often without appropriate stock medication, dilapidated health infrastructure. . . . And even if they can receive tons of pharmaceutical products as international donations, facing an unpaid personel, tons of medical products may be miraculously vanished.

Of course there are also private hospitals, but can go there only those who have means. How many can have access to these hospitals when we know that we can estimate within 30% of the workforce, those who may have a salary at the end of the month and receive medical care paid by the company. What about the rest of the population? "The health situation remains worrying wih high level of infant and maternal mortality and still limited acces to drinking water and sanitation. Unemployement remains high, especially among the young, and the average monthly salary in the public sector does not exceed Euro 100." [203]

---

202. US Department of State, op cit.
203. Congo Republic.

However it is a scandal regarding electricity. While Congo is considering connecting some African countries and even outside Africa to Inga, the need for domestic electrification is very far from being satisfied. Almost all of those who were fortunate to have the power content themselve simply with electrical established since colonial times. Some electrical transformers that were made for small loads, are now working to support loads far higher than expected as they face the extended locations, as officially there is no provision for electrification in most of extended location areas.

SNEL, a state company affected by the general crisis is below the expectations of the population. Some people seeing the impotence of SNEL to respond positively to their request for extension of transmission lines or because of lack of resources by the population to pay the fees charged for the electrification of their homes, engage in illegal connection but that is dangerous.

Because it may cause fire or be the basis of fatal accidents. Electrical wire bare at some of the line and uncontrolled can cause loss of life during the rainy season, electrical wires not well covered and uncontrolled from puddles in the streets can cause loss of human's life in places wetted by rainy water.

As you may have read in the pages above, the economy is disjointed. Unemployment is rising, the economic structures destroyed . . . Although unemployment is very high, dismissal in many industries continued to push the population into poverty. Because of this, many find themselves for survival in small business, shops, street trading, the general trade. People get together to find something to eat. However we can notice that many times to trade in Congo, people see themselves invited to lie.

For example, when you import goods from abroad, some negotiate with customs officials, they apply to taxing the informal method called "the rule of three simple" method informally customs posts of the country by some customs, taxing, which is to divide the tax payable by three. If the fee payable is $ 3,000, we will have three parts: one part to the state is $

1,000, one for the assessor and one for the merchant. Then we take the share that goes to taxing worker, divide by two, or $1000: 2 = \$ 500$. So the trader will pay $ 1500 or around. At least 1000 or slightly more for the custom's fees and 500 or slightly less for the customs worker. That is to say, instead of $ 3,000, the merchant will pay 1500 or slightly more.

And this is done only for insiders to the system. And there are many mechanisms in tax. For example when someone imports footwear "leather boots", to cover the merchant, the assessor can only write "boots" implying rubber boots used during the rainy season, which taxes are lower than the first category (luxury shoe-boots). The mechanisms are legion, and as here we do not do a study on customs laws, we limit ourselves to the examples cited above to support our assertion on the general crisis in Congo.

Let us assum that there are two merchants who will buy the same goods at the same place at the same price. At the customs, the merchant X does not know the system under-taxation, pays $ 3,000 as tax, while his colleague, introduced to the system pays $ 1,500. If they all use the same market for sale, the merchant Y can have its price lower than that of his colleague and will probably sell his merchandise quickly, have a faster turnover of stock, allowing him to go even buy his goods. While his colleague ignoring the system find difficult to understand how his friend can sell at a price so low, until connected to the system, discover what was a mystery.

And there he will be forced to choose between continuing to be honest, sincere or marry the informal method. The same for rail transport, as in the country one can see its cargo destined led after one, two or even three months behind if we did not substantiate the loadmaster giving some bribes. This may also be the case of inland water or even air.

Over 70% of the workforce is agricultural and it is growing because unemployment is increasing. And most of them are living in rural areas. These farmers can not be truly motivated to produce more if their products don't have a good market flow. Here means that urban environments containing almost all consumers must be related to rural areas (producers), by suitable road infrastructure so that products can be delivered in the city.

But the condition of roads in the Congo is to be deplored. That is how farmers are discouraged because how can they produce more if the decay products of last seasons in rural areas lack the means to deliver it to consumer markets, to urban? To reach the urban centers, cities, lack of resources in certain cases of necessity, people are forced to use means that some countries have used in past centuries: they use bicycles, carry loads on their heads or backs, for long distances but at high risk because of insecurities. In these conditions how much can reach urban centers and how long?

Because of this, because of unlike city/country, because of the attraction of cities compared to rural areas, insecurity in rural areas because of heavy wars in the country and because of many other factors, the rate of rural exodus is becoming increasingly growing.

After all these pages on the chaotic situation in Congo, let now talk about the causes of this situation. There are internal causes (which may be immediate or distants) and external causes (immediate or distants). Speaking of internal causes, none has yet need arguments stating that the DRC has suffered mainly selfish interests of men in power.

The political behavior of men in power is weak. In this state of affairs, the attitude of the population has much to do. Because in this chaos some people assist indifferently saying that as Christians they can not participate in making units at politically. For them it is only necessary to confide in God who will do anything for them. Here we say that the collective psyche of the population in Congo is also very important in the chaotic situation of the country. For if the collective thought is dominated by fatalism, very dangerous symptom destroying any hope for change.

The lack of national consciousness for some sons of the country, because they let themselves be used by foreigners to destroy and keep the country in chaos. Poverty is also an obstacle to genuine democracy, because in a country where the majority of the population is poor, it takes a conscious effort to avoid problems such as buying conscious, corruption . . .

Social disintegration, lack of social cohesion, tribalism . . . have their share in the chaos of the country.

In view of the political regimes in the Congo, starting from President Joseph Kasavubu to Joseph Kabila, through Joseph Desire Mobutu and Laurent Kabila, none of these presidents had received a formal high academic education and graduated. We wish here to consider the hypothesis that adequate education is one of important factors, significant in the management of a country. However is not absolute as it must be associated to others like the consciousness. To improve management requires a thorough knowledge of issues related to management of states. You need to know to understand some issues, sensitive political phenomena. Here we must say that the knowledge, understanding of state–phenomena is one step in preventing the political crisis.

Still speaking of the causes of the chaos in Congo, of course we can point out the internal causes. But there die from internal causes, the keen eye can see the net spread by international politics, mostly Western politic in which, unaware politicians from underdeveloped countries may find themselves swept away, and lead their respective countries in a crisis long-term politic.

Also, one of the concepts that can hold our attention about the chaotic situation is globalization in which the center (which is made by the Western powers) is leading the periphery (which consists of the underdeveloped countries). The center dominates the periphery politically, economically and even culturally.

Sometimes, globalization finds itself consolidated by natural disasters. For example there are countries affected by floods, earthquakes, volcanoes . . . The countries without strong economies can not cope with these unfortunate events to help their people. And they ask for assistance or incur debts to rich countries. These underdeveloped countries assume large debts so and do not know that as the debts are taken, they found themselves hostage and pledge their political independence, economic and even cultural life of their country.

And rich countries are seizing these opportunities to expand their spheres of influence, their spaces of domination slowly but very surely without attracting too much attention.

To understand how underdeveloped countries are pledging their political independence, economic or cultural, take the example of someone who has contracted debts to the bank and who can no longer pay them. The bank will seize his movable or immovable property in value of its debt. It is much the same way that the underdeveloped country not knowing what to pledge, empties into the Wolf guell giving political independence pledge.

These rich countries try to justify it by saying that they are not responsible for natural disasters that cause poor countries to get these types of debts. And what happens is in the will of God. This may be true but curse is the one through who this bad thing is accomplished. *

The western countries mainly U.S., France, Belgium and others who supported Mobutu when he assumed power, have played a significant part in accelerating the destruction of the Congo, ill progress they have subsequently abandoned him when he was almost no more important to them as physically exhausted by the disease and only waiting for death.

Should they still expect services from someone who had no future in terms of physical health? And then a big question looming on the horizon: what would be after Mobutu? These Western powers feared that after the death of Mobutu, the democratic process could evolve positively for the country (after the collapse of his national barrier number 1).

It was then up a plan to derail democracy or misslead it.That is how was developed the plan of AFDL and Laurent Kabila, which had long sought to overthrow, but without success-the Mobutu regime, found the right moment, prompted by national and international political environment, to return to Congo. Then he had confidence in its allies wanting to seize the opportunity to complete the liberating work he had undertaken since

---

*   Lamentations 3:37-38, Matthew 26:24

1964. But he did not know that the supply of its allies of circumstance was a poisoned chalice.

First it is necessary to understand that the ADFL not having a weapons manufacturing plant could not have the weapons which could allow them to seize power in Congo. Some may say that the weapons are purchased. But which rebel group can purchase the weapons for him to win the war without the support, endorsement, blessing of the circle of decision makers in international politics? Everyone knows how the ADFL took power in Congo.

But as unfortunately social facts change, and man is a complex of relationships, Laurent Kabila which westerns thought to have under control had begun to show signs of inflexibility, revolutionary's tendency, trend problematic for the group of those who want to control Congo. From there, the West had begun to show their opposition to the man they had initially supported. This is understandable in so far as the West including the USA, through banyamoulengués, had used Lawrence D. Kabila as an occasional support to prepare a political system that can replace the Mobutu regime, who had gone to extremes, a regime which criticism exposed his supporters because it was a regime where it was easy to detect that it was in the pay Westerners.

To understand that the ADFL was sustained in the war in the Congo by western powers including the United States, one must use his intelligence. For example, one could observe the passivity of the Security Council during the period of occupation of towns by the Congolese Banyamulenge's rebel in the ADFL. But as Gilbert Ngijol says: "after government bombing's aircraft of cities occupied by the rebels in February 17, 1997 at 16 hours, the Security Council passed unanimously and urgently the next day February 18, 1997 a resolution calling for an immediate ceasefire . . . , . [204]

204. GILBRT Ngijol: AUTOPSY OF GENOCIDE RWANDA, BURUNDI AND THE UN 1998 Paris Editions Presence Africaine.

Rwanda, allied to Burundi, Uganda and supported by western powers, is involved in the Congolese conflict. Rwanda is a small disadvantaged by geographical factors, an area of 26,338 km2, is one of the smallest countries in size, with densities highest in Africa. With the majority of the population 90% living on agriculture, the country's revenue is derived mainly from coffee, tea and also tourism.

To understand the alliance of Rwanda with Uganda and Burundi, some facts not unimportant among members of the Tutsi ethnic group can be useful. For example, President Yoweri Museveni could not objectively take power by force in Uganda than by relying on the Rwandan Tutsi fighters led by the late Major General Fred Rwigema, the first president of the RPF. The RPF in turn was supported by elements of the regular Ugandan army to take power in Rwanda. Also long time ago Rwanda and Burundi were centralized monarchies that separated only at independence on 1st July 1962.

And the speech of the Rwandan president, Pasteur Bizimungu declaring in October 28, 1996, i quote: "the current Kivu region belonged in the past to Rwanda and if DRC no longer wanted to make peace with Banyamulengue, should give them to Rwanda with their land, "[205] reflected the will of the ruling RPF to see this rich province of Kivu to return to Rwanda. Although the message was from the lips of President Pasteur Bizimungu, there are strong reasons to believe that the message came from the high military command authorities. We know that Pasteur Bizimungu was the official president of Rwanda, but in reality the President could not take any decision without prior approval of the Vice-President of the High Military Command, Maj. Gen. Paul Kagame.

To realize that this project is not the less, or a chance, see the following statements: 1. of Mr. Daniel Simpson, U.S. ambassador in Kinshasa at the time "i will tell you that Rwanda is well equipped and came to settle in Zairian territory for long". 2. of Mr. Nicholas Burns, spokesman for the

---

[205] GILBERT Ngijol: Ibid

Department of State at the time: "we want to warn banyamoulengués and those who might support them that the world watches them." [206]

Also let see what happened in the history between Russia and Eastern Europe[207]: to be sure that Russia will be safe against attacks of the capitalist countries of Western Europe, Stalin decided to have around himself the countries that could be under Russia's control. For this it was necessary to introduce communism in these countries, but how to realize this? That is how the following steps were to be followed:

1. COMMUNIST'S INFILTRATION

As is the case in many countries people living at the borders of countries often share a number of values (language, way of greeting, names, habits . . .) and thus it may be easy to get them move across borders if a systematic monitoring is not required. And the men animated by selfish interests can use these weaknesses to make evil plans.

2. COMMUNISTS SHOULD HAVE THE POLITICAL POST

After being infiltrated and after successfully posing as indigenous, the next goal was to manage to have a political post and it was also guided by the whole machine, the political monster.

3. THE ELECTIONS WERE HELD BUT FAVORABLE TO PRO COMMUNISTS

Elections were organized in a way to favor a sole political party that was mostly the Communist Party.

4. THE STRUGGLE FOR ANTI COMMUNISTS potentiate

[206.] The world of December 5, 1996 n0 16 130 quoted in AUTOPSY OF GILBERT Ngijol genocide in Rwanda, Burundi and the UN Edit Presence Africaine, Paris 1998.

[207.] Namibian Senior Secondary Certificate (NSSC) . History's book grade 11-12. Module 1 Part 1, ordinary level. ISBN n0 99916-65-61-7.

One final step was to potentiate, to hinder the non-communist government to reassure the majority. That is to say that if one wanted to keep his anti-communist position, should resign or other wise abandon its old ideology.

From the foregoing, it is necessary to understand what is happening in the Congo in connection with the plot of the score or the taking hostage of the Congo. For example since 1998 and even before, Rwanda, Uganda and Burundi occupied territories in Congo. During the time that these lands were under their control, they were not only exposed to widespread looting of natural resources, but also to likely infiltration by populations from these countries.

Also the government of Joseph Kabila is using what they call mixage of elements of so called rebel's army troops with the Congolese Army forces. This is happening as we can read: "in a peace process facilitated by Rwanda, Congolese President Joseph Kabila and Nkunda negotiated the integration of Nkunda's men into five brigades within the National Army through a process known locally as mixage." [208]

Later on a UN report in November 2009 "described how former CNDP officers, now integrated into the Congolese army, continue to profit from their deplotement in area in the east." [209]

But no one can assure the Congolese opinion that Nkunda and his men are Congolese when we can read: "although Kagame denied involvement with Nkunda, the UN Security Council released a report in December 2008 that found evidence that Rwandan authorities were complicit in the recruitement of CNDP's soldiers." [210]

---

[208] UN Report on Congo raises the possibility of Genocide. September 9,2010.

[209] UN Report on Congolese raises the possibility of Genocide. Idem

[210] UN Report, ibidem.

Even before that, some enlightened minds have seen the beginning of the realization of a gigantic plan against Congo, partition, or the taking hostage of the Congo under the passivity or complicity of some major world powers. In the wake of the events we see the regime of Joseph Kabila and his allies take advantage of the naivety of some Congolese, political environment to create the partition of the Congo. And for that, different approaches have been, are being, or are about to be realized. Among others:

–The regime of Joseph Kabila in coordination with its allies has already begun to make the infiltration of Rwandese gained to their cause, their plan in Congo. Many excuses are used for infiltration.

This infiltration was made to justify the presence of Rwandese on Congolese territory, who would go to Congo for Rwanda at the right time to implement the plan as we said in the preceding pages.

Over the time these will be infiltrated plunger to have political responsibilities in Congo. Meanwhile the ruling regime in conjunction with its allies can develop mechanisms to monitor and systematically undermine the real opposition.

And when the time comes, in case elections are held, the ruling regime and the infiltrators can influence the elections in their favor and keep the Congo in the status quo.

On the other hand, in addition to the search for Lebensraum, other objectives were considered. Used by Western powers, Rwanda has thought and think to solve the problem of Rwanda by involving Congo. And Rwanda had engaged in this adventure thinking that in addition of economic interests in Congo, Rwanda, Burundi and Uganda even will still gain by taking eastern Congo. This would secure them against their rebel groups which use part of the country as rear base.

But if you look at the dice here with all these considerations, it should be understood that Rwanda has been and is used as a scapegoat. This leads us to say that Rwanda is not primarily responsible for the war in Congo, especially when we know that in addition to its own problems, this country does not have very strong economies that may enable it to face real war in Congo. Also this country depends largely on fundings from outside (World Bank, IMF and other financial institutions) to supplement the money in his budget.

Here it is proper to say that the war in Congo is an asymmetric war, war between the rich nations against a poor nation economically, unlike a symmetrical war, war between nations that have roughly equal status, the economies and military powers nearly equal. This can be supported by what is said by Wayne Madsen, an americain journalist researcher, author of Genocide, who covered operations in Africa 1993-1994: "the U.S. military have long been involved in the clandestine war in Congo. On May 17, 2001, Madsen said that U.S. companies, including one that has links with former President George Bush, is about to ignite the Congolese conflict for monetary gains." [211]

What is happening in Congo today is largely a conspiracy of international powers mainly the U.S. This is reflected by men who work, arrange for evil plans against the Congo on behalf of Western powers. This group has the advantage of having the resources and personnel for their services. That's how they build relationships with certain individuals of the Congo who are at their service.

Underlying all this, industrialized countries desperate to go one hand to secure control of the country's resources and also to monopolize the market for selling their products. The wealth of countries determine the actions of international powers in the existence of conflicts. The misery, suffering, war, loss of human lives do not matter to them as their interests are met. War seems to be very favorable for them (world powers) until it (the war) can bring them great benefits they may have than in peacetime or during the regime of legal political institutions.

The war is very favorable to the enemy's well-being Congolese. Especially if it's low intensity war, during which time a cease-fire seems to be observed,

---

211. WAYNE MADSEN, cited by Antoine Roger Lokonga in Media coverage of the invasion of Congo: in the footsteps of Western Interests?

but where the danger of a possible war is not completely removed or a system that opens the door to a possible war as it is the case in Congo. During this time we do not really know who controls whom, who controls what and where the wealths of the country are cut off from the country by looting. For example, a frequent speaker on the issue of "open line," said on the 07/06/2005 that it has been observed that small aircrafts land in forests, in different places far from towns in the DRC. What are these aircrafts looking for if it is not that they are going to plunder the resources of the country? [212]

Here we can differentiate resources. First there are resources said leading edge resources such as diamonds, gold, oil, uranium, copper, cobalt, bauxite, natural gas . . . which are resources that take years to be renewed, then they are rare. On the other hand diffuse resources such resources as soil, water, timber, livestock . . . This will help to understand why the Congo is one of the countries most threatened by the greed for money. For there is a relationship between wealth resources and the existence of political conflicts, wars in most third world countries.

As also said Clarence Tshitereke [213], there is a strong correlation between countries with abundant resources and advanced existence of conflicts in relation to countries that have primarily diffuse resources. In a table under the title: CONFLICTS IN AFRICA AND THE ROLE OF NATURAL RESOURCES, Clarence Tshitereke shows that in most of the following countries (Algeria, Angola, Cameroon/Nigeria, Congo-Brazzaville, DRC, Liberia, Sierraleone, Sudan) countries which were involved in conflicts possess at least the following leading edge resources :oil, gas, diamonds, uranium, copper, cobalt, gold, iron, rubber, bauxite.

In the same vein, the interest of natural resources like oil is not new. For example, we read in AWake: "to the end of 1940, when the war between

---

212. "Uncle Paul," an avid participant of the programme "open line", a programme of the Namibian National Radio. The show of 6/7/2005 from 9 to 10hoo am.

213. Clarence Tshitere (senior researcher at the ISS) cited by Nyambali Sem in On The Origins of War in Africa.

Romania and Hungary seemed imminent, Adolph Hitler was quick to act as arbitrator. A goodwill gesture apparently. But what Hitler wanted was to prevent the oil from falling into Romanian Russian hands. Oil was still a major factor in the invasion of Kuwait by Iraq in 1990 and the entry of other nations in the cons offensive. [214]

We have also said that the major powers want to control the market for selling their products. What says Noam Chomsky can enlighten us on this: the U.S. had opened Japan to American trade with a lot of warships and threats. They introduced the open-door policy in China, to make sure that they enjoy the same opportunities as other imperialist powers in exploiting China's resources. Finally, they had sent troops to Beijing with other nations to assert the supremacy on western China. While the U.S. demanded that the Chinese market is fully open to trade, they insisted in revenge that Latin America remains a strong market-closed to everyone except USA. [215]

Africa in general and the Congo in particular has been exposed to many negative experiences, the Congo has experienced the slave trade, colonization and the brain drain. About settlement in Congo, of course there could be positives. But they are surrounded by many negative points which we continue to pay the consequences until today. If we start with the beginning, it must be said that the official mission as presented by the colonizers was an alibi to be accepted. Often the international powers come behind humanitarian considerations to justify their actions, while the real reason lies elsewhere. Fortunately we know that we must use two functions (manifest and latent) to better interpret a fact or a social phenomenon. Let's talk about these two functions:

1. the manifest function: one that looks good in the eyes of the world, but which is not the real motive behind the action.

[214.] Awake of November 8, 2003, page 11.

[215.] NOAM CHOMSKY: THE WAR OF U.S. FOREIGN POLICY AS Howard Zinn, 1999.

2. The latent function: that is the real reason for the action but that is not exposed to the society as it does not seem good in the eyes of the world. An example will illustrate this. Someone goes to church to meet a friend as he knows he/she will be there. When asked why he goes to church? The man replied that he goes to church to pray (manifest function), because this seems good in the eyes of the world. But in reality, he goes there to meet his girlfriend (latent function). He hides it because it does not seem good in the eyes of the world.

Colonization has better prepared Congo in one side and another as a country dominated by contradictions that make it a fragile and fertile political manipulation of any kind. Indeed, as Gilbert Ngijol said: "the colonial administration replaced a traditional social organization with certain economic and political aspirations of the people by an administration for import but inappropriate to modern structures and generating conflicts, and broke the vital natural cord that maintained the precarious peace and stability in black Africa that is now completely devoid of its social cues and abandoned to disorder and violence. Therefore, the potential social conflicts remain in all states of black Africa including the DRC, the colonizers had compromised the security by establishing a history deliberately regional, tribal or even claniste. [216]

In their strategy of divide to conquer, the Belgian colonialists put emphasize on some qualifications misleading arbitrarily valuing certain regions, tribes, clans . . . They cherished, favored some provinces in terms of school infrastructure, production, public interest as hospitals, health centers, road infrastructure . . . without a fair allocation. It was not uncommon to hear sometimes overestimate natural economic potential of certain provinces. This could not go without reinforcing the widening gap between regions, tribes . . .

Bewildered of its scheme, its mode of production, pre-colonial ideology, the Congo was found wrapped in the internationalization of the economy, it found itself engulfed by the power politics. Yet while every nation-state

---

[216.] GILBERT Ngijol: Ibid.

as a National economy, part of the wider global economy, must set itself certain preconditions to participate in the world system as a partner and not as a periphery. But in economic relations with international economies, Congo is used as a source of cheaper raw materials, a consumer market for Western products which are often sold very expensively, a market of cheaper labor. The Congo is so packaged in the political, economic and even cultural international, dominated by the superpowers.

Speaking of superpowers, Ngijol Gilbert said that the U.S.and Russia remain the only superpower which conducted the first to the explosion of their first thermonuclear bomb in 1952 and 1953. Both countries wish to ensure they legitimated by the force leading the world by the Treaty of 1 July 1968 for the non proliferation. By this treaty, the rest of the world outside the nuclear club, is purely and simply excluded from military competition and thereby the economic and political decision-makers worldwide. [217]

The world is almost led or influenced by one superpower, the U.S., which is provided with international institutions like the Security Council to support its efforts. That's how we are witnessing both, contradictory phenomena where the Security Council failed to hide his bias exposed by playing a passive complicity. This is without counting the veto recognized to the five countries nuclear club including the U.S. It is not excluded from seeing the U.S. go to against decisions of the Security Council confirming its superiority over the world. Moreover, we can perceive through the speech by Madeleine Albright, as U.S. ambassador to the United Nations at the time: "the U.S. would act multilaterally when possible but unilaterally if necessary, repeating the message of the President Clinton". Thus in messages to Congress, said his government had the right to unilateral use of military force to defend the vital interests of the country. [218]

---

[217] GILBERT Ngijol: op cit
[218] GILBERT Ngijol: op cit

From the foregoing it appears that Congo is a victim of internal and external mechanisms that can only accommodate and maintain continuous underdevelopment.

We appreciate the work of the UN to a certain extent, because we can see that through its specialized organs, it seems determined to participate effectively in the democratic process in Congo by intervening in a timely manner. For example by sponsoring independent radio, the case of Radio Okapi, that is of great importance.

We must recognize that once the pressures of the UN, the international community to the delegates at the inter-Congolese dialogue for the signing of the agreement were a "great contribution" in the Congolese conflict. There may be other actions that we do not quote here.

However, we fear that this is a recovery strategy, called the law of the falling rate of profit (social dilatation) that is to lose some but to win big. Here we believe that the activities of the United Nations through its specialized bodies will have unforgettable effects, when the United Nations in his capacity as a peace activist organization, get involved with a comprehensive strategy also that point in the democratic process by framing the will of the Congolese people is to see the Congo to build democratic political institutions.

It is said that the accession of Joseph Kabila as president has accelerated the peace process in Congo. This may be true if we consider the various retirement programs of countries' armed forces directly involved in the Congo war, the arrival of the MONUC troops, their deployment in rebel-controlled territories, the territory under control government, visits to various international figures to accelerate the democratic process, the beginning of program execution DDRRR (Disarmament, Demobilization, Reintegration, Repatriation and Resettlement) fighters identified as negative forces in the Lusaka agreements including the Interahamwe and mayi-mayi, initiated by MONUC, ...

All this is to be classified as safety and security, but will have a very positive echo in the country only if it culminates in a successful transition, achieving the five key points, main objectives of the ongoing transition as also said by Anzuluni Bembe:

1. Reunification, pacification, State authority and territorial integrity restoration and possibly the construction of the country.
2. The national reconciliation.
3. The formation of a restructured and integrated national army.
4. The organization of free elections.
5. The establishment of structures to reach a new political order. [219]

From examination of the five points mentioned above, you will agree with us that not only until 2006, but until now, restoration of State authority throughout the national territory is not yet fully realized. National reconciliation, the formation of a restructured and integrated national army are far from being realized. The national identification should be done systematically but had not been performed. Signs that do not mistaken did and does not guarantee the holding of free, fair and transparent elections. All this showed and shows that the regime is far from realizing the hopes of the Congolese people.

Although all this, most Western countries have shown that their interest in Congo is not peace and well-being of the Congo, but the continuity of a regime in their pay, ensuring selfish interests. Yet this was enough for not only the government of Joseph Kabila, with its institutions, but also his supporters, to understand that the Congolese have suffered so much that they are entitled to human dignity and a life.

But the regime of Joseph Kabila, in keeping with the policies of his masters, has ruled the country as archaic in full sight of almost everyone. That's also the words of Amnesty International's report: "The election period was marked by numerous violations of human rights, including disappearances, arbitrary arrests, ethnic violence, the excessive use of force by security forces to break up political protests, restrictions on freedom of expression

---

[219.] Anzuluni BEMBE ISILONYONI: Ibid

and assembly. Worse the announcement of the first round of presidential elections on 20.8.2006, had provoked protests in the streets of Kinshasa, between soldiers loyal to President Joseph Kabila and those loyal to Vice-President Jean-Pierre Bemba, the result was 23 dead." [220]

Determined to play his card, President Joseph Kabila went on with his play to defy the Congolese people, and started another term as head of the country in February 2007, assured by his supporters, the "strong" of the time. Because of this, there were protests, disputes about the poll by representatives of political parties and even civil society, who found themselves duped. And in March 2007 this led to tension for a few days in Kinshasa, and it degenerated into clashes between personal bodyguards of Bemba, and elements of the army of Joseph Kabila, said the regular army. [221]

Contrary to that, President Joseph Kabila with the army, the country's finances, some Congolese, its toolkit and reassured by his masters, he only mocked the Congolese people. It is from here that some Congolese dozing since 2001 when Joseph Kabila was parachuted from the top, began to understand that from the inter-Congolese dialogue to say these days, political maneuvering were organized to entertain the people and find how to legitimize their pawn.

Determined to exploit the Congo, the group of pimps regime of Joseph Kabila, is investing its efforts for international opinion to believe that President Joseph Kabila won the "democratic" elections and, provides strategies and tools for looking up the economy of the country. For them, once there is a so-called recovery of economic growth, a most naïve population can forget (the) condition (s) for a new era in Congo. This group could use a bit of his means to earn a lot (the falling rate of profit), to further strengthen the bonds in which the country finds itself already.

---

[220]. AMNESTY INTERNATIONAL REPORT 2007
[221]. AfDB/OECD 2008

It's based on what we said above that we can include the following: "since 2001, with the support of the Bretton Woods institutions, the government began to implement economic reforms, financial and structural to stabilize its macroeconomic situation and create an environment conducive to development driven by the private sector. He managed to stop the cycle hyperinflationary and stabilize the exchange rate.

The inflation rate stood at 511% in 2000 fell to 135% in 2001, then to 18% in 2006. [222]

It is to be an asset in the regime of Joseph Kabila, however ephemeral if not accompanied by political guarantees reassuring. For every wise man knows that if the economic is not supported by the developmental politic favorable to a rational, efficient, and profitable interaction is ephemeral. We may also realize that the relative difficulty although the "economic growth since 2002, the DRC remains one of the poorest African countries. About 80% of Congolese live below $ 1 per day. In 2007, the country ranked 168th out of 177 countries in human development." [223]

With Kabila as head of the Congo since 2001 as it says: "Various programs created in recent years have not improved the security of the population, but social inequalities have increased. The rate of poverty of the Congo is very high, it was around 70% in 2006." [224]

There are private initiatives that are building or think to build Congo by building infrastructure (hospitals, school complexes, houses . . .), which is a good thing to encourage. But all this can be meaningful only when the politic reassures the next day, because if it presages a day in crisis, conflict, current building efforts would risk to be wiped out.

---

222. http://Web.   World   bank.org/WBSITE/EXTERNAL/ACCUEILEXTN/ PAYSEXTN/AFRI . . . 28/08/2008
223. AfDB/OECD 2008
224. AfDB/OECD 2008

So there are some government initiatives such as China that are already involved in the Congo by building roads, bridges, communication lines (telephone) infrastructures . . . , which are laudable initiatives, but to put in specific intervention strategies (punctual strategies). But for these initiatives to be meaningful, comprehensive intervention initiatives are necessary. It is here that politics can not be shelved as to give meaning to these specific initiatives, insurance policy envisaging a peaceful day, is more than a condition. And this can be done only when there are credible political institutions.

On the other hand, we must understand that these countries like China are not in Congo because they like Congo and seek its development, but to establish business contracts that will bring them money and lots of money. Here is an intervention in a broadcast "open line". [225] of 07.07.2008, deserves attention. The speaker gave the example of the DRC to show that the investment that China is doing in Africa are at great advantage of China. "China has given nine billion U.S. dollars to Congo for the construction of roads. And in return China has a free hand on copper for 15 years. And with the free hand of China on copper in the DRC, China will earn 72 billion U.S. dollars. If that is so it is sad for Congo.

And here we do not totally condemn China for its approach, it will still leave something visible (infrastructure), because there are countries or organizations which stop by giving money only. And we know that there are governments who ask for money (foreign aid) on behalf of the people, ostensibly to develop the country, but use this money as their private property. And all this only adds to the external debt which will ultimately weigh on the country.

What is unfortunate here is that China can not find a contract in which, although that it will build the Congo, will earn profits of that order. This is only possible in a time of political confusion, as is the case now where

---

[225]. Open line: is a radio broadcast program with open line with diverted Namibian stakeholders involved.

Joseph Kabila's main channel does its share and that of its allies, and ignores the crucial regarding the country's political future.

Yet when we look at several elements and factors, it appears that Congo is a country where if well-organized, well managed, can make huge income from all sources of income. We can cite as examples, customs, tourism, in addition to other resources of the country. But the Congo today have more to foreign aid, or +−51.4% of GNP in 2006 as an example.

Already in 2001 only to see how Joseph Kabila was parachuted into the head of the country, some enlightened men, had stirred the alarm bells to warn the people and international opinion on the conspiracy mounted against Congo. And today we do not work on assumptions to evaluate the integrity, efficiency and profitability of the regime of Joseph Kabila as since 2001 that Joseph Kabila heads, there are more speeches than the performance for nearly ten years.

For example we read: " ... the Congolese government had ordered a review of 60 mining contracts separated, granted during the war 1996-2003, to reassure themselves they are legal and fair. "The government will no longer tolerate fantasies in the management of its mine" had commented Martin Kabwelu, Congolese Minister of Mines.

Global Witness, an international organization that has investigated the links between the exploitation of natural resources, conflict and corruption, claiming that from 1996 to 2006, the large amounts of mineral wealth of Congo were committed in the obscure business that provided huge benefits to multinational corporations, but little or no benefit to the country as a whole. "Senior politicians, military officers, rebel leader and other individuals also took advantage of these individual agreements to the detriment of the population," Global Witness accuses." [226]

On the other hand "the new government had prepared its program in early 2007, including a governance pact, also reaffirming its determination to

---

[226] NEW AFRICAN (New African) page 46-47. October 2007

strengthen macroeconomic stability, fight against corruption and implement sound policies to promote good governance. [227]

Very good intention, as was the case in the regime of the late former President Mobutu . For the months did not pass so that people could begin to live the opposite: "in 2007, this new exercise in democracy was undermined when government institutions seemed at times exceed constitutional boundaries." [228]

Violations of human rights are recorded as one reads: "the national army, police, military and civilian intelligence operate with little or no regard to the laws of Congo or international law, and commit the majority of violations of human rights that it reported. A growing number of violations were attributed to the police. The lack of discipline and lack of command of these forces, and widespread impunity enjoyed by them remains the barrier to improve the enjoyment of human rights. The Congolese state security forces as well as foreign armed groups are committing hundreds of illegal killings.

The acts of torture and mistreatment committed by the routine of government security and armed groups, including strikes, wounds with knives, violated in the dungeons. The detainees are held without communication with their families, often in secret detention sites. In Kinshasa the presidential guards and special services of the police have, arbitrarily tortured . . . those who are perceived as opponents of the government. Some are referred because they are the ethnic group of Jean-Pierre Bemba, a native of the province of Equateur. The defenders of human rights receive death threats from anonymous and are harassed by the authorities." [229]

Given the foregoing, a significant policy change is more than necessary. Because the findings are consistent about the failure, as can also be

---

[227] http://Web. World Bank. Org/WBSITE/EXTERNAL/ACCUEILEXTN/ PAYSEXTN/AFRI . . . 28/08/2008.

[228] http:// URL. World bank.org/WBSITE/EXTERNAL/ACCUEILEXTN/ PAYSEXTN/AFRI . . . 28/08/2008

[229] Reports of Amnesty International 2007

read: "the chances for DRC to achieve the Millennium Development Goals (MDGs) by 2015 are seriously compromised. It will significantly increase public spending in key social sectors and continue to depend on non-governmental partners to provide services. [230]

This brings us to the next chapter, Chapter 4.

230. http: Web. World Bank. Org/WBSITE/EXTERNAL/ACCUEILEXTN/ PAYSEXTN/AFRI . . . 28/08/2008.

CHAPTER 4

THE INTEREST TO CHANGE THE POLITICS IN CONGO

After having red the chapters 2 and 3, you can realize that the fate of the Congo is decided more than 70% by westerners. And for that, democracy is democracy only if it is in their interest.

It is with almost their resources (financial, material, organizational) that the westerns organize the elections.

They are the ones who approve or not the elected. For if by the force of things the elected is from a genuine opposition that wants to work and has genuine interest in the country, the Western will ignore him up to come to political isolation, and create a so-called opposition favorable to them, which is in their pay. It is that they will support, seeking to mislead the people by all means, doing everything to frustrate, block the change that the country may have. For example they may refuse to support any program from the elected regime although yet needed to start the country.

They will rather maintain the so-called opposition they have created to sabotage, oppose the program of the newly elected. They can even try to infiltrate the advisors to the newly elected to disorient his vision, his program, his political philosophy to destroy any hope for the start of the country. And they have the means, even to manipulate the population to bring her to ignore his responsibility to change the country. And for that all means are good, they are able to create such chaos in the economic and financial policy that can cause social chaos and return the political machine at zero.

Given the foregoing, it is undoubtedly the West that is also an obstacle to political change in Congo. It must be however said that when we speak of the West, we do not involve all citizens in this region because we believe that among them there are some who have a heart, which have a sense of humanism who have a heart of compassion, who see things differently than those who support the systematic looting of our country not knowing that they create an imbalance that they will not control that will turn even against them sooner or later.

However, although we know how it is often said that the country must rely on its own efforts, supported by the international community is important be it even a political support.

But as man is driven by interest in this chapter we will answer to the questions:
−What is the interest of political change in Congo for the Congolese?
−What's best interest, which may lead the world, including the group of those who support the status quo, protective policies, institutions, monstrous ideologies Machiavellian for purely selfish interests, to understand the need to support political change in Congo?

Let's start with the interest of the Congolese to change political institutions. At this point, everyone should know that it is a responsibility for every human on earth, Congolese included to make the world better and that starting with his own country. What more natural than to understand that we must participate in building the world by offering what we have, to build our country and thereby contribute to the construction of the world? It is obvious that to develop a society, it must foster a balance between its various components, its infrastructure, superstructure and structure above.

The world is dominated by interest and men act on interest. Let's talk as examples the case of the USA and Japan. History tells us what happened in 1945 (world war II): "Japan was under occupation of American troops led by General Douglas MacArthur. Under his control the Japanese people had worked hard to rebuild their country. The money, to live and equipment from the U.S. were released in Japan in aid. [231]

The author continues by saying that there was good reason for this American aid "as the reason was that in 1949 the Japanese giant neighbor, China had fallen under the control of the Communist government of Mao Zedong with the policy of the Cold War apparently spirited to expand into Asia, the Americans decided to have a strong ally and friendly in this country. For this they did everything they could to rebuild and fortify a new Japan as quickly as possible". [232]

And the Japanese have quickly seized the opportunity to make Japan what it is today in the world. Here we can say that there were as Olivier Dollfus said: "in Japan the standard of living was one third that of Argentina. But in 1992, according to the CEPII, per capita product of Argentina was half that of Japan ($ 10,000 and $ 20,000) and a ratio of 1: 10 according to the World Bank (2,300 to 23,000). [233]

It is also the case in Western Europe having lived through difficult times, had to rebuild after the Second World War, benefited the assistance from the USA through the Marshall Plan. And the support was not given to Europe without interest. History shows that through this assistance, the U.S. wanted to keep its ideological influence policy against the Soviet threat as was also said by Bry Ó Callaghann. [234]

We can continue with South Africa which was under the yoke of apartheid but relatively significant change was fostered largely by Western powers including the United States through the international institutions of the UN.

[231.] BRY Ó CALLAGHAN: Understanding history. The World and Africa. Longman Namibia (Pty) Ltd 19 Joule Street, Southern Industrial Area, Windhoek, Namibia. P.O BOX 6025, AUS-NPAN PLATE, Windhoek, Namibia. Longman Namibia, 1997.

[232.] BRY Ó CALLAGHAN: op cit

[233.] OLIVIER Dollfus: The new world map. What do I know P.U.F 1995.

[234.] BRY Ó CALLAGHAN: Ibid

We want to point out here that the change in South Africa was possible not only by the national struggle but fostered by the actions of Western powers including the United States who above the interests of South Africa, had seen their own interests.

As stated by HJ and RE Simons, "the independent Republic of South Africa was constituted as a first post for the spoils of imperialism in general and has always played this role. In this global role, South Africa facilitates the transfer of values from neighboring countries with their consent, at the same time to benefit from all the sides in their investment effects that characterize these relationships with the capitalist world economy. The imperialist interests in general and that of the State of South Africa coincided. This explained why the representatives of imperialism in general (including Reagan and Thatcher) shamelessly supported the South African regime.

The profit of the capitalist investment is not the only reason for this alliance. Imperialism justified its support for the South African state and its economy based on its fight against communism.

That is why South Africa was seen as strategically important. For example during the ending 1978, South Africans ports had provided logistic support and repair vessels of 12,552 capitalist countries, an average of 2,500 vessels sailing around the cape every month. [235]

> Returning to the interest that the Congolese have to promote change in the Congo, saying that Congo should encourage a balance between space (ecosystem) and society (men belonging to this space). The prosperity of this society depends on how the man manages his society. And here the politic is certainly a place for we know that the politic as a

---

[235]. HJ and RE Simons (1969) cited by DERRICK Chitale: THE POLITICAL ECONOMY OF RESPONSE SADCC and Imperialism.In SADCC Prospects for disengagement and Development in Southern Africa. Studies in Africa Economy politique.

management of public affairs, largely influences the others (the body economic, the cultural authority, ideological). For example, economic policies, social policies depend largely on the general politic, mother politic. Here we say that a developmentalist politic is essential or a condition for the development of Congo.

For the world to respect us, treat us with dignity, we must first treat us with dignity ourselves. If in certain countries when talking about the Congoleses, it is not often in terms of dignity, among other reasons it is because when we speak of the Congo in political terms, it is negative, it is very ridiculous. While worldwide, some Congoleses who live outside Congo, prove their rationality, efficiency, profitability, in terms of human potential.

For those working in public institutions like the presidency, government, parliament . . . when they go for inter-State meetings, meetings of inter-governmental international organizations, the dignity, respect they can receive in these forums is not related to the wealth that has accumulated evil honestly, shamefully, but they respect you especially because of the credibility you have in your country and the credibility of your country in the concert of nations.

Some times, congoleses are unpopular and hardly accepted in some foreign countries, not because they are the subject of personal bad relationship, but because of the image that this country Congo is in politic. For example, some citizens of foreign countries observe the life led by some Congolese ambassadors and staff working in embassies and consulates representing the Congo.

It's no secret that this staff representing the country is some times forced to become a businessman, because of unpaid time. Some times some see their homes without electricity due to lack of payment. Short life leaves something to be desired compared to the ambassadors of other countries. How can you force someone to have consideration for the Congoleses when he sees those who represent them, living a miserable life and times of evil honest?

All this should concern us and sincerely bring us to correct our mistakes to change the situation in our country. We must reject this situation, must resist as always, but this time adding another dimension.

The foregoing shows that it is no mere spirit of humanism that the West can make gifts. To return to the Congo problem, we say that the fate of Congo depends now in part on Western powers including the U.S., for example to discuss a take off in Congo, it is imperative that there be peace first . And true peace can not be without the consent of the great powers through the UN, the Security Council. Without their consent the Western powers through their relationships in the world and positions across the Congo's neighbors, are able to create insecurity in Congo, and they can afford.

But we know that for the Western powers, democracy in Africa in general and the Congo in particular is democracy if and only if accepted by them, whether it is favorable. It is in this sense that many Western nations have supported dictatorial regimes, even maligned by the public, but fighting the regimes from the popular will, the real elections, credible elections.

The time has come when Western countries supporting the status quo in the Congo must understand that their politic has repercussions not only in dominated countries, but also in their own country. For proof, let us consider:

1. THE CASE OF GLOBAL WARMING: is a global threat

Today we know that one of the main causes of global warming is the emission of gases including carbon dioxide of pollutants in the atmosphere and the destruction of flora, including forests, which are however the main actor in absorption of gases including carbon dioxide that destroys the environment seriously. It has already been demonstrated several times by biologists that plants are of paramount importance in the absorption of gases including carbon dioxide.

And it is no secret to anyone that Africa in general and the Congo in particular, well-managed can be a significant reserve of rainforest, and participate with great potential in the balance of the biosphere nationally, continentally and globally. It's not for nothing that David Willet and Deanna call Congo, the "Amazon of Africa". [236]

Once you have realized the importance of forests in Congo, it is also important that you can account for the increasing threats to these forests in terms of their destruction. According to data (*) from 1990-2000, data in a form of a diagram published by Fact on File, in: in just ten years, Africa lost over 12 millions acres, Asia nearly 10 millions acres of their natural forests. Only Europe managed to increase its forest cover. According to these data, Africa is the first, South America the second, Asia the third, North America the fourth and Oceania the fith to have registered loss in this matter.

Based on the above chart, you can realize that Africa is the continent most threatened, followed by South America under the destruction of the forest. And if you look seriously the chart above, it should be noted in general a correlation between the volume of forest destruction, the economy and politics. And as you can see, Africa is the first continent threatened by

---

[236.] (2) DEANNA Swaney, DAVID WILLETT: Africa, Lonely Planet is a shoestring. Lonely Planet 1995. National library of Australia Cataloguing in publication.

(*) Published by Facts on File, in.

destruction, has as you know, political problems first, then economic as is the case in Congo.

The threat of destruction or the destruction caused by wars aside, it was estimated that 80% of people in Africa use wood as fuel to prepare food. In addition Africa has the highest population growth rates in the world. And it follows that the land around certain cities in the Sahel, a wide belt of semi-arid land in the southern edge of the Sahara desert had its trees cut on more than 100 km in all directions. [237] And Professor SAMUEL NANASINKAM to say that the majority of African citizens destroy their own environment simply to survive. [238]

The foregoing does not spare the DRC, and you know it takes many years, even 50 years for a seedling to reach the size of logs and large trees that are cut almost every day and in unknown quantities. At the root of this destruction, mainly poverty that is directly related to the economy and economy at her turn is affected by the politic. Western countries can say that they have nothing to do with it. When you destroy the Congo, where and how this affects also other countries, the western countries?

Here it is important to understand that if for example the air pollution in a particular continent may cross political boundaries and go to other continents, can some how affect the lives and bring the pollution, causing acid rain destroying plantations, affecting men's health, affecting life in general. Similarly the forests in a particular continent may, by absorbing carbon dioxide gases which reduce the amount of toxic elements in the air of this continent, at least reduce the total amount of toxic elements that are across continents.

And as we know that the major producers of greenhouse gases are the major powers including USA, is there no great interest in these powers, to encourage effective, rational, efficient management and therefore protect the environment, especialy as they are among the first officials to polute

---

[237] South African Magazine Get away, Wake you quoted in the January 8, 2005: The planet earth can it be saved?

[238] Professor SAMUEL NANASINKAM, quoted in the same Wake up.

the environment ? And a rational, efficient management can not be done without consent, without the complicity of people in the respective countries through credible institutions established in accordance with their wishes. And when it comes to managing the country, we see mainly political institutions which are shaping the way for other institutions. It is here that the Western powers, great powers must understand, given the importance of Congo in terms of forests and biosphere elements, the need for Congo to have stable political institutions, from the popular will, not only for the interest of Congo but also of the world.

The Congo with credible political institutions that are supported by the population, will promote the rational, efficient and cost effective public affairs. We have highlighted the forest, but in addition to forests, Congo has mountains, lakes, rivers and a diverse fauna that are part of the complex chain of life.

However, although few efforts are arranged by international organizations for the protection of flora, fauna . . . , the threat of extinction of these different lives in Congo continue to grow.

Also, it may seem that Congo is not so threatened because there are efforts, there are international organizations working for protection in this area, and on the lists may be Congo is not the first to be threatened in this area.But what is true is that if Congo enjoys democratic political institutions, efforts to protect flora, fauna as well as others, will find willing and protection, will be significantly enhanced because not only accepted but also granted by population.

Still speaking of the destruction of the country, the destruction which the poor population is mainly responsible aside, the most awful, most cynical destruction, is the one organized by various business circles in connivance and blessing of the government of Joseph Kabila.

This destruction is to set by the program account of the systematic plundering of the country. To realize that let us read as follows: "opaque in the days of colonial occupation, was the plunder of the ivory for Europe in the depths of the jungles of the DRC that formed the heart of the operation. One hundred years on, the looting continued, but this time in the form of wood and other strategic natural resources. According to the survey conducted by GREEN PEACE INTERNATIONAL (a pressure group for environmental protection), international companies are slaughtering woodland spirits to roll, rip forest communities with simple things like a beer trap, sugar and salt to access the rare and juicy hard wood worth hundreds of thousands of dollars.[239]

But onr thing real is that "the Congo rainforest is the world's second largest tropical forest after the Amazon and one of the planet's essential defences against global climate change. Global emissions from tropical deforestation alone, contributes up to 25 % of the total annual human-induced CO2 emissions to the atmosphere." [240]

While such a flora's favour deserve to be taken ccare rationally for the benefit of not only DRC but also the world, "a new report launched by Greenpeace today exposes that international logging companies operating in the Democratic Republic of Congo are causing social chaos and wreaking environmental havoc.Tthis business encovers endemic corruption and impunity.

"21 million hectares of rainforest are currently allocated to the logging industry, an area nearly seven times the size of Belgium. Most of DRC's timber is exported to Europe, with France and Belgium currently the largest importers." [241]

And Greenpeace proceeds saying that "it is crunch time for the DRC rainforests. The international logging industry operating in the country is out of control. 'Unless the world Bank helps the DRC to stop the sell off of these rainforests, they wil soon be under the chainsaws' said Greenpeace International Africa Forest campaign co-ordinator, Stephan Van Praet." [242].

[239.] New African, October 2007.

[240.] Greenpeace International.
Greenpeace exposes that logging in the Congo rainforest is out of control.
Press release—April 11, 2007.

[241.] Greenpeace International: idem.

[242.] Greeenpeace International: ibidem.

Apparently worried about the situation, the world Bank has taken some positive steps to reform the timber industry in DRC for example by pressing the government to cancel certain existing contracts, and revoke 6 million hectares of concessions allocated illegally.

"However, international Bank documents obtained by the Rainforest Foundation reveal that the Bank's ultimate intention is a massive expansion of the country's timber industry. A 60–100 fold increase of timber per year is foreseen, with an area of some 60 million hectares (some what larger than the size of France) being put up for grade. The Bank documents refer to the creation of a favourable climate for industrial logging." [243]

Although apparently all this good will,the "Bank and FAO have failed to take in account the highly unstable situation in Congolese politics and the serious weakness of the government. The authorities in Kinshasa, are as yet, unable to exercise any meaningful control over the activities of logging companies. Secondly, the world Bank approach to the development of DRC's forests look like based on the assumption of economic benefits to the country's poor people." [244]

But if one can read further the revelations of Greenpeace, will find that in this business, Congo as a nation looses socially, economically,and especially environmentally. That is how every day no one knows how many trees are cut down in the name of improving the life of Congolese.
But the world should be aware and in alert about this: "the DRC rainforest contains 8 % of global carbon stores. It is estimated that forest clearance in the DRC will release up to 34.4 billion tones of CO_2 by 2050, roughly equivalent to the UK's CO_2 emissions over the last sixty years." [245]

Yet many biologists believe that the preservation of biodiversity is a necessity for humanity. Several meetings were convened on this. From

---

[243.] World Rainforest Movement.
   Democratic Republic of Congo: after the war, the fight for the forest.
[244.] World Rainforest Movement: idem.
[245.] Greeenpeace International: ibidem.

these meetings, these conferences revealed, among the resolutions experts such as Barbara Ward and Rene Dubois say
"A broad consensus, that environmental threats are becoming increasingly a global problem and requires a comprehensive approach. But two consultants from two Asian countries have suggested that little progress will be saved, be it in terms of economic or environmental terms until each individual country learns to manage its own ecosystem. And an ambassador, Adlai Stevenson said that the earth can be compared to a small spaceship on which we travel together, depend on vulnerable supply of air and soil. [246]

Considering the hypothesis given by the ambassador. If people traveling (living) on this spacecraft decide to manage adequately the vulnerable soil and air supplied by this vessel, two possibilities can be envisaged: the first is when people living on one of the plots that make up the ship, set themselves up as master to control besides their plot, the other plots. To do this, they justify their decision by saying that the missmanagement in other plots affect the environment.

The second possibility is when all the plots being aware of the situation, agree that the residents of each plot can be controlled first in their respective plots (Intra plot control) and on top of that have a coordination (a international control plot) to assess the effectiveness of control within plots. Of these two possibilities, the second has much chance of success, because the first practice which not only recquires more means and also that it works on the principle of imperialism.

Let us return to our planet earth by saying that what we said above can be valid for our planet. It is well to remember that every country on earth is composed of a space and society. The space (ecosystem) and society (composed of men and their institutions). The survival of each country

---

246. BARBARA WARD and RENE DUBOS: ONLY ONE EARTH.The care and maintenance of a Small Planet. Report on the Human Environment, Inc. 1972.

depends largely on the political, economic and social differences between men and between men and their institutions on the other.

But we can not ignore the relations between countries. Our problem is to understand that the political, economic and social behaviour affects largely the ecology, the environment of each country and also to some extent the lives of people living in other countries. From the foregoing, it appears that the action, the human behavior is largely the basis of environmental problems. It is therefore necessary that in every country, people can take measures they will be forced to comply with. And men can not meet the measures only if they feel really concerned, associated with them, knowing that it is good for them, their interest. This does not exclude the international coordination based on transparent and balanced principles.

In view of the foregoing, the definition of politics as Rod Hague and Martin Harrop can challenge us: politics is an activity where groups reach a consensus agreement by making a selection decisions trying to reconcile their differences. [247] It should be noted that this is a positive policy, designed to operate only when there are credible institutions to which people adhere, to which the people have confidence, faith, this miracle word which, brings more than what we think.

2. TERRORISM:

If at the moment, global warming is a global threat as we have said in the preceding pages, it is not the only one to threaten the world. There are also global other phenomena that also threaten the world. Among them, there is terrorism, which as they say, puts people on alert. Almost everybody believes that we must find ways to eradicate terrorism, a scourge of the century. On the contrary, the facts show that the world terrorism is to drive more and more scope and spirit to become increasingly sophisticated. For example, the U.S budget expenditures against terrorism alone were over $

---

[247] Rod Hague and Martin Harrop: Comparative Government and Politics. An introduction. 6th Edition. England.

10,000,000,000 in 2000. [248] But one year later on 11 September 2001, the U.S. had registered the shock ever registered, caused by terrorism.

These acts were condemned and treated as horrible crimes against humanity. Senior politicians like George W. Bush, Ronald Reagen have so eminently condemned these acts they described as the "barbarism," and urged the international community to fight them wherever they are. And then everyone believes that terrorism is not a good thing in itself and therefore must seek to end. To end it we must first find its root causes in order to find effective solutions. And we must take time to think at the causes because success depends on it.

But it is often on causes that thoughts differ. Mainly two groups are emerging: on one hand there is those who think that terrorism is merely an act caused by hatrate, jealousy . . . without seeking the root causes of this hatrate, this jealousy . . . On the other hand, there are those who think that terrorism is an act of claiming, a reactionary measure against evils like injustice, discrimination, systematic violations of human rights, imperialism . . . The latter happens often when the man has a disappointment on the part of institutions meant to protect him.

An example will illustrate this: someone is the victim of a package organized against him by his neighbor. Wounded in his conscience, he accused the criminal to the court which unfortunately plays the game of the criminal and protect him, knowing that behind the perpetrator is hidden the interest of the men heading the court.

Surprised, the victim discovers that the court has played the game since the perpetrator is his friend. Overwhelmed, the victim addresses to use lightning thunder. Unfortunately the lightning thunder kills not only the wrong doer but destroyed the house and even affects the family members who were yet inonçants.

[248.] Awake of May 22, 2001.

And on terrorism, one can observe that the 21st century is characterized by, among others the development of advenced imperialism, by the growth of violations of human rights on one hand and terrorism on the other. Imperialism is still present in the underdeveloped countries including the DRC.

Regarding violations of human rights combined with imperialism, one example is that of Iraq where the U.S. once they became aware of the capacity of the military potential of Iraq—because in addition to other ways the U.S. could use the mission of UN inspection in Iraq for data, information that could help to decide on military means to destroy it—challenged the Iraq up to besiege it, despite the resolution of the Security Council banning the U.S. from resorting to arms to resolve this conflict.

In DRC violations of human rights are daily. Yet the DRC, like many other countries, has the right to self-determination, independence, freedom as defined in the UN Charter. Western powers including the United States should know that what they do in terms of violations of human rights, imperialism, affect the world around them. And the world around them looks at them, watching them, and this can bring this world to react to his martyred way.

Certainly the Western powers are reassured by the defenses they have. But we must know that everything that is made by man has limits, and that man is a complex and inventive genius. When you think you have closed all roads, unhappiness, suffering can make to discover others, especially when we become aware of our situation and that God is on our side.

We believe here that the Western powers including the USA, understand that maintaining Congo in chaos, is to heat a bomb that they have created themselves but which will turn against them. May the westerners, including the U.S.A know that the DRC is gradually becoming aware of the responsibilities of Westerners, including the USA in his misery, his plight, his hell.

This awareness is growing enthusiasm slowly but surely in the hearts of the Congo until the day it will explode, maybe not in the direction expected by Westerners. Perhaps the xenophobia against the U.S.A for example and their interests is far from being observed in Congo, but prevention is better than cure they say.

May the world understand that poverty, too much injustice, imperialism, innoua exploitation of peoples . . . may lead people to develop a reactionary, such as terrorism.

Because what is happening around the world about anti-american demonstrations, may be interpreted as a warning. This is the case of what happens in Iraq, is also the case among others of what happens in Afghanistan where to see pictures of May 29, 2006 on the television[249], the protesters said they did not want Americans in Afghanistan.

Given the foregoing, we hope that the countries responsible for miseries, of imperialist policy in some countries including the DRC will be vindicated by the following: "in December 2001 a few Nobel Prize winners were agreed and signed a statement that says that the only hope for the future lies in cooperative international action, legitimized by democracy." [250]

3. THE AIDS

To continue the list of global threats, AIDS is now regarded as the global risk and the world is challenged to find solutions. Sure, International Organizations including the United Nations through its specialized organs play a prominent role, not only in reducing its spread but also in the treatment of those who are already infected.

Yet we can observe the influence of imperialist policy in the spread of AIDS. We may think here of countries where because of wars, girls, women are raped. There is a strong correlation between the wars, poverty, conflict in underdeveloped countries and the high rate of AIDS. And wars,

---

[249]. The images shown on television (NBC Namibian Broad Casting) of 05/29/2006.

[250]. Wake up from 8 March 2004.

conflicts, poverty . . . are related to the policy of Western countries against the underdeveloped countries.

We can agree with Gilbert Ngijol saying that in case of collusion between the major powers whenever their interests are at risk in developing countries, it can be observed the "indirect confrontation, opposing indigenous peoples of countries concerned by pulling the strings by distance. (3[251]) This reminds us of what Martin Valmaseda called puppet's theater (4[252]), in which the great powers rule the world through a system similar to a doll size standard articulated by the woolen. This doll is on display in the Museum of Puppetry in Lyon in France.

If we assume that wars are correlated with increased infection rates of AIDS and the imperialist policy is correlated with the wars in underdeveloped countries in general and the Congo in particular, can–we not say that international politics (imperialism) is largely responsible for the increased infection rate of AIDS in the Congo?

Let us think of many families that because of the general economic situation, see, let their daughters into prostitution to find something to eat. And if we understand that the economic crisis in Congo is caused by the political crisis, it should be understood that somewhere politic has a responsibility in the spread of AIDS. And if this policy is the result of an international plot, it is very contradictory to want to fight against AIDS while we support the politic that promotes the spread of AIDS.

However, Congo has the potential in human besides its other recognized more potential. If well framed in a condusive development political system, can participate effectively in the search for a cure against AIDS. We know for example that people finds its medical products primarily based on natural ingredients from the vegetable world, animal . . .

[251.] Gilbert Ngijol: Ibid

[252.] Martin Valmaseda: "Getting free of manipulation." Involvement 8. Publishing on Epiphany BP 724 Kinshasa Limete-1994.

For example, as can be read in Awake: it was estimated that the top 120 drugs that have occurred in 150 prescriptions used in the U.S.A are from natural ingredients. Then when losing the world's flora, the man loses opportunities to find new drugs and chemicals, we are losing the potential cure against AIDS and against a virus-resistant planting." (1[253])

And the world knows that Congo hasn't shortage of potential in terms of flora, fauna . . . , which may help in pharmaceuticals that can help not only the Congo but also the world. Also features the Congo could tear the curiosity of tourists and is a fast convenient to answer a lot of genuine scientific curiosity. But the Congo is not only in political crisis, but growing in political uncertainty.

4. POVERTY

The major powers are meeting sometimes to discuss the thorny problem of poverty. In 2000, for example, leaders of countries have agreed to fight against poverty. In their meetings, they often take time to discuss possible ways to reduce the poverty rate. And you can see that the under-developed countries whose political institutions are generally in crisis, are most affected, those most affected and among them the Congo.

Among the means to fight against poverty, the major powers are considering financial aid that is important but almost useless in countries where political structures, political institutions are unjust as Congo, because this helps to only enrich advantaged men in power. We know that in these underdeveloped countries including DRC we must work very hard to change the situation. But how can one works hard when the political structures are not favorables?

The world must understand that we must first assist, promote the establishment of democratic political institutions. And the Western powers including the United States have the means to promote the establishment

---

[253.] Ghillean France, Director of Kew Gardens in London (UK), quoted in the Wake up 22/11/2001 Who Will Protect the web of life?

of credible political institutions, democratic, but rather look at their selfish interests. For example, it is not easy for countries that profit from war, knowing the benefits they derive from the arms trade and related activities. Here is the view of some Western countries seem short because the other side would not contemplate what the era of genuine partnership can produce in terms of quality of life.

5. THE CREDIBILITY OF POLITICAL INSTITUTIONS

Finally, let's finish this chapter by saying that it is appropriate when there are meetings, international conferences on peace, security . . . to deal with credible institutions from the will, the popular consensus, than dealing with unjust institutions, because they have no popular mandate, they are from tricks, dictatorship, nepotism . . . . These institutions because they don't have the people's confidence will not be easy to make resolutions become reality and that will reduce the problem to square one. Because a program where people do not feel concerned is a program dedicated to failure.

CHAPTER 5

PROPOSAL FOR A POLITICAL SOLUTION IN CONGO

After have carefully read the preceding chapters, a man of sense can not hesitate to challenge the current regime in Congo. What is important for us not only to challenge existing institutions, but want more of this, to present a model of transitional institutions which supported, provide a qualitative political change in Congo.

In this chapter, we propose a political solution to end the political confusion that exists so far in the country for many years.

And we were able to realize that the Congo is suffering not only from the lack of respecting the constitutional texts (and speaking of the constitutional texts let say that there has been so many). But above all, men in whom the people can put their confidence to handle on behalf of people because the success of the transition depends not only on institutions but also on the respect of the texts by the leaders and people. The people's confidence as well as the support of international opinion, the world powers must remain essential at the present time. All these elements are interdependent and will contribute to the success of the transition.

It is in 1990, under conditions described in Chapter 1, that late Mobutu, President of the Republic at the time, launched the so-called political transition in Congo, but since 1990 until now Congo still in the dark political confusion, without having democratic political institutions.

Today, the Congolese overwhelmingly believe that the current government has only prolonged the suffering of the population. Moreover, since the mandate that the overall agreement (inter-Congolese agreement) had entrusted to Joseph Kabila, one could observe skepticism in the majority of the population. But Western powers have shown their support in this scheme, justifying themselves to support political peace, national harmony, the welfare of the Congo.

But today the international community can see that in almost all cases, the government (government of Joseph Kabila) proved weak and incompetent, inappropriate to give the treatment needed to Congo.

There are more than five years ago that the government of Joseph Kabila, could convince no one, apart from the status quo group. He offered and still offers no guarantee for democratic elections. But althougth apparent inability of the regime of Joseph Kabila to bring the country to the real election, the group of Joseph Kabila and his supporters, determined to achieve their wicked plans, had moved heaven and earth to convince in 2006 that elections will be credible and democratic.

That's how in circumstances that the world knows, some Western countries had taken—although the multiple voices, testimonies that had criticized the massive fraud that characterized the sad events called "elections"—the country back to square one but with Joseph Kabila as head of the country, as desired by the "strong" of this world. For imperialistic reasons, countries have considered these so-called elections to have been transparents and credibles. This is understandable especially when you consider that in this political confusion, Joseph Kabila has now over nine years at the helm of the Congo.

Even when we observe what is happening in Africa about the change of political regimes, too few chairs—from the tip of your fingers—hold democratic presidential elections, although they do know that the time is no more favorable for next term for them. What about Joseph Kabila especially when you know how he was dropped on top of power in the Congo?

But now the world can testify that the Congolese people is driven to flee the Congo because of insecurity among others reasons, the uncertainty about the future, political problems, economic problems . . . , Congo is still live the political crisis. What to do to save this country from this chaos? Should it be despite all obvious facts showing that what had happened and still continued to Congo, is a trick to hide the Western imperialism, leaving the country in this chaotic situation?

In response to these questions, everyone who has a heart, might have the opinion that we must help Congo to have democratic political institutions. And this can only be achieved through democratic elections, but how to arrive to credible, transparent elections in Congo? This is where we say that the political institutions needed to support transitional are essential for a real change in the Congo. And this is where President Joseph Kabila can challenge the Congolese people by accepting a neutral government to lead the transition and organize elections.

And instead of continuing to extend the misery of the people, the government of Joseph Kabila and related institutions must honestly recognize their failure, and support the new transition program. We must praise the patience of the Congolese people, without which the government could not even do half of his so-called mandate, without knowing the clashes, the popular resistance of the highest caliber. But now the people are tired to hear more than demagogic speeches of those in power and its sponsors (Western powers) because he has already seen all the colors in addition to the economic, politic and social Calvary.

With regard to this, we can not remain insensitive, indifferent, because the situation in Congo is deplorable. We rather need to be challenged. It is in this order of idea that, we propose a political solution for this country. And as people in great majority insists on change, if it adheres to and supports our thesis, certainly that Congo will see a new era. And Congo needs not only institutions but also facilitators to lead these institutions.

Speaking of leaders of major political institutions of transition, the country will need to find:
1. A personality that will take care of the Presidency of the Republic.
2. A personality that will occupy the prime minister office.

3. Men who will constitute the parliament.
    But the challenge is that these men must be men in whom the people
    can identify themselve.

If today we have problems to run the country, can we not look into the
country's recent history, if there are not men in whom the people can trust,
whom the people can have had been directly or indirectly downstream to
represent? Of course it is. For proof, let take a time to question the events
at the start of the transition and how it was extended until today.

The concept of political transition in Congo began with the historic speech,
delivered April 24, 1990 by late Mobutu, President at the time. One of
the highlights of this period is the national conference that began Aug. 7,
1991. While some have criticized the National Conference saying that it
has shown itself only by endless quarrels between rival political leaders,
the Sovereign National Conference however, had exceeded this level of
learning to perform to the creation of the High Council of the Republic
(HCR) which will now balance the Presidency of the Republic and the
government, and replace the parliament. Bishop MONSENGO PASSINYA
was its president.

As it was already said in the previous chapiter in agreement with the opposition,
Mobutu announced January 14, 1994 the government's resignation and
the dissolution of the High Council of the Republic-Transitional Parliament
(HCR-PT). It should also be remembered that the ADFL had begun its
offensive in September 1996. And all the while Mobutu continued to
disturb, confuse the democratic process until trapped by the advancing
rebels, had been obliged to meet Laurent Kabila on board Louteniqua, a
South African ship.

As Ngijol Gilbert also said, this meeting organized by the South African
President Nelson Mandela, was unfortunately a "failure", precisely because
of the divergent views between President Mobutu and Laurent Kabila. In
fact during the meeting, Mobutu announced that he would no longer be
a candidate to succeed himself, and promised to hand over power to a
candidate who would be democratically elected. To this end, Mobutu

called for the creation of a transitional body to lead to democratic elections (presidential and legislative) in less than a year, which body should be headed by a neutral.

Finally Mobutu demanded an immediate ceasefire. Laurent Kabila for his part, accepted the establishment of that transition organ and the ceasefire, but on three conditions:

-First, the political forces that should be part of this body of transition are exclusively selected by the only AFDL
After that, the transitional authority is entirely run by the same AFDL
—Finally Mobutu resign permanently.
Front positions as antimony, this meeting could not settle as a failure. The second meeting which was scheduled in the same place for 14 May 1997, was simply canceled at the last minute, Laurent Kabila failed to attend.
(254)

Let continue saying that after the failure of the meeting of May 14, 1997 and before the irresistible advance of the troops of the rebellion to Kinshasa, some Western powers like the U.S. and France in particular, had pressure on both the rebel leader Kabila and President Mobutu, whom they asked to negotiate in order to avoid unnecessary bloodshed in Kinshasa.

The final communiqué of the Heads of State urged the Zairian political forces, under the direction of the High Council of the Republic-Transitional Parliament (HCR-PT), to conduct the election of the president to allow the smooth functioning of institutions and thus promote a democratic transition in accordance with the Transitional Constitution. The Heads of State also took note of the statement that Mobutu, because of his health problems, will not be a candidate to succeed himself.

Following the recommendations of the Heads of States and pressure from Western powers, the High Council of the Republic-Transitional Parliament (HCR-PT) met May 10, 1997, and elected as president, the Archbishop

---

254. GILBERT Ngijol: op cit

of Kisangani, bishop Lawrence Monsengo Passinya despite the refusal of the radical opposition represented by Etienne Tshisekedi. Bishop who thus became the second person would replace Mobutu Sese seko in case of a power vacuum.

But until then, Laurent Kabila continued to reject what he called scenario and demanded the departure of Mobutu first, before ceasefire. May 16, 1997 President Mobutu humiliated by the advance of the ADFL, left Kinshasa with members of his family to Gbadolite, his hometown, and went to his exile in Morocco.

Laurent Désiré Kabila proclaimed himself President of the Republic May 17, 1997. While he was loved by much of the population when he began his offensive, he disappointed a significant proportion of the population some time after he became president. He became hostile to any democratic trend, but prevail a kind of one party, the ADFL. All means, any excuse at hand were brandished to justify. That's how he could say, among other reasons: "you can not keep clean water in a dirty calabash", in the words of an old African adage. [255]

The ADFL was so strongly opposed to any political force, even a peaceful one, and even the transitional body, the HCR-PT, that however, was the result of a long process that took water and blood to the people and was an important step in the process towards democracy. President Laurent Kabila, who was nevertheless loved by the people at the start—because of the fact that he had put out Mobutu from power—suddenly desappointed however much of the population, challenging the election of Bishop Monsengo elected president of High Council of the Republic-Transitional Parliament.

It should be recalled that "there were many Congolese opposition to both the Mobutu regime and the rebellion (ADFL), considering that Kabila who had conquered the country by force with the support of foreign troops, was not a democrat, and could even be more dictator than Mobutu, who also took power in a military coup. This category also in the words of

---

[255.] Laurent Desire Kabila, quoted by GILBERT Ngijol: op cit

Gilbert, preferred a neutral to lead the country, and it is in this context that Bishop Monsengo Passinya was elected President of the High Council of the Republic-Transitional Parliament." [256]

As a reminder, we said that the Congo needs leaders of the transitional institutions. Here we are:

1. THE PRESIDENT OF THE REPUBLIC FOR THE TRANSITIONAL PERIOD

From the above, we can remember that before Laurent Kabila to conquer the country, there was someone who was indirectly elected by the people. And there the Congo and international opinion will agree on the fact that since the election of Bishop Monsengo head of HCR-PT, there is no one who has received such confidence, such a downstream of the people to represent him in such a position.

And given that the position of President of the Republic of transition remains vacant after all these patterns experienced without success, it is reasonable that the cardinal MONSENGO PASSINYA hold this position to lead the people in elections. And we believe that Cardinal Monsengo Passinya is aware that there is nothing that is so difficult, like taking over the leadership of the country to bring a new political order. Fortunately he will have the people behind him and the international support to lead the people safely.

Moreover, in view of what we have said above, it is exactly as if we were already on the track leading to the main road that, lets see who does what, why, for how long . . . ? But a few meters from the main road, while the people hoped to move towards the main road to progress towards democracy, the country has been diverted from the first track to another that has pushed several kilometers away from the main road.

But later the people found that the track on which the country is driven now is not the one on which he was, and that the country is on the wrong track.

[256.] GILBERT Ngijol: Ibid

Here we propose to return to the first track, but with some rearrangements may be to avoid hitting against some of the traps set by political leaders at the time, the case of President Mobutu, who took his time to put obstacles to delay or derail the democratic process.

And here we urge all political forces, those faithful to the former regime of Mobutu, the loyal to the regime of Laurent D. Kabila, those of the current regime of Joseph Kabila, those loyal to former rebel parties, those loyal to the peaceful opposition, civil society, all the forces, to recognize this, and honestly support the program because the future politic of our country depends on very greatly.

2. THE FACILITATOR OF THE PARLIAMENT OF TRANSITION

In principle parliamentarians are elected by the people. They are mandated to represent the people, to talk on his behalf. And for that we need to organize elections, for it is through elections that the people expressed confidence. However, as the current parliament can not inspire complete confidence, since it is the product of the regime, the plot of Joseph Kabila, another mechanism to find those who can represent people, may be considered.

Because we are facing a need to find the leaders of the parliament without going through the elections, then the question is, are there not men who can earn the trust of the people? In response to this question will be answered positively by saying yes. In the absence of elections, there are men who deserve the confidence of people. For proof, let see if we can not find legitimacy in the traditional leaders (chiefs).

In many cases, traditional authorities do not derive their legitimacy from the fact that they were elected directly by the people, but their descent in the royal family, their ability, capacity, availability to take to heart the destiny of their people respectively. There is a philosophy of representation, a notion of consensus on the person to earn the trust of the people, because if the head betrays, he betrays the aspirations of a people, it undermines itself and undermines the future of his people.

Customary power reflects to some extent to a political representation because there are standards, a number of pre-established rules for access to the customary power.

Let us borrow an example from the Bible in Exodus 3: 16 where lack of gathering all the people, the Lord asked Moses to go and gather the elders of Israel. We discuss this passage because it shows that a default to gather all the people together, they were able to take a sample of the people consisting of the elders.

And power based on traditional customary law is not very far from the model presented in the setting of the ancient people of Israel. Often it is by inheritance that one can acquire the customary power. Before becoming a tribal chief, the deceased before his death should pass to the successor, the secrets, some principles for the welfare of the clan, the tribe . . .

Even if the tribal chief dies in circumstances that have prevented sudden placing normal power, there are always mechanisms to ensure that the successor may be in possession of information that occurs during normal power tranmission. And the represented population will recognize him/her as her traditional chief, to whom she confides her mandate.

When trying to understand the elections, we realize that the philosophy of elections is primarily based on the notion of representative mandate. Certainly in the elections, the representation is stronger than that observed in the appointment of chiefs. However by lack of the high representativity (the elections), the representativity found in the traditional, customary power, so low it might be, can help in this transition period to avoid endless wrangling. For peaceful political parties, civil society, political parties, armed . . . will be recognized through the traditional chiefs.

Although not from the polls, the customary power may be valid if accepted by the society which can guaranty its legitimacy, playing the role of parliament in transition.

But we know that there must be a minimum of conditions such as minimal educational background to be qualified to become a member. In this respect the traditional chief who meets the criteria can become member transition or otherwise qualified to nominate a significant fate for him.

It is in this sense that we thought of using traditional leaders. But in a philosophy of consensus, the current parliament will be reduced by 50% of its members according to the votes obtained by each component of the National Assembly. Thus the 50% offered will be occupied by representatives of the people found, through the mechanism based on the traditional authority.

Certainly we can take into account in determining the quota of MPs by province, things like the number of people in each respective province, based on a previous reliable census. This will be the work of an ad-hoc technical team under the responsibility of the President of the Republic of transition.

There will also be details such as the composition of the transitional parliament office, the election of President, Vice President of the Parliament by members of parliament, the rules of procedure . . . , which are secondary details. Thus, the transitional parliament will be formed. In fact in the political history of Congo we see that there were not only MPs voted and those who were co-opted, but there were also traditional leaders (chiefs). So far that's not all because we have yet to find a host of the prime minister.

3. THE PRIME MINISTER

Having established the parliament, to find the Prime Minister, becomes a bit easier since we already have two institutions (the Presidency of the Republic and Parliament). Political forces, political parties and civil society will organize to find some candidates for prime minister that they will propose to the parliament and the parliament will elect the Prime Minister from among nominated candidates.

Once elected, the Prime Minister should know that there is a challenge and must get to work.

In the absence of credible institutions to lead the country towards a democratic era, we offer these three institutions around which a consensus may be emerging to lead the country to qualitative political change. Without claiming to have found the most perfect, most ideal, we trust that, understood and supported, it will bring real change in the Congo. These are the three main institutions of the transition. But in addition to these, the institutions supporting the transition are necessary:

1. The Independent Electoral Commission.
2. The High Council of the media.
3. The National Observatory for Human Rights.

These institutions to support the transition such as those of the inter-congolese agreement (257) had planned, but have unfortunately not been effective.

The presidents of all three institutions to support the transition will be elected by the transitional parliament. Independence for each of the last three or the first three institutions must be dedicated. But this independence would not rule out of cooperation, collaboration.

After the issue of leaders of institutions, now let us turn to the texts governing the transition. In this regard we propose that the country can adopt existing texts, as regards the texts the country has known so much, but the problem is more the lack of compliance. And after adopting an existing text, it may find rearrangements in parliament to suit the current situation.

As for the length of transition, a consensus will be around a year and a half, two or three years.

In light of the foregoing in paragraphs above, it appears that the gains of the souverein national conference (SNC) held in 1991, we seem to be

---

257. Global and inclusive Agreement on Transition in the Democratic Republic of Congo. Signed in Pretoria (Republic of South Africa). Decenber 17, 2002. Sun City, adopted April 1 2003.

acquired which the country can use. And then there is a need to talk a little about it. It is true that the SNC was convened by the late Mobutu, President of the Republic at the time, but to the will of the barn most of the people at all costs wanted to change. The world may remember that the president at the time was not for the advent of such an institution, but it was obtained by force of events. From its convocation until the elction of the President of High Council of the Republic–Transitional Parliament, it was not an easy thing. People lost their life to claim the holding of this forum.

Against his will, Mobutu President at that time had to sign the opening of the Sovereign National Conference (SNC). That is how 2800 delegates from the country's political parties, civil society and government came together to prepare the future of their nation.
"However the President Mobutu managed to stem the rising tide of opposition, blocking the demands of the Sovereign National Conference (SNC) for far–reaching concessions including elections. In hindsight, the Sovereign National Conference was a squandered opportunity. But despite its failure to oust Mobutu, the gathering remains a fundamental point of reference for Congo's pro-democracy movement in that it generated several initiatives for far–reaching change, including the introduction of a federal political system. The SNC produced a constitution, but it would never be implemented such that the 1994 constitutional Act applied until 17 May 1997." [258]

The SNC came to the point where the country could find itself with three transitional leading political institutions. Besides President Mobutu, the nation through delegates at SNC elected the Bishop Monsengo President of the High Council of the Republic–Transitional parliament, and the opposition leader Etienne Tshisekedi wa Mulumba, Prime Minister. And with

---

[258.] Hauser Global Law School Program
Globalex. The legal System and Research of the Democratic Republic of Congo (DRC): An overview by Dunia Zongwe, François Butedi and Phebe Mavungu Clément.

these transitional institutions, if supported by the international community, Congo would have started a new era.

But unfortunately, the super power nations leading the world did not see the things in that way. By contrary, blinded by their motto in most of the Less developed countries: "let us care about looting of resources (found on the soil, subsoil, . . .), regardless to people living on that soil, area".

That is how DRC missed once again to take its train for the development. Like in 1960 when the UN and other super power countries at the time decided to let the Congo to walk on a wrong way. And as if it was not enough, they (super power countries) decided to let rub down, from the memory of Congolese, the brave work done by the SNC, by organizing other political forums alluring to be worried about the political crisis in Congo, while beyond all, it is political confusion that is taking place in the country.

CHAPTER 6

EFFORT' SUPPORTS TO MAKE THE CHANGE
IN THE CONGO

After chapter 5, in which we proposed a political solution for Congo, we now turn to Chapter 6 where we talk about the efforts needed to support change in the Congo, because this change can only be effective if it is supported first inside, then outside. These two requirements taken as part of a system where the malfunction of one affects the functioning of the other, from malfunction of one affects the functioning of the system. That's how this chapter focuses on what to do to support change in the Congo by Congolese and by international community, international opinion?

For the Congolese, something must be done about the involvement of some Congolese in politics. We must understand that an action affecting the politic not only helps the person involved and his family but that person being involved is involved in building the country and thereby benefits all the country.

Contrary to many people who retreat from politics—by saying: "I am a Christian, politics is not my business, besides i am not a politician, politicians are criminals, i can not participate to political views, . . . , i hope only in God who will do anything for me, the political influence affects our society. And even the above is said by the lack of deep understanding of what a Christian means, or lack of deep knowledge of what it means politics because politics is often reduced to negative politics. Maybe to some Christians, politic is not in agreement with the will of God.

To them, we ask the question: how can we be Christians, but agree to condone injustice, abuses against our fellow human beings by our peers, without feeling concerned? While as we live in this society have a responsibility to build it, make it better.

Since being a Christian does not just implies reading the Bible, fasting and prayer, worship and praise God . . . but to sacrifice ourselves for God, starting with self-sacrifice for others, for men. How can you preach people to overcome poverty by encouraging them to work, while the political structures have killed the job? We must involve ourselves where we see the obstacles to the well-being, be it in politics, and avoid saying that i am not a politician, i leave politics to politicians, i' m not particularly concerned as this does not affect me. It is here that the famous poem by Bertold Brecht [259], from which I quote some extracts, can build:

"they arrested the workers, religious, unionists" etc, but this could not mean anything to some people because they thought not interested because they had nothing to do with the different groups arrested, until they found themelves arrested, and it was too late for them torealise that they were suppose to be together and resist as a block.

A Christian must know that he must be free of manipulation not only spiritual but also material because both are in inter–influence somewhere. Our thoughts determine our actions and can determine, as our actions can too. If you know that God can use you to save your country, as he did with Moses, for example, it goes without saying that your behavior towards the politic will be influenced. We must try with God, we must pray that God bless our work but not expect him to come to do it for us. When you start something right, God is with you, he protects you, he adds intelligence, wisdom, courage to face events. Sometimes we die, but when you die for a just cause, that is 10,000 times more than dying without leaving a trace, no memory for the country.

[259.] sBertold Brecht, quoted by Martin Valmaseda "Getting free of manipulation". Social Commitment 8. The epiphany Editions BP 724 Kinshasa Limete-1994

The slogan of the journal Europe Magazine–which was banned at one time by the President Kasavubu–published in Brussels: "if you do not mind the politics, the politics deals with you" [260] means that if you do not know the problems of your country, how your country is run, you will leave easily deceived. It does not say that everyone must work for political office, what is required is that everyone working in his field should participate in nation building and therefore must know how to manage his country.

There is a challenge here on Christianity as well as practitioners of other religions because it can be observed also in the Congo that as Professor Patrick Laubier said "who call themselves Christians become numerous, but the enthusiasm and heroism does not characterize them all". [261]

Another challenge is to respect its commitments to the country, through constitutional provisions. This is a requirement of democracy, because democracy depends not only on the proper functioning of the institutions but also and above all trust and respect for these institutions by the leaders as well as by the ruled. And institutions from the will of the people work to manage efficiently, effectively for the benefit of the country. They do their best to ensure fair and equitable redistribution of income and opportunities, ensure safety, a better future for the country.

If the government institutions that are yet to come to the popular will stand out, divest themselves of these principles, they gradually lose the confidence of the people and leads the people to disown them using the means he officially recognized by the constitution.

It will require a dialogue between the governing institutions and the people. A good flow of information will send the echo of public governance to the people. Democracy itself is not an end but a means to ensure the equitable

---

260. PATRICK OF LAUBIER: The escatologie. What do I know? PUF 1998 108, boulevard Saint-Germain, 75006 Paris.

261. The journal Europe Magazine, quoted by Professor KITENGE-YA in the course of family sociology in the first license Sociology 1991-1992 University of Lubumbashi (DRC).

redistribution of national income, opportunities, ensure the well-being and a better future for all.

And here the constitutional text is a must for one can not confuse the country with his family, clan, or even his farm. We want the Congolese to understand that some countries even in Africa where a group of people can not arise with weapons to gain power. To them a simple question will be posed: what are you looking for? If they say they seek power, the answer will be given to them to cut short their dreams. Because they will be told that the power is acquired through elections. If you want power you have to wait for the elections, and this is written in the constitution that everyone must respect.

But in Congo none of this, by contrary Congo is a real political jungle. To be heard is when you take up arms. That is how through the so-called nationalism, many took up arms rightly or wrongly to liberate the country without knowing how often to take power by arms and stay as such, it is to legitimize his departure by firing squad or a dishonorable manner.

That's how Congo is up to these days without institutions voted by the people. And during this period of political confusion, there are those who either want to obstruct any possibility for the realization of genuine institutions, or to pass so-called trapped institutions but whose purpose is to perpetuate the status quo. It is often politicians collaborators, an institution tailored whose key terms are never explained to the people. A rigged up where the people do not understand why such or such other clauses.

But the country must seek a constitution which guarantee authentic change, which guarantee a better future for Congo. So early that the country has such a constitution, it will know it needs the means to achieve it, knowing that the first means is the people's trust.

In the Congo armed groups claim to have the love of country and take up arms in conscience to liberate the country. But as these armed groups have failed to find a solution, we believe that in the name of the people they love, they bow to the need, supporting the transitional government as we have proposed. And like all think they have the confidence of the people, they can expect to earn fair elections office.

One can not speak of efforts to support the change and miss to mention the military whose role is not to be overlooked. Already it is noted that the military should be apolitical. It must serve the entire nation, all citizens, not serving a person, group or political party. While supporting outstanding efforts, efforts by international organizations including MONUC for national integration of the army, we can consider the permutation of the military by making a mixture.

That is to say that we can take some of the soldiers in Kinshasa, they are sent for example in North Kivu, another in Eastern Kasai, Western Kasai, Katanga, Equator, Upper Congo . . . provinces. And the same is done for each region across the country. But this is not easy when we consider the expenses that may incur (eg. must be found where to stay, the cost to move them . . .) But democracy is guaranteed where the military is aware of their role (ensuring national security, defend the laws of the country).

On the other hand, an effort must be made in the direction to overtake us in terms of internal quarrels related to regionalism, tribalism.., to promote the national interest that is dear to us to build our country being in the unit in diversity. As such, we can use examples of developed countries, to develop, had to minimize the ridiculous things that block, hinder development.

More than one known in the history of Europe, the Hundred Years War. This war can not be mentioned today as a positive factor which has been used to develop. We must understand that in every generation there are things that change, there are elements which the future generation must divest itself without rejecting all elements of the previous generation. Here we must make efforts to divest ourselves of things like regionalism, tribalism . . . We must put the nation so that we can move forward for development.

The politicians must seize the opportunity to do better because they say, men live only once and each time we see them, they should mark a new step in the sequence of events. And know that in life, the best thing you can do is to nurture, caring group of people that are at your responsibility, because if you do not make it during your living, the future will judge you.

Policy makers together with the people, at their respective levels, must rebuild the moral values that have been destroyed for years. Patriotism, a feeling for the motherland is one of those values. As stated by Professor Michel Borgetto: "it comes from the latin word meaning land of patria, it indeed has the same root as patter that means father". [262]

Patriotism in Congo has become a myth, because: "there is no country and patriotism than where men are free, equal and happy. Do we have a patriotism if the powers of distributive injustice destroys any freedom"? [263] Certainly not. And here we can understand why the Congolese run from their country, are driven to flee, abandoning their homeland, because the patria meaning the patter is no more functional in Congo. People no longer feel secure in their own country, their homeland. Some feel even more alien than foreigners.

For positive change, we must admit critics because from clash of ideas comes the light, they say, and criticism allow to be measured against key objectives. The motto of the French newspaper, the Figaro, motto borrow to Bon Marché challenges us "Without Freedom to blame, there is no flatterer's praise". [264] To say that if the press is muzzled, what the press well you said is not true. To be happy when the press said well about you, you should give to this same press the possibility to blame you. Because what you do when you are in power, affects positively or negatively your future.

---

262. Professor Michel Borgetto: Currency: "Liberté, égalité, fraternité". What do i know? P.U.F 1997.éééé

263. Professor Michel Borgetto: op cit.

264. Le Figaro, quoted by Professor Ya-Kitenge in the course of Sociology of the Family in Sociology 1 license 1991-1992, University of Lubumbashi, Faculty of Social and Administrative Policies. Lubumbashi R.D.C

For proof, you can see that many presidents of the less economically developed countries in general and Africans in particular do not want to relinquish power, especially when they think about their future after power, after leaving the halls of power. Some think that their life after leaving office, will be an ordeal, a life at risk.

However, there are presidents who, after having left office, continue to have the confidence and esteem of the people and government. They are thus regarded as wise and are not far from those that affect the country's politics. Examples in Africa include former President Nelson Mandela of South Africa, former President Ketumile Masire of Botswana. . . .

And all this depends on how it was managed during his reign—if during his reign was managed efficiently and effectively in the interests of the people, they brought the country to good economic growth, the country will be very grateful even after departure from power, as a reward for what they have done for the country.—But if while they were in power, they did push the country into the abyss, they may be treated very harshly by the country. Despised by the people, they risk being at the merci of the government. This is to say that what you sow is what you reap.

In the world there is almost nothing that is done without interest. Almost every action has an interest either immediate or distant. But what is needed is that while having an interest, that the national interest is greater. While the whole nation will invest great hope in the transitional government, it is not excluded that there is the fear that this government abuse of power.

We therefore believe that some favors could be guaranteed to that government besides their wages. But these concessions may be applicable only in the future, provided that the said government through its commitments will honor people and will fulfill the expectations of people. That is to say that after the transitional period, members of this team might get the favor related to Good Citizenship, politics, for having faithfully performed the duties, responsibilities entrusted to them.

And these favors will be budgeted for a certain period. All this should be seriously considered by the parliament after the democratic elections held not by the transitional government, but by the government, the second government of the Third Republic. This is to ensure that the parliament did not consider these favors direct links in the transmission of power.

That is to say that the transitional government prepare and conduct elections to the first government, first term of the third republic. And the first government organizes elections for the second government, second term of the third republic. It is this government that will consider giving favors to the transition team. It may be that until the second term of the third republic, some of the team members of the transitional government die. In this case, the person or persons entitled to receive this benefit will be given that right.

Regarding the African's interest for political change in Congo, we believe that Africa is aware that the problems of the Congo affect in one way or another the african continent. Given that the DRC is a country in the middle of Africa, a strategic position, to free the Congo is not only a necessity for Congo, but also for Africa because Africa will not want to be weak from his heart, Interior. .

And wanting in the future a strong Africa, it provides political supports to Congo for the establishment of credible political institutions. Althougth the country must address itself first to be released, still the effort of other countries is needed. This help can be of any kind and even ideas. However in terms of ideas, before biting an idea, we must analyze it systematically so as to avoid to swallow an idea whose objective would be to keep us in the state of underdevelopment.

For example in 2004, some Western politicians, particularly some Belgian politicians had suggested that if Congo could not hold elections as planned, the international community will entrust the management of the country to an organization like the EEC, the United Nations to bring it to the elections.

This has happened in some countries in the past, the case of Namibia. Indeed, the League of Nations withdrew the German control of Namibia, Namibia entrusted under the control of South Africa. But the world will remember that it had yet to Namibia to lead armed struggles for liberation from South Africa. What of Congo whose greed by the Western powers are further proof?

Certainly there could be an opinion that could bite in Congo to the idea of Western powers (make Congo under the control of such organizations as the EEC, the UN) without knowing the hidden agenda behind this horrible plan. Throughout the world there is not one country that has developed because it accepted the return of the settlers. Nevertheless, the Congo can be open to a scheme that together, white, black, yellow . . . all together for an ideal can build a modern society. And why it takes precedent, the constitution, the expression of the people. Consider placing the Congo under the control of organizations controlled by the Western powers that the rest are ultimately responsible for much of the chaos known in Congo, would be officially to put Congo in the mouth of the wolves.

International organizations like the UN, must wonder about the honesty of their decisions, their actions mostly in underdeveloped countries. Because due to ever increasing suffering of the developing countries affected by imperialism, various political manipulations and domestication, economic exploitation, the role of organizations such as UN is questioned.

The Congo was invaded twice by Rwanda, Uganda and Burundi, although under the guise of some Congolese acquired to their cause (an alliance with some Congolese), this in full view of the United Nations which has shown complice indifference.

We invite Rwandan, Burundian and Ugandan governments to understand that border security they seem to claim, can not be resolved effectively and efficiently by the current government in Congo or by any government to their preference. But this issue can be resolved effectively and efficiently only by a responsible government, that meet Congolese consensus first before it is enjoyed by foreign governments which will be partners. And this government will need the international understanding, given the importance and distinctiveness of the question. Such a government may result only from trustful election.

Probably after the government is formed there might still be some pockets of resistance, perhaps even some neighbor governments which are actually involved in this conflict. In this case, Congo will have no choice but to first let know that fact to the international community and take responsibility.

CONCLUSION

After all the preceding chapters, we come to the conclusion. You've realized, after reading these chapters, that Congo is in chaos. And that the politic is largely responsible for the chaos of Congo. As one of the instances, it has seriously affected the other two instances.

As a country, nation, Congo (DRC) needs to develop. For this it needs a strong government, backed by the people and the international community. It's such a government that can meet the challenge of security, carried out among other things, the project as the reform of the army and police into an army and national police. Such a project can take time, but it is true that a government whose democratic principles, justice are updated, can speed up to achieve a rational, efficient and profitable societal project.

To achieve such a government is through elections. Elections are a means to well-being, not an end in itself. Here it should be understood that if the elections do not result in a democracy and democracy does not promote the welfare, development of the country, it is a wasted effort.

We said that the DRC needs the elected political institutions. But who will organize the elections? Here as you reported in the preceding pages we can not count on the Kabila regime to hold democratic elections. And we have proposed in this book to find a transitional government.

It is true that Congo had a very long transition period and the people are tired. Because even after "the most expensive elections in the world" [265],–the Kabila regime has failed to bring democratic political culture, peace and national harmony expected–DRC is still in a transitional phase.

[265.] World is Witness. Voices on Genocide Prevention.

And speaking of the political transition in DRC, people are tired. And because of this, the wish is to go for elections by all means. Here we must understand that there is no need to run, a transition is needed to level mountains, valleys created by the previous regimes. For example, "the most common level of extreme poverty in Congo, can create a favorable climate for the emergence of corruption." [266] If it does not establish safeguards, it can affect to some extent the mseaning of elections.

It is true that internally, there are challenges such as tribalism, regionalism, fatalism etc. But all this will be minimized by building strong structures open to development. For example, if job offers are published in a set time limits, and that there is a structure, a skilled team in employment, composed of worthy people to ensure efficiency, effectiveness in the passage of employment tests.

The world is witness that in 2006, "Congo scored 5.8/100 for the World Bank and indicators of accountability. And in the Global Integrity report, the Congo was classified in 144th/158 position." [267]

But in "2011, DRC is classified the 5th of 177 nations based on the indexes of the countries that failed in the substance of peace. This indicates a high level of dysfunction of the economy and politics and a country that is not capable of providing the basic needs of its population. It is ranked at 2.4 out of 100 according to the indicator for monetary policy in the World Bank.

In 2009, the DRC was ranked 176th of 182 countries according to UNDP HDI.

In 2008, it was ranked 158th out of 180 nations in Transparency International and the index of perception of corruption." [268]

[266.] World is Witness. Voices on Genocide Prevention.

[267.] 126 Idem

[268.] Google, What is the score of DRC in 2011 for World Bank's indicator is Goverment transparency. [PDF] Democratic Republic of the Congo.

Yet as we have said before, not only that the DRC had organized elections in 2006, the most expensive in the world, but also received significant financial support in addition to the reduction of external debt.

If after all the billions paid in the DRC, the majority of the population still lives in misery, poverty beyond description, how can we not say that if the majority of money was not received by the people, the money went into the pockets of corrupt politicians and leaders? [269]

It is here that anyone can understand that "millions without reforms will have no impact on poverty and sustainable development" [270], except if it is for maintaining the law of the falling rate tendentielle profit.

In this situation, every man of human sense should be questioned to provide a solution to save the many lives sacrificed in the Congo, definitely do something to change the political situation in Congo. What to bring about change?

In response to this question, as we have already said, we must lead the people in elections so that he chooses men who can run the country efficiently, effectively for the benefit of the country first and then the world. It is here that the majority can be of the opinion that we must organize the transition. For this transition to succeed, there must be support not only of the transitional text but also of men who have the confidence of the people. Without the men responsible, credible, framed by a constitutional text, we will experience a transition which only extend, offering no warranty that may lead to reliable and honest elections.

Given the above, it is contradictory and unrealistic to expect the regime of Joseph Kabila to bring the country to peace, national harmony, well-being Congolese. Since it appeared in the preceding chapters that the so-called elections in 2006, the rest was nothing transparent and therefore could not

---

[269]. Gustavemoke's blog: Fathers to sound: a Dictatorship Rising game. Page 287.
[270]. (6). China in Africa: the real story. Page 280

be credible, reliable, were cunning, the masquerade of the West to extend the term of Joseph Kabila, who was dropped at the head of Congo under conditions in which the world has witnessed. Far from bringing the solution this trick has only put the Congo on a gear tooth in the vicious circle of underdevelopment. And the country is yet again in the political confusion.

There is therefore a need to find a solution for a confident transition that can end this long and protracted transition that began in 1990. This is where we put our contribution to the Congolese nation, proposing how to find people that can direct the presidency of the republic, the prime minister, parliament, of the transition.

Instead of asking for arms to liberate the country, we opted instead to raise awareness of these great powers on the necessity for them to support political change than supporting the status quo in the Congo.

Our book is to take in the perspective of promoting the happiness of the Congo in particular and the world in general than in a view of trial. But we know that happiness which we speak is a relative happiness as absolute happiness not only of Congo but also of the world will come only from God.

Perhaps our proposed solution is not the only route to take leading to a political settlement in Congo, but it is however realistic, and the future can give us reason.

Apparently the Western powers through some speech say they support peace and the democratic process in Congo. On the other hand through the facts that do not lie, the same Western powers leave the ambiguity in their positions with respect to the DRC. This although many years of suffering endured by the people. But these so-called Western powers have no right to continue to suppress human lives in Congo, for God who is the creator of those lives is able to confuse these nations by raising the spirits that can cope against the powers that oppress the poor lives.

REFERENCES

1. André Mbata B MANGO (Professor at the University of South Africa) and MPRARISENI Budel (responsible for education at the same university) Democracy and elections in Africa in the Democratic Republic of Congo: Lessons for Africa.

2. ALAN WHITE and ERIC HADLEY: Germany 1918-1949.
    c Collins Educational, 1999, 8 Grafton Street, London W1X 3LA.

3. ALEX DACIDSON and PER STRAND: the path to democracy in 1993.

4. Barbara Ward and Rene Dubos: Only one Earth.The care and maintenance of a small planet.

5. BEN WHITAKER: Minorities.   A Question of Human Rights ?

6. Britannica. Book of the Year events of 1995.
    C 1996 Encyclopedia, inc.

7. CLAUDE LEVI-STRAUSS, MARGARET MEAD, LAILA Shukry, EL Hamamsy MN SRIMIVAS discussions on war and human aggression.
    Mouton Publishers. The Hague. Paris 1976.

8. CHRIS Osbon, JAMIE STOKES: Towards Creating a sustainable culture of human rights.

9. CHRIS Osbon, JAMIE STOKES: Environmental issues on file.
    C Diagram Visual Information Ltd 2002.

10. CHRISTOPHER CLAPHAM: African guerrilas. James Currey Ltd., 1998.

11. DAVID VITAL: The survival of small States. Studies in small power great power conflict.
C Oxford University Press 1971.

12. DEANNA Swaney, DAVID WILLETT: Africa Lonely on shoestring. Lonely Planet 1995. National Library of Australia Cataloguing in publication.

13. EDUCATIOIN ADULT AND DEVELOPMENT. N0 45, 1995. Institute for International Cooperation of the Confederation for adult education.

14. FLORY KAYEMBE: Weapons and democracy.

15. GILBERT Ngijol: autopsy of the Rwandan genocide, Burundi and the UN. Editions Presence Africaine, Paris 1998.
16. Dr HF Verwoerd: one crisis in world consciousness. The road to freedom for: Basutoland, Bechuanaland, Swaziland.

17. HENRY DAVID THOREAU: Civil Disobedience and Essays. Dover Thrift Editions, 1993.

18. Ibbo Mandaza: peace and security in Southern Africa. 1996.

19. INTERNATIONAL HISTORICA STATISTICS, Africa, Asia and Oceania. 1750-2000 4th Edition B.R MITCHELL.

20. INTERNNATIONAL HISTORICAL STATISTICS, the Americas 5th Edition 1750-2000 BR Mitchell Palgrave MacMillan, 2003.

21. INTERNATIONAL HISTORICAL STATISYICS. EUROPE 1750-2000

22. JEREMY LEGGETT: global warming, the Greenpeace report. Greenpeace Communications Limited 1990.

23. JOCELYN MURRAY: Cultural Atlas of Africa.

24. JOHN J. KATZAO, Nangolo Mbumba, BRYN O CALLAGHAN, PA Helgard PATEMANN, I EDDIE Van Staden, DAVY H, A TAIT: Spots History of Mexico in the third book of the humanities in Namibia. Taken from the English.
C Cass/Longman Namibia Namibia Project and 1993.

25. JOHN DUNN: modern revolutions.
C Cambridge University Press 1972.

26. JURGEN Schmandt JUDITH CLARKSON: the regions and global warming.
Impacts and response strategies. New York Oxford.
Oxford University Press 1992.

27. KENNETH D. WALD: religion and politics in the United States.
Congressional Quarterly, Inc. C 1992.

28. Lumumba Kasongo TUKUMBI: Towards Creating a sustainable culture of human rights.
C Individual contributors 1998. WHK: Gamsberg MacMillan 1998.

29. MABEL FRANCIS ELLIOT and E. Merrill; social disorganization.
C Printed in the United States of America 1961.

30. MELINDA LIU: China/USA the real clash of civilization. News International week. Com April 24 2006.

31. MARTIN Valmaseda: break free from manipulation.
Editions Epiphany BP 724 Kinshasa Limet 1994.
Original issue: Alandar. Folleto n0 20 c/Armenteros, 13 28039 Madrid (Spain). Original title: para que no los Hilos our Tirena. Translated from Spanish by Conchita Vicente, Juan Antonio Yrazabal, Emmanuel NTEL Bizezila and Theo.

32. NAOMI CHOMSKY: the war and U.S.   foreign policy.
C Howard Zinn, 1999.

33. PATRICE E. LUMUMBA: Congo land of opportunity is at risk?
Office of advertising, S.A Editors.
Marcq street, 16, Brussels 1961.

34. Paul Raymond Bérenger: seas, oceans and small islands. UNEP Our
planet in volume 15 n0 1.

35. PETER H. MANN: Methods of Sociological Enquiry. Oxford Basil
Black Well, 1971.

36. PETER STIFF: Warfare By Other Means. South Africa in the 1980s
and 1990s. Galago publishing 1999 (Pty) Ltd PO Box 404 Alberton
1450 RSA.

37. PETER STIFF: the silent war. South African Recce Operations
1969-1994. Galago publishing 1999 (Pty) Ltd PO Box 404, Alberton
1450 RSA.

38. PIERRE MERLIN: Africa can win. Paris Karthala 2001.

39. Phil ya Nangoloh: the politico-military conflict and human rights
violations in Angola: International conspirancy and Complicity.

40. Professor Isango IDI WANZILA: being the first political history of
Congo graduate Political Science and Administrative 2000, University
of Lubumbashi in the DRC

41. Professor Kaleli KABILA: sociological methodology course, the first
license Sociology 1991-1992 University of Lubumbashi Zaire.

42. Professor KITENGE YA: During sociology of family sociology 2nd
license 1993-1994 University of Lubumbashi Zaire.

43. Professor O. LONGANDJO: During 1993-1994 sociometry 2nd license Sociology University of Lubumbashi Zaire.

44. REGIONAL SURVEYS OF THE WORLD. Africa south of the Sahara 2001 30th Edition Europa Publications.

45. Wake up the May 22, 2001.

46. Wake up from November 22, 2001: Who Will Protect the web of life?

47. Wake up from the Mar. 22, 2005: the mountains, which will save them?

48. Wake up from 8 January 2005: can planet Earth Be Saved?

49. Wake up from 08 September 2005: Cooperation vital for life.

50. RICHARD MACKAY: The Atlas of endangered species.
Threatened plants and animals of the world.
C Myriad Editions Limited, 2002.

51. A ROBERT LISTON: the United States and the Soviet Union.   A book on the back ground stuggle for power in 1973.

52. ROD HAGUE and MARTIN HARROP: comparative government and politics.
An introduction 6th edition, 1982, 1987, England 2001.

53. SAMIR AMIN, DERRICK Chitale and Ibbo Mandaza: SADCC Prospects for disengagement and development in Southern Africa. Studies in African political economy.
C the United Nations University, 1987.

54. The wokrld yesterday and today. Social studies.
C 1990 Silver Burdett Ginn and inc.
Printed in the USA.

55. The other side. How Soviets and Americans Perceive Each Other.
    Halperim, Jonathan J, 1958.
    E.   183. 8. S 65 084 1987.

56. Watchtower 1 May 2004: should the clergyman preach politics?

57. Watchtower 1 January 2005: Can religion unite humanity?

www.ingramcontent.com/pod-product-compliance
Lightning Source LLC
Chambersburg PA
CBHW070103290526
45789CB00005B/1899